The
FRIENDSHIP
BOOK

of Francis Gay

D. C. THOMSON & CO., LTD.
London   Glasgow   Manchester   Dundee

A Thought
For Each Day
In 1978

The world is so full of a number of things,
I'm sure we should all be as happy as kings.
Robert Louis Stevenson

NEW BIRTH

However great our troubles
Time will ease the pain;
However long the winter—
Spring breaks through again!

DAVID HOPE

JANUARY

SUNDAY—JANUARY 1.

A NEW commandment give I unto you, That ye love one another.

MONDAY—JANUARY 2.

FOUR years ago, some of the old folk in the Caithness village of Mey decided to form a club. It would meet monthly, and they would be able to have a chat, hear the news about one another's families and so on.

Well, it was a great success. Then someone suggested, " Why don't we ask the Queen Mother to join us when she's living at the Castle of Mey? After all, she's a pensioner herself." They were thrilled to hear she'd be delighted to come.

And, just a few days after her 76th birthday, she came and met every one of the 56 members. She was given her membership card by old Mrs Lee and said she'd like to hear about all the meetings, even if she couldn't be at them.

Now, two of the pensioners in the club are completely deaf. How sad, thought the others, that they wouldn't know what the Queen Mother said. They were wrong, though — for when she learned they could not hear, she put down her handbag, and spoke to them in sign language! I'm told she taught herself many years ago, and though few are aware of this, she has used it over and over again to speak to those who cannot hear — in hospitals and homes, to children and old people. And how their faces light up with joy!

Do you wonder that, yet again, my hat comes off to her with sincerity and affection?

TUESDAY—JANUARY 3.

SOME people carry their sunshine around with them. In Boston a paragraph appeared in a local newspaper, " Yesterday was a dull day in Newspaper Row till Philip Brooks, the poet and preacher, came along the street and the sun shone again."

We can see ourselves mirrored in the eyes of those we meet, lighting up or darkening at our approach. Try carrying a bit of sunshine around with you today. It doesn't weigh a thing—but it's more precious than gold!

WEDNESDAY—JANUARY 4.

"ALWAYS jump at the chance to do somebody a good turn. You'll never regret it," the minister had been telling his congregation. On the way home he saw a small boy trying to reach up to a rather high doorbell.

" Let me do it for you, sonny," said the minister, giving it a good peal.

" Thanks, sir," grinned the youngster, who then took to his heels and disappeared round the nearest corner, leaving the minister to face the music!

THURSDAY—JANUARY 5.

THERE'S much to be said for a place in the sun
Where cares seem to float clean away.
No worries, no sorrows—just laughter and fun
From morning till close of the day.
But a flower will shrivel and wither and die
If the rain never darkens the sky,
And the soul that knows none of life's shadows, my
friend,
Is the soul that life's true joys pass by.

MANY years ago, Mayor Fiorello La Guardia of New York City said, " I seldom make a mistake, but when I do, you can count on it being a beaut!"

The world loved him for that. We all make mistakes. But how many of us ever admit it?

NEW YEAR is a time for new beginnings. But this story starts with a quarrel. A Glasgow man, his wife and two children walked out of his mother's house. A comment by Granny on the children's manners had led to a bitter row.

After that, though Granny wrote to apologise, Mary, her daughter-in-law, couldn't forget what had been said, and her husband, though sore in heart, felt he had to back her up.

On Christmas Eve a parcel arrived. In it were two wee coats for the children, sent with Granny's love. They were beautiful, but Mary saw at once they were no use—they were much too small. And then she realised why. In the lost year the children had grown taller—but Granny still pictured them as they had been last time she'd seen them. That made Mary think, and brought home the sadness of it all.

So, on New Year's Eve, as the clock crept up to midnight, she got out the car and drove across the city. She knocked on Granny's door, stretched out her arms, and, with tears in her eyes, said, not " Happy New Year," but " I'm sorry . . ."

A Christmas present that was no good. The first-foot who said, " I'm sorry." Together they brought about a new beginning to the happiest New Year a Glasgow granny could have.

TENDERNESS

There's nothing so gentle,
Nothing so mild,
Nothing so kind
As the hands of a child.

DAVID HOPE

THE FRIENDSHIP BOOK

LET not your heart be troubled: ye believe in God, believe also in me.

TOM CLARK'S greatest ambition had been to leave something of value to his children when he died.

But when his family of six sons and three daughters looked through his treasures, they found an old watch, a photo, a letter, an old spoon — bits and pieces worth a few pounds at most.

Yet one of his daughters, who lives in Old Farm Parade, Leeds, tells me that as they looked at them, these things brought not only tears of the grief they felt in their loss, but a new understanding of the real riches a man may possess.

For each worthless knick-knack brought back a host of memories of him — of his gentleness, his kindness and his wisdom. They remembered how they never turned to him in vain for help or comfort; how, with the passing years, their respect for him grew; how, because of him, the whole family remained close and united.

The treasures Tom left, says his daughter, would leave the richest man in the world envious, and the greatest gift of all that he gave, not only to his children but to the many who mourned him, was simply the gift of knowing him.

" I'm truly proud," she says, " to be part of this family — the six sons who carried our dad, with unashamed tears, to his resting place, and the three daughters who could only try to comfort one another. No money on earth could buy what he gave us — himself."

A fortune, indeed.

THE FRIENDSHIP BOOK

WHEN the Rev. George Gunn was minister at Juniper Green in Edinburgh, he was invited to a dinner held in honour of Winston Churchill. In the course of conversation the great man asked Mr Gunn, " How many turn out to your church on Sunday?" " About three hundred," was the reply.

" What, every Sunday!" said Churchill, astonished. He pondered for a minute or two and then exclaimed, " We politicians couldn't do that. It must be your *theme*."

DID I ever tell you about the elderly gentleman who greeted his neighbour with a cheerful, " Good-day !"—although it was cold and pouring rain.

The neighbour, a younger man, glowered. " What's good about it?" he demanded.

The old man smiled and winked. " Son," he assured him, " when you reach my age, *every* day is a good day !"

A GROUP of teenage girls who were shortly to leave school were being shown round a clothing factory by the personnel officer.

It took the best part of two hours to show them the machinery and describe the latest production techniques. At the end of their tour the personnel officer asked if they had any questions.

One girl pointed to a handsome young mechanic and coyly asked, " What's his name?"

First things first !

NEW LIFE

In shady woods and under banks
The modest primrose gleams,
As Nature stirs and comes to life
From out its winter dreams.

DAVID HOPE

FRIDAY—JANUARY 13.

MY friend Jim was telling me that his wife was not in a very good humour the other evening. Jim is very fond of home-made brown bread and usually she bakes it for him twice a week. She had had rather a busy day and was complaining about the extra work involved in making bread at home when it would be so much easier just to pop out to the corner shop for it. Kneading and pummelling away, she declared it was the last loaf she would ever make.

So did they have a row? Not a bit of it. " I went and made her a cup of tea," said Jim, " and we sat down and had one together. She was all right after that. And do you know," he grinned, " all that extra pummelling she gave the dough paid off. It was the best loaf she's ever baked for me!"

SATURDAY—JANUARY 14.

THERE was no official ceremony when the first stone of the new St. Paul's Cathedral was laid in 1675, but something occurred which greatly impressed the onlookers.

Stones from the older cathedral, burned out in the Great Fire of London in 1666, lay by the site. One of them was to be used as the first stone of the new building. Sir Christopher Wren, the architect, gave a sign and a workman lifted a huge slab from the old pile. As he laid it in place, the bystanders saw, carved on it, the Latin word, " resurgam "— " I shall rise again."

SUNDAY—JANUARY 15.

I AM the good shepherd: the good shepherd giveth his life for the sheep.

THE FRIENDSHIP BOOK

IN the show *The Music Man*, Meredith Willson tells of a professor who is trying to persuade a girl from the library to meet him at a footbridge across a stream in the park. Although in her heart she really wants to meet him, she finds herself saying — " Please — some other time — maybe to-morrow."

The professor's exasperated reply is worth noting — " Pile up enough tomorrows and you'll find you've collected nothing but a lot of empty yester-days. I don't know about you, but I'd like to make *today* worth remembering."

DARK days there'll be for you and me;
No doubt we'll grouse awhile.
But courage and a bit of faith
Will help us all to smile.
Be strong ; let not your spirit fear,
And you will have a happy year.

IN the school playground, a group of six-year-olds were discussing what they'd do when they grew up.

Two or three of them, of course, wanted to be professional footballers. One declared he'd be a jet pilot. Another, a racing car driver. Then it was the turn of one little boy.

" I'm going to be a lion tamer," he declared. " I'll go into the cage with six fierce lions, and I won't be scared."

He looked at his chums' disbelieving faces. " Of course," he added. " I'll have my mum with me."

THE FRIENDSHIP BOOK

GARRY SKEA was four when Mrs Ledder, who lives across the road from him, was taken to hospital seriously ill. Garry was very concerned. He had heard his parents talking about it and knew all was not well.

One day, as Mrs Ledder's sister left the house, Garry ran up to her and demanded to know why she hadn't taken him to hospital with her. " Should I have come for you, Garry?" she asked. " Yes," said Garry firmly. " I heard you telling my daddy I'd be a tonic for anyone who was ill."

So Garry was duly taken to see Mrs Ledder, and he *was* a real tonic to her, and to the others in the ward, too. So much so, he went back next day — and who should he meet there but someone else who'd also come along to cheer the patients, Sir James Robertson, the former chief constable of Glasgow ! I'm told it was quite a picture to see Sir James shaking hands with the patients, and behind him, the little lad with the golden hair gravely following suit.

A distinguished knight of the realm and a wee boy who wanted to see a sick neighbour . . . Both, in their way, left behind them comfort, joy and the blessing that always comes from knowing that someone cares.

THIS little prayer has brought strength to many. I print it here, in the hope that some will see it for the first time, and perhaps find in it a message for themselves :

" Give me the courage to fight for what can be remedied, the fortitude to bear what cannot be taken away, and the ability to know the difference."

PERFECT

The snow fell softly in the night;
On every branch and twig it lay,
Revealing with the morning light
A scene of sparkling artistry.
No hand could paint, no fingers trace
The perfect beauty on Earth's face.

DAVID HOPE

SATURDAY—JANUARY 21.

IT is often said that something worth saying can be expressed in a very few words. The Lord's Prayer in the full Authorised Version has a mere 65 words. The Ten Commandments have 297 words. The American Declaration of Independence has just 300 words. But now here's something to think about. A directive of the Common Market on the import of caramel and caramel products runs to 26,911 words.

Was that worth saying? I ask you!

SUNDAY—JANUARY 22.

HE maketh me to lie down in green pastures: He leadeth me beside the still waters.

MONDAY—JANUARY 23.

COMFORT can come in unexpected ways, and from unexpected places.

When the Rev. Joe Philp, of Busby, died in Glasgow Royal Infirmary, his wife went to collect his things from the hospital. A young doctor handed her a piece of paper. " Some people call this a death-certificate," he said. " But I am a Christian, and I do not accept that. I believe that life goes on." He paused, then added, " So, Mrs Philp, here is your husband's life certificate."

For some, death is the end of everything. For all of us, losing a loved one must bring sorrow. Yet the words of that young doctor, who shared the faith her husband served for more than thirty years, brought great comfort and healing to Mrs Philp. They gave her the courage and strength she needed as she walked out of that hospital with no one by her side.

ON a mantelpiece somewhere in Edinburgh is a unique clock.

It has a brass face, with a galleon in full sail engraved on it, and I have no doubt it is still keeping perfect time. I heard about it from Mr James Briggs, of Mountcastle Terrace, who's interested in repairing clocks and was given this one by a friend to see if he could do anything with it.

It had lain in the garret for years. But once he'd blown the dust off, and cleaned it up, Mr Briggs could see it was the work of a craftsman. Carefully he stripped it down, repaired the fault, put it together again, and wound it up. At once it began to tick, and he returned it to his friend, commenting that it was a fine piece of work.

His friend nodded and, to Mr Briggs' amazement, told him it had been made by a man with no hands. The man was a soldier who had been badly wounded in the war, and, among other injuries, lost both his hands. He was sent to Erskine Hospital, near Glasgow. There he found both a home and work, and learned the skill he needed to build that fine clock, with all its hundreds of intricate moving parts, its polished case and burnished brass face.

Next time you're tempted to shrug your shoulders and say a thing can't be done, remember that clock, and the man with no hands.

TWO Bradford mill-owners were paying their first visit to York Minster. Looking around in wonder at the vast and beautiful nave, one of them whispered to the other, " By gum, Joe . . . tha could get a fair few looms in here!"

THE FRIENDSHIP BOOK

SPELLING, I admit with quiet pride, has always been one of my stronger points.

But others aren't so lucky. The other week, Angela, who's six, stood up in class and tried to spell " banana." Halfway through, it seemed she was stumped.

" Would you like to try again?" her teacher suggested helpfully.

" Oh, I know how to spell ' banana,' " said Angela. " It's just that I don't know when to stop!"

I THINK we all smile a little when the name of Mrs M. is mentioned. I won't give her full name for it wouldn't be kind to risk hurting someone we all admire very much.

Why do we smile about her if we admire her? I think it's really because she is so completely engrossed in what she is doing for " my old folk " as she calls them.

She helps with " Meals on Wheels." She runs parties at an old folks' home. She organises groups of young folk to help pensioners in their gardens and with their decorating. Whenever she hears of a newcomer to the district, she's there trying to interest them in her schemes.

Perhaps the reason we smile is that we know very well that when Mrs M. speaks of " my old folks," she herself is older than most of them. She's eighty if she's a day!

Sometimes I hear people say: " She's lucky to be so active at that age." But the Lady of the House and I have a strong feeling that it's the other way round — that it's being so interested in other people that keeps her so young.

THE FRIENDSHIP BOOK

A YOUNG friend was preparing for an important business exam and the other night I watched him rattling through a complicated problem that involved some very long multiplications and divisions.

He knew I had been watching him and, when he had finished, he held up a little book of tables he had been using. " Logarithms," he said. " Wonderful things. I wonder who invented them."

Now, I've forgotten almost all I ever knew about logarithms, but I do remember quite a bit about the remarkable man who worked out the principle that is used by mathematicians in every country.

He was John Napier, a Scottish country gentleman, who lived about three and a half centuries ago. His were troubled times, and during the years he spent working out his system, there was always at the back of his mind the fear that illness or a robber's dagger might prevent him completing it.

But one day, in the year 1614, he was able to present his book to the world. Scholars all over Europe recognised in it the work of one of the greatest original thinkers of all time. But for all the brilliance of his brain, John Napier was a man of rare modesty. Science and mathematics were not enough, he said. A man must work for the glory of God.

Three days before he died, in 1617, he made his will. In one sentence he showed the kind of man he was: " I have not done perfectly as I would, but zealously as I could."

What man could do more?

WHAT is man, that thou art mindful of him?

THE FRIENDSHIP BOOK

MONDAY—JANUARY 30.

> *SOME jobs are dull, no doubt of that,*
> *   And yet they must be done.*
> *There's nothing like a happy song*
> *   To make them seem like fun.*
> *And when they're finished we can say,*
> *" Was that a task? It seemed like play!"*

TUESDAY—JANUARY 31.

MRS BROWN, of Hartlepool, is a widow, and she was feeling sorry for herself.

She and her husband had lived a good and decent life, and tried to be good neighbours. But when she was left alone, Mrs Brown would often sit thinking nobody cared.

Then one day her niece Annie asked her to come and stay for two or three days. She cancelled the papers and milk, but that's when the trouble started —for, by mistake, the milkman left milk on the step the second day.

That did it. Later that afternoon, someone called, saw the milk, and could get no answer at the door. There were phone calls from one to another —no, nobody had seen Mrs Brown go out, and no-one knew where she was. So they contacted her son, and he came round at the double. He couldn't get an answer either, so he broke a window to get in, cutting his hands and tearing his coat on the broken glass, dreading what he would find inside.

Then he thought—maybe she's at Annie's. And when he arrived and saw his mother sitting there —well, he almost wept with relief. As for Mrs Brown, she didn't know whether to laugh or cry, for it told her in a way nothing else could that people really *did* care about her after all.

She's glad the milkman made that mistake !

FEBRUARY

WEDNESDAY—FEBRUARY 1.

NOT long ago, I visited the Wesley museum in City Road, London. I saw lots of interesting and amusing things that the Wesleys had used and worked with during their lives: the great man's christening gown, a lock of hair, spectacles, chair, desk, pen, hymns and written sentiments.

When I had seen everything, I left the high old house next to Wesley's old chapel, and walked across the road to Bunhill Fields, the Dissenters' cemetery, to see the grave of Susanna Wesley. Bunhill Fields is one of London's pleasant green sanctuaries, so I was pleased to sit for a few minutes under a big tree.

I smiled to myself at the thought of John Wesley and his collections of " this and that " and I couldn't help remembering those recipes he had collected and marked TP (Tried and Proved). My thoughts went to the little prayer room at the end of his bedroom which then looked out over green fields. If Wesley had arranged the museum himself, I thought, he would have probably put a notice on the door " For Prayer and Meditation —TP."

THURSDAY—FEBRUARY 2.

ONE door shuts, another opens,
  Future beckons with a smile.
What's in store round life's next corner?
  Patience for a little while!
Though we cannot always see
  The reason for what's waiting there,
Something's taken, something's given—
  The scales of life will balance fair.

THE FRIENDSHIP BOOK

SOME American politicians have a reputation for long-windedness—for using several words where one would do. But ex-President **Harry Truman** was not a bit like that—he had a simple, no-nonsense approach to politics, and indeed to life in general. When discussing the rigours of political life he said, " If you can't stand the heat, keep out of the kitchen." In other words, don't expect life to be a bed of roses—it never is. The more you want to do in life, the harder the battle will be—and the hotter the kitchen !

IT'S a wonderful gift to be able to put ourselves in somebody else's place and understand the difficulties he or she is facing. When we do that, we're much less likely to make cruel snap judgments.

I'm thinking especially of the late Fred Streeter, whose gardening tips delighted and helped so many. Fred was a lifelong churchgoer and one day he was asked to preach a sermon. I'm sure Fred would give some inspiring advice but it's what he said *after* the sermon that impressed me.

" I always thought it must be pretty easy to preach a sermon," said Fred. " But I'll tell you this much. Everything looks very different once you're in the pulpit. All those faces looking up at you and you're just one little fellow looking down at them."

It was a humbling experience he was never to forget.

THE righteous shall be glad in the Lord, and shall trust in him.

THINGS WE REMEMBER

A stitch or a sole, a heel or a nail,
John was a craftsman and never would fail.
But what I liked best, when I was a boy,
Was the way his strong fingers could mend an old toy.

DAVID HOPE

THE FRIENDSHIP BOOK

FRED FERRIS, of Sawley, Nottingham, was helping a friend to clear his grandmother's home. Now and again his friend would hold up a piece of bric-a-brac, mention how his grannie had treasured it, and what it meant to her.

That's when Fred came on an old man's boots beside the fire, creased and worn with age, but still shining as if newly polished. " Surely you'll throw these old things out ?" he said. But his friend shook his head. " No," he said, " I'll keep them." Fred was mystified. " But why?" he asked. " They're no use to you."

Then his friend explained. Some years earlier, after his grandfather died, he and his grannie had been clearing out some of his possessions and came upon the boots. " I'll put these out, Grannie," he'd suggested. But Grannie smiled and took them from him. " I'll never part with these," she replied.

Why? Because, she said, when she saw them she could retrace the path they'd trodden down through the years—a path of joy and love, of honour and faith. " Aye," she said to her grandson, " if you could go back over the road they've come you'd understand what happiness really is." And so, to her dying day, Grandad's boots were kept polished and shining by the hearth, as they still are today.

SAMUEL PEPYS, who kept a famous diary, was also a very important man at the Admiralty in the reign of Charles II. Though he became wealthy, he never lost sight of what things were really important. " Mighty proud am I," he once wrote, " and ought to be grateful to God Almighty that I am able to have a spare bed for my friends."

THE FRIENDSHIP BOOK

SERENDIPITY is a clumsy kind of word. But I like its meaning. It is the art of stumbling upon happy, pleasant or lovely things by chance.

Recently I came upon this poem which I have gladly added to what I call my serendipity box:

The long, dark street was poor and drab,
Yet I shall not forget
That stirring moment when, by chance,
A little girl I met.
For in her tiny hand she held
A bunch of snowdrops white,
She smiled in passing, and I thrilled
At such a lovely sight.
I thanked God that although today
The world is often sad,
There yet are things so pure and sweet
That we may still be glad.

A QUIET-LOOKING elderly lady moved into a house at the end of our road a few months ago, and in no time at all she seemed to have dozens of friends. People were always popping in to see her — young and old alike — but it wasn't until I came home one afternoon and found her having tea with my wife that I realised the secret of her popularity. Quite simply, she's such a good *listener*! She didn't have a lot to say herself, but she listened with such *zest*! Her eyes sparkled, she clapped her hands with joy, her eyes filled with tears, she frowned in concentration, she bristled with indignation — every topic mentioned was received with the same enthusiasm.

Clearly there's so much more to being a good listener than simply listening!

THE FRIENDSHIP BOOK

GRANDMA and Jennifer were having a heart to heart talk. Mostly about cats. " I've two cats, Grandma," said Jennifer. " Susie and Topsy. How many cats have you, Grandma?"

Grandma couldn't compete. " I've no cats at all, Jennifer," she answered.

Jennifer said nothing for a moment but she was thinking hard for something kind to say. " No, Grandma," she said at length. " But you've got Grandpa."

ANDREW GRANT and his wife moved house in January. Their new home has a garden in which the previous owner wasn't interested.

The grass is overgrown and the borders are choked with weeds. As he surveyed his wilderness, he looked over the fence at his neighbour's garden, as neat as a pin, and couldn't help comparing it with his own. " I wish it had been *your* house we moved into !" he said to his neighbour.

The other man smiled. " Well," he said, " it's funny you should say that—because it's exactly what *I* said when we moved in here five years ago !" And he told Andrew that his garden, too, had been a wilderness when he arrived, and only years of hard work had transformed it. Andrew's garden had been beautiful then—the first owner of the house had spent all his time in it. It was only when the second owner moved in that it became neglected and unkempt.

" You see," said Andrew's neighbour, turning back to his digging, " *if the grass looks greener on the other side of the fence, it's often because they take more care of it there !*"

THE FRIENDSHIP BOOK

FOR God so loved the world, that he gave his only begotten Son.

AFTER the funeral service for the racing driver Graham Hill in St Albans Cathedral, late in 1975, the funeral party were on their way out when his widow, Bette, saw a woman she knew sobbing quietly. She immediately stepped out of the procession, went over to the mourner, took her hand and whispered one word — " Courage."

It was a small act, but of such is the Kingdom of Heaven made.

YOUNG Peter was being given what I believe is called an assessment test by the headmaster at the school where he had just started.

Peter, bright as a button, answered all the headmaster's questions in a way that drew an approving smile. Till the headmaster asked: " Peter, tell me, what colour is your jersey?"

" Green," said Peter, like a flash.

The headmaster was puzzled, for the jersey was bright red. He decided he would try one or two more questions and come back again to the jersey. But, when he asked a second time, Peter's answer was still very firmly " Green, sir!"

Very puzzled now, the headmaster said, " Are you quite sure your jersey is green, Peter? I think you're wearing a red jersey."

" Yes, I am — but this jersey isn't mine," said Peter. " It's my brother's. *My* jersey is green."

You can't beat the logic of a five-year old, can you?

THE FRIENDSHIP BOOK

CAST your bread upon the waters and it will come home to you. I heard the other day of a strange way in which this belief worked out.

During the last war, lifeboatmen from Ramsgate rescued an airman whose fighter plane had been shot down in the Channel. The airman was Richard Hillary, who later wrote that brave and moving book *The Last Enemy*. And he was a descendant of Yorkshireman Sir William Hillary. It was Sir William's vision that had made his rescue possible, for, over 150 years ago, he had founded the Royal National Lifeboat Institution.

Truth is stranger than fiction.

THURSDAY—FEBRUARY 16.

I KNOW two " doggie " stories which show infinite devotion and courage. The dogs were Chuffy and Bede.

Chuffy belonged to a Wesley Deaconess, Sister Joan. He sat through services quietly, and after the benediction would greet the congregation. Sister Joan used him as a subject for her talks, and to the delight of the children would produce Chuffy to illustrate her message. He brought pleasure to elderly people, too. " A useful little evangelist," his mistress called him.

Bede, a setter, had been on holiday in Cornwall with his master, and strayed away. Father Louie had to return home to Essex without him. He was heartbroken. Six months later, the priest's postman recognised Bede struggling home, thin, footsore and bedraggled. He had walked hundreds of miles to find his master and for that epic journey he was selected as " the most courageous dog of the year " by the Kennel Club of Great Britain.

FRIDAY—FEBRUARY 17.

THERE'S a lot of sense in these lines from Mrs Kate Luce, St Clement, Jersey.

It's fun to go shopping with someone you like, a friend who won't mind if you stop, and gaze in the windows and wander about, looking round in each different shop;

It's so nice just to stare at the things that you'd like, though you haven't the money to buy — pretty hats, shoes and gowns, books and furniture, too, lovely pictures you have to pass by.

But I'm sure I'd be bored if I had all these things, and a mountain of money to spend — for the wishing and wanting is half of the fun of a day round the shops with a friend !

SATURDAY—FEBRUARY 18.

I EXPECT you'll have heard of Grandma Moses, the American lady who, in her seventies, started painting pictures, and soon became famous for her colourful and charming scenes of American life. Fame didn't go to Grandma's head, though — not a bit of it !

In her autobiography, *My Life's History*, she wrote, " I look back on my life like a good day's work. It was done and I am satisfied with it. I was happy and contented, I knew nothing better and made the best of what life offered. And life is what we make it, always has been, always will be."

Grandma Moses knew about other things besides how to paint attractive pictures !

SUNDAY—FEBRUARY 19.

LET all those that seek thee rejoice and be glad in thee.

THE FRIENDSHIP BOOK

THE favourite hymn of many people is "Abide With Me." But few know that the man who wrote it, Henry Francis Lyte, also wrote a tune for it. It was difficult to sing, and somehow it never seemed quite right for the words.

Then one day a year or two later, a gifted London organist was standing with his wife at the window of their home, gazing out at the sunset. They were heartbroken, for their little girl, aged only three, had died not long before. As her father looked at the sinking sun, the words of Lyte's hymn passed through his mind — " Fast falls the eventide . . . the darkness deepens . . . when other helpers fail and comforts flee . . ."

Suddenly, tears in his eyes, he turned away and sat down at his desk. He took up his pen, and, ten minutes later, a new tune lay before him. He called it simply " Eventide ", and it is the tune to which we still sing " Abide With Me " today — at seaside missions, evening services, as a coach tour wends its way home, at Wembley internationals, as we bid farewell to loved ones.

A tune born in a father's broken heart, yet it has blessed millions.

TUESDAY—FEBRUARY 21.

WHEN he left Yale University, the famous author, Sinclair Lewis, was asked by his professor what he intended doing with his life.

Lewis, then unknown, said that more than anything else he wanted to earn his living by writing.

" Then you will starve," replied the professor.

" I don't care if I do," retorted Lewis.

" Then you will succeed," said the professor. And he was right!

" I SOMETIMES wonder if life is worth living?" mused the pessimist.

" It is," replied the optimist — " And it is worth living much better than most of us live it."

THURSDAY—FEBRUARY 23.

MRS MARSHALL had been away for a week or two.

Her husband had died at the end of January, quite suddenly, and her daughter had suggested she should come and stay with her for a few weeks.

But here she was, back home again. She stood with her hand on her gate, thinking of the empty, cold house, and the empty, cold years that stretched away in front of her.

Then, just as she put her key in the door she saw them—three small white snowdrops by the side of the step. She stared at them for a moment, then went inside, closed the door, sat down in the kitchen and wept. Through her tears she pictured Jim planting them the previous April, on a sunny Sunday evening. They'd brought them home from a drive, just a clump of limp green leaves, turning yellow as they withered. " They don't look much just now," said Jim as he wiped his hands on an old bit of sacking. " But just wait until spring . . ."

Mrs Marshall had forgotten those snowdrops. But now, here they were, the little flowers struggling up to begin a new life with their heads turned to face the sun.

Just three snowdrops. But in them Mrs Marshall found the message that helped her to face her new life, too.

THE FRIENDSHIP BOOK

ONE of the main themes of Lent is temptation, and how to master it.

There is an amusing tale — a parable, one could call it — of a man asleep in a tent when a strange face looked in at the flap and said, " Good evening, sir." " Good evening," said the man. " I see who you are: you are a camel." " Yes," the camel said, " I am, and a very cold camel. Please let me put just my nose inside till it gets warm."

The man allowed it to put its nose in. But next, it wanted to put its neck in, and then one leg, and then another, and then its hump. " This is too much," said the man. But the camel only came farther in, till even its hind legs and tail were in, too. At last, as there was no room for both of them in the tent, the man had to get out.

The moral is plain: don't let temptations put even their *noses* inside. Turn them out at once!

SATURDAY—FEBRUARY 25.

CLARE FRANCIS is just a slip of a girl — 5 ft. 2 in. and seven and a half stone, and she is certainly the smallest person ever to have sailed the Atlantic alone. She entered for *The Observer* Royal Western Single-Handed trans-Atlantic Race in her thirty-eight-foot boat " Robertson's Golly." In her book, *Come Hell or High Water*, she graphically describes how she survived two violent gales, thirty-five-foot waves, two weeks of continuous fog, and waking up one morning to find she'd just sailed past two massive icebergs.

So you don't need to be six foot of masculine brawn to achieve great things in this world—Clare Francis has proved that what you may lack in quantity you can certainly make up for in quality!

HURRY-UP!

How long will he keep us waiting?
Our master's awfully slow:
Pity we have to wait, but that's
A dog's life, you know!

DAVID HOPE

THE FRIENDSHIP BOOK

GOD is a Spirit: and they that worship him must worship him in spirit and in truth.

ONE of the nurses in the great Johns Hopkins Hospital in Baltimore was approached by Dr Grenfell of Labrador when he was looking for someone to run a hospital there. He told her that there would be no remuneration for the job, and that she would have to pay her own expenses, but he promised her, " You will feel a love for life you have never before experienced."

The nurse found that Grenfell was right. After she had been working at the hospital for some time she wrote to a friend, " I never knew before that life was good for anything but what one could get out of it. Now I know that the *real* fun in life lies in seeing how much one can put into life for others."

WE hear a lot these days about new methods in education. But I wonder if the purpose of education has ever been better put than in these few words from that deservedly popular writer, Angus MacVicar. He wrote them in a delightful book of reminiscences entitled *Rocks In My Scotch*. He says:

" My own idea of a teacher's sacred duty is that he should endeavour to establish in young minds not only knowledge and how to use it, but also a higher concept of living, an ideal of discipline, with love and full consideration for other human beings. And surely the best way he can do this is by personal example."

MARCH

THIS is the tale of three hyacinths in a bowl. One looked as if it would produce a very large bloom, but instead it grew stunted and bent. The other two grew up straight, and their colours were lovely to behold.

Yet despite its handicap, the stunted plant slowly continued to grow. It had many florets; and finally when the other two hyacinths had passed their peak, the stunted flower became increasingly beautiful, and eventually had twice as many florets, as well as being taller.

Their owner had watched a sermon before his very eyes. He had seen a plant gradually overcome its handicap to grow even more beautiful than its fellows which had no handicap to face.

THERE is an old story of a Chinese mandarin who fell upon evil days. He lost all his money, his health suffered and he had much personal sorrow. One day he pleaded with local men to provide him with a motto which would help him in good times and bad.

In the weeks that followed, the mandarin received many suggestions. None of them succeeded in raising his spirits. Then the mandarin's daughter presented him with an emerald ring. Inscribed on it he read the words " This too will pass." It was the message he was looking for. From that day forward, he was able to face up to his troubles, knowing that they could not last, and in facing up to them he overcame them.

THE FRIENDSHIP BOOK

IT was a sister in one of our biggest hospitals who told me the secret of a nurse's smile — " As a new young nurse I felt so sorry for a patient in pain I couldn't stop tears coming into my eyes. An older staff nurse saw what was happening and straight-away sent me off on a message.

" Later, she took me aside and explained firmly, but kindly, how a patient's last strength, maybe even his recovery, often lies in his nurse's smile. And how a tear in a nurse's eye can undo the good of a whole course of treatment. It's a lesson every nurse has to learn, I was told.

" There are few of us who have not had to take refuge in a changing-room and cry for a while. Then we wash our faces, maybe put on some fresh make-up, straighten our caps and step briskly back to the ward.

" We don't fool each other, but we must not give way to our emotions. It never becomes easy, though with the years it does become less hard."

Nurses . . . how much we all owe them ! And what a poor place the world would be without them !

WHEN the going's getting tough,
And you think you've had enough,
And every day you take becomes a mile,
Don't forget, the road seems steeper
If you turn into a weeper —
You'll feel better if you wear a sunny smile !

TEACH me thy way, O Lord, and lead me in a plain path.

MOTHER'S DAY is over again.

But I would like to share with you a letter that came to me from a young woman. She writes :

" One very happy day eight years ago I was handed a tiny bundle—the baby boy my husband and I had just adopted.

" I will never forget that wonderful day, or that other unknown mother who gave her baby to me. I think of her often, and wonder what she is like. I wish I could tell her all about our child, how he is getting on at school, and of the day when he said how much he loved me and his daddy, and his other mummy and daddy.

" I hope all the mothers who have given up their babies for adoption realise how precious their children are to couples like us who cannot have their own. On Mother's Day they must all be thinking of the child they gave away, and I want them to know that I am thinking of them and asking a special blessing for them."

TUESDAY—MARCH 7.

THE Rev. Dick Sheppard was once in church as an ordinary member of the congregation, and during the morning service something happened of which St Francis of Assisi would have approved.

At the Holy Communion, a dog walked up the aisle into the sanctuary, and just when Mr Sheppard was worried in case the celebrating minister should call the verger to get rid of the dog, he came down from the altar, patted the dog, and persuaded it to lie down within the altar rails.

The congregation smiled — and then continued in prayer. Their worship had not been spoiled; a kindly gesture had helped to enrich it.

THE FRIENDSHIP BOOK

*LIFE ticks away in my quiet room, the days go
  slowly by,
A hundred memories stir my heart and sometimes I
  must cry,
But Spring peeps through my window pane, awakes
  within my mind
The happiness of days gone by, the joys I left behind.
The one I loved would never wish me drowned in
  endless pain,
So I must weave the threads of life in pattern once
  again;
I'll open doors and windows wide, I'll let the sun
  shine in;
Maybe from ashes of the old a new life can begin.*

LIZ THOMAS was fourteen when she decided she
wanted to go to Vietnam. At an age when other
girls were thinking of schoolfriends, outings and
holidays, Liz could not get the terrible sufferings of
the Vietnamese people out of her mind. Her
determination never wavered and when she had
finished training as a nurse, she applied to over thirty
organisations to be sent to work in Vietnam. To her
disappointment, they all told her she was too young
and inexperienced. But she kept on trying and at last
a small charity group accepted her.

The story of Liz Thomas's work in Vietnam —
amongst orphans, street-girls, prisoners, the sick
and refugees — is told in her remarkable book *Dust
Of Life*. It is a heroic story and her outstanding
bravery and compassion shine from every page.
Few have done in a lifetime a fraction as much for
suffering mankind as did Liz Thomas, the nurse
from Sussex, in those three selfless years.

FRIDAY—MARCH 10.

MRS COE, 82 years old, colour blind and deaf, made a patchwork quilt for the missionary bazaar. It was her pride and joy—but despite every effort it failed to sell. Sadly she said, " Send it to the Mission Field."

It went—and caught the eye of an African chief who wanted it so much that in exchange for it he reversed a three-year-old refusal to let the local mission build a little chapel near his village.

Old Mrs Coe died soon after the bazaar—but thousands of miles away her homely patchwork quilt performed a little miracle that was to transform hearts.

SATURDAY—MARCH 11.

I CAME across a piece of paper the other day with eight lines of poetry on it, written fifty years ago by Hyman Robinson of Glasgow. He never thought of publishing them, but he sent them to me, and I think you'll find in them a message worth pondering.

Life is worth a little sorrow,
  Life is worth a tear or two;
From the flowers a lesson borrow,
  In the rain they shine anew.

If the sunshine cast no shadows
  We'd be blinded by the glare;
Life is worth a little sorrow
  If you've friends to share your care.

SUNDAY—MARCH 12.

RENDER to Caesar the things that are Caesar's, and to God the things that are God's.

THE FRIENDSHIP BOOK

ONE half-forgotten memory
  Comes back by chance to you,
And brings a wistful sadness
  That could break your heart anew.
Yet would you be without them, friends,
  Those thoughts of yesterday,
That send a sunbeam through the clouds,
  Some gold amidst the grey?

TUESDAY—MARCH 14.

NAN MACDONALD of Haddington has a small friend called Danny, who lives with his parents in a flat on the edge of Edinburgh.

One day, Danny came home from Sunday School clutching a bunch of daffodils. It seems he'd got them from his teacher. She'd asked if any of her class knew of someone old, who lived alone, and might like some flowers. Danny said he did.

His mother frowned. " Do you *really* know someone like that?" she asked, for she couldn't think of anyone. Danny nodded. " 'Course I do," he retorted. " The old lady who lives upstairs." Again Danny's mother's brow furrowed. " But you don't know her yet," she said. " She moved in only two weeks ago. I've spoken to her only once myself."

" I've been up to see her three times," he said. " I carry up her empty dustbin and she gives me a glass of milk and a jammy piece." He paused. " She says she thinks she'll be happy here, but she's lonely and she misses her garden," he added. " She likes me to go and see her, so I'll just take her flowers up now."

Danny's mother looked at him, and her eyes were bright. " Danny," she said softly, " would you ask her if she'd like to come down for tea today? It's time *we* got to know her, too . . ."

THANKS

We feed the birds when winter grips
And freezes land and rivers.
But oh! the pleasure they return
Makes them indeed the givers.

DAVID HOPE

THIS is the story of the third son of a Gloucester-shire country gentleman, who left the rolling hillsides of the Cotswold country to become an apprentice in the City of London. He hated the noisy, dirty streets, and many times longed for the freshness of the countryside. But he worked hard, and began to love the city and its people. Eventually he made a fortune from " cats "—boats which then were used to carry coal up the Thames and the Fleet. As a distinguished merchant, he became Lord Mayor of London four times.

Richard Whittington was very dearly loved. He gave away his wealth to build and improve churches, hospitals and almshouses, and he formed a foundation to provide apprenticeships for poor boys which still functions today.

Five hundred years later this generous man is still remembered, not just as a nursery story hero, but as a man who gave away love to his fellow citizens.

DR WILFRED T. GRENFELL rendered pioneer service in Labrador. A continuous stream of patients who came to his surgery sometimes called for more sympathy than he felt he had to give. But pasted on the wall were these words :

" *He did kind things so kindly—*
It seemed His heart's delight
To make poor people happy
From morning until night."

Dr Grenfell said that every time he looked up, those words spoken of Jesus were to him a clarion call that if he would find joy, the real way was His way.

WEDNESDAY—MARCH 22.

THIS is a confession.

It's by Robert Yssennagger, of Calgary, who hasn't always lived in Canada. He is Dutch, and this happened years ago, when he was a teenager in Amsterdam.

One stormy day, as he was about to cross a bridge in West Amsterdam, a little old lady sheltering behind one of the pillars begged him to help her across. Robert tells me, with shame, that he just muttered, " Don't be so silly," and left her there alone and afraid.

Some weeks later, with a friend, he crossed a similar bridge over which an old lady was struggling against the strong wind. His friend spoke kindly to her, took her arm, and walked her safely over. For the first time Robert realised the strong are here to help the weak — and it changed his whole attitude to life.

Today, the boy who refused to help an old woman spends almost all his spare time in eventide homes, visiting lonely old folk, comforting them, chatting with them, holding their hands and praying with them. The older and frailer they are, the kinder and gentler he tries to be, and their faces light up when they see him come through the door.

Truly God moves in mysterious ways.

THURSDAY—MARCH 23.

WHAT I love best about children is that they are so natural—even when they're of Royal blood. Margrethe is the popular and lovely Queen of Denmark today. When she was still at school, a new girl in class asked her, " What's your father?" " He's a King," Margrethe replied. " What's yours?"

FRIDAY—MARCH 24.

ONE evening, two small brothers were trudging across a snow-covered field to the cottage that was their home. " Come on, Hugh," said Tom to his little brother. " Let's see which of us can walk in the straightest line to the house."

So off they set up the hill, a little apart, towards the cottage. Ten minutes later they reached the gate and looked back at their footprints in the snow. And there was no doubt about it — the younger boy had won easily.

" I don't understand it," said Tom. " I kept my eyes on my feet all the time, but your track's much straighter than mine. How did you do it ?"

Hugh shrugged his shoulders. " I don't know," he said, baffled. " I didn't look at my feet at all. I just kept my eyes on the light in the kitchen window, and walked towards that."

I think they both learned a lesson in life that evening, don't you?

SATURDAY—MARCH 25.

HOWEVER troubled you may be,
However dark your night,
There always comes a dawn at last,
A morning clear and bright.
And life, though sad, becomes somehow
A precious thing again,
And there's a joy you would have missed
But for your grief and pain.

SUNDAY—MARCH 26.

GO quickly, and tell His disciples that He is risen from the dead ; and, behold, He goeth before you into Galilee.

THE FRIENDSHIP BOOK

MONDAY—MARCH 27.

TOMMY had been a good boy, so his mother gave him ten pence to buy sweets.

However, he didn't say thank you, so she said, " Tommy, haven't you forgotten something? What do I say to Daddy when *he* gives *me* money?"

" Is that all?" said Tommy innocently.

Well, she did ask!

TUESDAY—MARCH 28.

PENNY ELDRED lives in Port Hueneme, California. She sent me this list of words, nine in all, which for her are the most expressive of all :—

The most bitter word is — Alone.
The most beloved word is — Mother.
The most tragic word is — Unloved.
The most cruel word is — Revenge.
The most peaceful word is — Home.
The saddest word is — Forgotten.
The warmest word is — Friendship.
The coldest word is — Indifference.
The most comforting word is — Faith.

WEDNESDAY—MARCH 29.

PASSERS-BY in a Bradford street turned as a fire-engine raced to a halt outside a building. Out jumped a fireman, who hastily consulted a policeman on duty. Then an escape ladder snaked upwards and came to rest on a windowsill. The fireman quickly climbed up — and carefully released a starling that was caught in the wire mesh of the window.

That rescue never reached the papers, but doesn't it make you feel that it's not such a bad old world after all?

THE FRIENDSHIP BOOK

WHAT a lot our children can teach us !

Mr R. Galbraith, a young father, took his four-year-old son to the baths for the first time. When they got there, Mr Galbraith found he'd left his own trunks at home. Not to disappoint his son, he allowed him into the small pond by himself, giving him instructions to keep to the edge of the pool, and explaining carefully that he could be drowned if he didn't obey.

The little boy listened to everything his dad said. Then, with a puzzled expression on his face, he looked up trustingly. " But, Daddy," he said, " how can I get drowned when you're watching me ?"

Why did that young father's eyes suddenly fill with tears, and a lump come into his throat ? Only he can answer that, but he confessed to me he suddenly realised that somewhere along the line he'd lost the faith his son possesses — the knowledge that, no matter how far out of his depth he went, his father was watching and would not fail him.

" Yes, Francis," he adds, " I took my son to the baths for a lesson that day, but he gave me a lesson instead . . ."

A BLINDED soldier was recuperating in the Valley Forge Veterans' Hospital, Valley Ridge, in Pennsylvania. One day a visiting group came round while he was studying Braille. One of the group commented that he had " lost his sight in battle." The soldier turned his head in the direction from which the comment came, and, with a smile on his face, said, " You're wrong, my friend. I did not *lose* my eyes in Korea. I *gave* them for my country. My vision I will keep forever."

BACK TO BOYHOOD

When business cares are laid aside
Grave men their pleasures take
And pit their model boats to face
The countless perils of the lake.
Then barriers of age depart
For every man's a boy at heart.

DAVID HOPE

APRIL

SATURDAY—APRIL 1.

EVERY Sunday for some weeks, Irene and a friend, both in their early twenties, had been visiting wounded soldiers in a Belfast hospital. Most were too far from home for any of their families to come and see them, and the girls felt they could help by chatting and writing letters for those who couldn't manage.

One evening, as Irene sat by a soldier's bed, writing pad on her knee, her friend came up to her. " Irene," she said, " that young lad in the end bed wonders if you would please kiss him and hold his hand." Well, Irene's a shy girl. She blushed, and retorted, " We come here to talk and help — not for kissing !"

"Please," said her friend. Then, quietly, she added, " You see, he's dying, and they don't think he'll live until his parents and his fiancee arrive. He says you remind him so much of the girl he was going to marry . . ."

So Irene rose and crossed the ward to the soldier's bed. She sat down beside him, leaned over and gently kissed his lips. Then she took his hand and held it in both of hers. He smiled and whispered his thanks, and Irene stayed with him until he fell into a sleep from which he was never to waken, for he died that night.

Irene does not know his name. But she will never forget him.

SUNDAY—APRIL 2.

THE grass withereth, the flower fadeth: but the word of our God shall stand for ever.

THE FRIENDSHIP BOOK

MONDAY—APRIL 3.

AT times I'm glad I don't have too good a memory. Does that surprise you? But you see I have known people who had wonderful memories. They could remember all the slights and hurts that other folk had inflicted on them.

Such things are far better forgotten. And, you know, learning to forget is not all that difficult. It starts by leaving more room in our minds for the pleasant things our neighbours do and say.

TUESDAY—APRIL 4.

SHE was wonderful at cheering up anyone who was a bit low. The traveller A. W. Kinglake noticed that in the hospital room where operations were to take place, the maimed soldier would make sure that " the honoured Lady-in-chief was patiently standing beside him with lips closely set and hands folded, decreeing herself to go through the pain of witnessing pain, and he used to fall into the mood of obeying her silent command. Finding strange support in her presence he would bring himself to submit and endure." Such was the inspiring effect of Florence Nightingale.

WEDNESDAY—APRIL 5.

KING EDWARD VII once invited an up-country farmer to tea. No sooner was it poured out than the farmer tipped some of his into a saucer and proceeded to drink it that way.

The courtiers tittered, but they soon fell silent when the King gravely poured tea into his own saucer and drank along with the farmer. Ungentlemanly? No, the mark of a real gentleman who would not hurt his guest's feelings.

THE FRIENDSHIP BOOK

THURSDAY—APRIL 6.

A LEXANDER MacLEOD is a radar expert, with a hard and demanding job.

One night when he arrived home, he was feeling pretty fed up with himself. He confessed to his wife that, try as he might, things hadn't gone too well that day.

He'd been working with an R.A.F. flying team. Only four of the seven sorties were as good as he'd hoped. Alexander was downhearted, for he felt he should have got better results.

His wife smiled sympathetically and pushed a matchbox towards him. On the back of the box were these words:

A man who does his best today is a hard man to beat tomorrow.

Well, Alexander tells me the same trials were conducted by another team next day. They managed only one successful sortie out of seven, so Alexander hadn't done so badly the previous day after all. And now, whenever the going gets rough, he remembers the message on the matchbox — the message that the man who does his best *always* does a fine job.

FRIDAY—APRIL 7.

I FOUND this thought scribbled on a piece of paper in a drawer of my desk:

> *It is not easy*
> *To apologise for a wrong,*
> *To begin all over again,*
> *To forgive and forget,*
> *To control a bad temper,*
> *To keep a high standard,*
> *To remember that the sun will shine,*
But how worthwhile it is !

THE FRIENDSHIP BOOK

A READER in Australia has sent me this amusing story about a swindler who, when at last he was brought to trial, admitted that he always tried first of all to win the confidence of his victims by doing them a good turn.

The magistrate shook his head. " How could you swindle people who trusted you?" he demanded.

" Your worship," said the man in the dock, " how could I swindle people who didn't !"

WHERE there is no vision, the people perish: but he that keepeth the law, happy is he.

PETER BARR'S memorials are all around us — yet few have ever heard of this Govan man.

Born 150 years ago, son of a prosperous Glasgow mill owner, he could have followed in his father's footsteps, assured of wealth and position, but Peter knew in his heart this life was not for him. Instead he took a job as an apprentice with a seedsman.

When he had learned all he could there, he went travelling all over Europe, following the purpose to which he'd devoted his life — to give the world a bigger, brighter, lovelier daffodil.

He worked from early morning until late at night, selecting, matching and improving his flowers. At length, he became known as the daffodil king and to him, perhaps, more than to anyone else, we owe the splendid yellow trumpets of the daffies of today.

I like to think that each one blows a silent fanfare every spring to the Govan man who made them what they are.

HERE'S a word to husbands—written by a wife!
It's from Phyllis Bonser, of Alvaston, Cheshire.

It wasn't the wink from the milkman,
Or the smile on the postie's young face,
That made my autumn heart beat
So loud at a fast spring-time pace.
Just, " You look lovely in that, dear,"
As my husband went on his way—
These few words stayed lingering with me,
And brightened me all through the day.

WEDNESDAY—APRIL 12.

SOME years ago, an Edinburgh bus driver took
seriously ill on holiday in the Yorkshire town of
Barnsley. He'd to be rushed to hospital, and it meant
a stay of several weeks — hundreds of miles from
home, family and friends. He could have been in for
a bleak and lonely time.

But the local bus crews got to hear about him, and
when he was well enough to have visitors, they took
care of that. His wife was welcomed into their homes
as if she was an old friend, and when she had to
return to Edinburgh, she knew her husband was in
good hands.

And when the Edinburgh bus crews heard of the
kindness of the Barnsley bus men, they invited a
party of them for a week's holiday in Scotland, all
expenses paid. Such a splendid time was had by all
that it's now a regular annual get-together. In March,
a contingent of Scots bus crews go down to Barnsley;
In October, a party of Barnsley bus men come up to
Edinburgh, and many a lasting friendship has been
forged.

Just a simple bit of kindness — yet it gave disaster
a silver lining.

COME OUT !

Spring comes round again each year,
Kissing the sleeping world awake.
With eyes to see and ears to hear,
Beauty and joy are ours to take.

DAVID HOPE

THE FRIENDSHIP BOOK

IN Lydford churchyard, East Anglia, there is an epitaph which reveals a great deal about its subject:

Here lies in a horizontal position the outside case
of
GEORGE GROUTLEDE
Watchmaker

Integrity was the mainspring and prudence the regulator of all the actions of his life, humane, generous and liberal, his hand never stopped till he had relieved distress.

So nicely regulated were his movements that he never went wrong, except when set going by people who did not know the key. Even then he was easily set right again.

He had the art of disposing of his time so well, till his hours glided away, his pulse stopped beating.

He ran down November 14th, 1801, aged 57.

In hopes of being taken in hand by his Maker, thoroughly cleaned, repaired, wound up and set going in the world to come, when time shall be no more.

A GLASGOW pensioner dropped her message bag as she left a supermarket. A young housewife helped her to pick up the few purchases.

As the old lady turned to go, she realised her bag was heavier. Looking inside, she found a chicken and a packet of biscuits she hadn't bought.

" We're going on holiday tomorrow," said the young woman. " We'll not miss these — you have them." And with a smile, off she went.

Bless you, dear !

THE FRIENDSHIP BOOK

IN one of his most famous poems, Wordsworth wrote: " The world is too much with us." Many people, feeling that this is so, have discovered for themselves that by having an occasional " Quiet time " they can recharge their mental batteries and face life with new strength.

One such man was Sir Charles Peake, British Ambassador in Athens twenty years or so ago. Sir Charles was a man of great piety, and at certain times of the day he would announce to those around him that it was now the hour for meditation.

Any guests present would quietly continue whatever occupation they were engaged in, while, for about thirty minutes, Prayer Book in hand, Sir Charles would give himself over to meditation. Then he would turn back to what he had been doing, smiling and clearly refreshed.

SUNDAY—APRIL 16.

A WORD fitly spoken is like apples of gold in pictures of silver.

MONDAY—APRIL 17.

JOE SMALL was anything but a little man — he stood well over six feet tall. He was one of the cricket team from the West Indies which toured England in 1928, and in the Test match at Lord's he scored a half-century — his best score of the tour.

Joe was absolutely delighted at his score. But as soon as he left the field, he said to the umpire, " I shall have to let Mum know at once !" The friendly West Indian was eager to share his happiness with his beloved parent — even though it meant a message across the Atlantic Ocean.

DO you feel the sun will never shine again for you? Then here is a story from a miner who works in the depths of Ellington Colliery, at Lynemouth, Northumberland. There, tunnels lead from the foot of the pit shaft, for miles below you. Some right under the bed of the North Sea.

Recently he was making his way along a tunnel to the coal face when suddenly he stopped. There, growing on a water pipe, was a delicate plant, its green leaves stretching towards an electric light bulb. How it got there is a mystery. Perhaps a single seed had dropped from the coat of a passing miner.

The fact remains that, in this dark and barren place, five miles out under the sea, where no sunlight can penetrate and where no birds sing, that seed germinated, took root, and flourished, and the heart of a miner leapt with joy when he saw it.

In this simple and stirring parable, I believe there is a message for all who feel that darkness can hold no hope.

WEDNESDAY—APRIL 19.

EVERY wife knows that if she keeps on long enough at her husband she will wear down his resistance.

An elderly couple had been told by their doctor to go out more. He advised them to " Dig in the garden and sniff fresh air." So the wife kept on daily reminding her husband of what the doctor had said.

The meek man listened without comment, until one day he handed his wife a spade. " We'll take the doctor's advice, dear," he said. " You go out and do the digging and I'll come and do the sniffing !"

THURSDAY—APRIL 20.

WHEN St Anthony was alone in the desert, he grew to thinking that there could be no holier saint than he. Later, in the back streets of a great city, he found cobbler Conrad. Anthony asked him, a little haughtily, what he had ever done to please the Lord.

" Me ?" old Conrad replied. " Me ? I have done nothing but mend sandals. But," he said, raising his head, " I have mended each pair as though they belonged to my Lord and Saviour."

The simple cobbler taught St Anthony a lesson in humility he would never forget.

FRIDAY—APRIL 21.

ONCE a certain Duke of Norfolk happened to be at the local railway station when a little Irish girl stepped off a train with a very heavy bag. She had come to join the staff as a maidservant at his home, Arundel Castle.

Timidly she asked a porter if he would carry her bag to the castle, about a mile away. She offered him a shilling — all the money she had. The porter contemptuously refused. Then the Duke stepped forward, shabby as usual in appearance. He picked up her bag and walked beside her along the road to the castle chatting to her as they went.

At the castle gate he took the shilling she offered him and waved her goodbye. It was only the next day, when she met her employer, that the little Irish girl knew that it was the Duke of Norfolk himself who had carried her bag from the station for a shilling.

The truly great man does not think of his place or prestige. It is only little people who think how great they are.

WOODLAND MAGIC

Is there a sweeter music
To be heard along the way
Than the stillness that you hear
On a sleepy, sunny day?

DAVID HOPE

E

SATURDAY—APRIL 22.

SOME folk are born miseries.

Given half a chance, they'll pin you up against a wall while they reel off tale after tale of their misfortunes. Perhaps they're hoping for sympathy. Maybe they genuinely believe they've more to complain about than most.

Well, here are four lines to think about from John Scott, of Eday, Orkney —

> *If you talk about your troubles,*
> *And you tell 'em o'er and o'er,*
> *Sure, the world will think you like 'em,*
> *And proceed to give you more !*

SUNDAY—APRIL 23.

A SOFT answer turneth away wrath: but grievous words stir up anger.

MONDAY—APRIL 24.

SINCLAIR LEWIS, the American writer, once told a lovely little story about a blind mother who asked her daughter, " What can you see outside today, Kathy?"

" Oh," said Kathy, " nothing much. Old Mrs Brown is doing her washing, and Jim Farquharson is setting out to sea again, and young Adam is ploughing the low field with the white mares . . ."

" Ah," said her mother, " how beautiful !"

" Beautiful?" asked Kathy gently. " What do you mean, Mother?"

Her mother smiled. " Well, it is beautiful ! *Love* washing at the tub. *Love* sailing the seas. *Love* holding the plough."

Sometimes the eyes of the blind see things the rest of us cannot.

THE FRIENDSHIP BOOK

TUESDAY—APRIL 25.

TODAY many youngsters can't get work and many have jobs they don't want.

Well, 160 years ago a young lad worked as a blacksmith with his father in White Horse Close, Edinburgh. Some people might not consider it a very inspiring start in life. But Willie Dick listened avidly to old horsemen, trying to learn all he could to help horses and other animals. There were no classes for vets then. Nothing daunted, he attended classes for student doctors, and adapted for animals what he learned. He had to put up with many jeers — a blacksmith, speaking broad Scots, attending medical classes to doctor horses !

Yet Willie Dick went on to become vet to Queen Victoria's animals and professor at his own veterinary school. He charged the rich and treated poor people's animals free. Eight years after he died in 1866, the school he founded gained the Royal accolade, and now the Royal (Dick) Veterinary College is possibly the foremost of its kind in the world.

There's still a lesson in the achievement of a great man who started life in a humble smiddy.

WEDNESDAY—APRIL 26.

THE general manager of the Royal Bank of Scotland was recalling one of his early experiences as a branch manager.

" One woman had never been to a bank in her life. She had always kept her money hidden away in the house. But the day after she got married she came and opened an account with us. I was curious, so I asked her why.

" ' Well,' she said, ' it isn't wise to have all that money around with a stranger in the house.' "

THE FRIENDSHIP BOOK

A YOUNG couple in Motherwell, Mr and Mrs McKay, adopted a baby boy only ten days old. They christened him Denver Crawford McKay, and he became their pride and joy. When he was five, they told him he was adopted, and Denver seemed to accept it quite naturally. But often Mrs McKay wondered what his thoughts really were.

Then one day a year later Denver came home from school and said his teacher wanted to see her. Mrs McKay's heart sank. What had he been up to ? Thinking the worst, she went down to school next morning. There the teacher explained she'd asked her pupils to write a short story about themselves. " Here's Denver's," she said :

" My Mummy told me I was a very special child because I'm adopted, and I want always to say thank you to Jesus, specially because he made my Mummy and Daddy love me so much. Because when I was born I had nobody to look after me and my Mummy and Daddy adopted me. When I grow up I will look after them."

Of course, the spelling was that of a six-year-old, some of the letters were the wrong way round and, by the end, the writing was blurred because Mrs McKay was reading it through tears. But so thankful was she that, there and then, in the classroom, she bowed her head and said a silent prayer of gratitude.

I'm sure she cherishes that simple testament as one of the richest treasures of her life.

THE nasty word we can't recall,
The anguish caused can't be undone.
Far better not to speak at all
Than say the words and hurt someone.

FRIENDS

We're the best of pals, as you can see,
In fact, we never disagree.
He's ready when I want to play
And always lets me have my way!

DAVID HOPE

THE FRIENDSHIP BOOK

WHEN I showed a friend the 25 black dots pictured above and asked him what he thought they were, he was quite mystified at first.

" Is it a puzzle of some kind?" he asked. In a way it is, but it's a good deal more, as you'll see. It all began two years ago when an Orkney girl on North Ronaldsay, Mary Muir, was sent a slip of paper with these dots on it by a friend of her mother's, an old lady, also called Mary Muir, who is blind and lives in Dollar.

At first Mary couldn't think what it was. Then she found the dots spelt her name in Braille. Mary was fascinated. So much so she asked old Mary for a copy of the Braille alphabet. Soon a letter followed, all in Braille, and Mary tells me it was just like a secret code.

Indeed, she was so thrilled she decided to learn Braille—and now she can write letters just like her old friend in Dollar. Not only that, she also has eight young pen-pals at the school for the blind in Edinburgh, with whom she exchanges letters and tapes.

Only 25 black dots to most of us, but for one old lady and nine youngsters they opened a way into happiness and friendship which has benefited them all.

GOD is our refuge and strength, a very present help in trouble.

MAY

MONDAY—MAY 1.

JIMMY KIRKPATRICK, of Lincluden, Dumfriesshire, a dustman, used to see dozens of empty lemonade bottles among the rubbish put out with the bins. So he asked the householders if they'd mind keeping their empties separate, as he planned to use the money from the return of the bottles to buy sweets, comics and so on for children in Dumfries Infirmary.

That was over 12 years ago. And though Jimmy is no longer a dustman, he's still faithfully doing his bottle-collecting round, still raising money — as much as £4 a week for youngsters in hospital. Hardly a day passes that his cheerful smile isn't seen there.

He sits beside the lonely ones, and tells them stories. He shares secrets and sits beside the beds with no visitors at visiting time. In short, he helps them to realise hospital isn't such a bad place after all!

Three cheers, say I, for the man who, with little more than empty bottles and a big heart, has brought happiness to hundreds of children.

TUESDAY—MAY 2.

WE know the sweetest comfort
When we wear the oldest shoes,
We love our old friends better
Than we'll ever love the new.
There's a kind of mellow sweetness
In a good thing growing old,
For each year that rolls around it
Leaves an added touch of gold.

WEDNESDAY—MAY 3.

TITO GOBBI, the great Italian opera singer, explained on a television programme how he helped students to achieve success in the world of opera. He told them that obviously not all of them could take leading parts and be an Othello or Desdemona, but there were many other parts to be filled. "People are required for lesser parts; someone is always needed to come in to serve the dinner," he said.

All our gifts and talents are needed, and who are we to judge the importance of our roles?

John Wesley felt he had been saved for some special purpose after his father's parsonage went on fire and he was rescued from the blaze.

John Knox also felt he had been spared for a purpose when a bullet struck his study chair a few seconds after he had risen from it.

Most convinced of all was Lord Clive, the founder of the Indian Empire. Wild and dissolute in his early life, he determined to end it all by shooting himself. The gun misfired twice, and he threw the pistol down exclaiming, " It appears I am destined for something; I will live."

Why should I go on living when so many die, we wonder, when a dear one goes from us. But with time and thought we can often see the purpose.

THURSDAY—MAY 4.

DON'T dwell on the much that is bad —
Or soon you'll forget how to smile.
Give thanks for the little you've had,
Of the joy that makes living worthwhile.
Moans and complaints build walls all around you,
Smiles open doorways so friends can come through.

LUNCHTIME

Ducks are always hungry
And when they see me come
They waddle, quacking round my feet
— And there goes every crumb!

DAVID HOPE

FRIDAY—MAY 5.

SHORTLY before his death in 1954 Duff Cooper, at one time British Ambassador to France, looked back on his life in his book *Old Men Forget*. I have read many times the almost prophetic last paragraph :

" Life has been good to me and I am grateful. My delight in it is as keen as ever and I will thankfully accept as many more years as may be granted. But I am fond of change and have welcomed it, even when uncertain whether it would be for the better; so, although I am very glad to be where I am, I shall not be too distressed when the summons comes to go away.

" Autumn has always been my favourite season and evening has been for me the pleasantest time of day. I love the sunlight, but I cannot fear the coming of the dark."

SATURDAY—MAY 6.

A SCOTSMAN dropped a five pence piece in Piccadilly Circus, and despite the help of a policeman, failed to find it. He gave the policeman his name and address with instructions to send on the coin if it was found.

A few months later the Scotsman was in Piccadilly Circus again and happened to meet the same constable, who was standing watching roadmen digging up the street.

The Scot gazed at the great hole in amazement. " Man," he said, " I didna expect ye to tak all that trouble !"

SUNDAY—MAY 7.

THE Lord is my rock, and my fortress, and my deliverer.

MONDAY—MAY 8.

WHEN little Andrew arrived home from Sunday School with a picture of a harvest field to put on the kitchen wall, no one could have guessed what he was starting.

Like so many, his parents were kind, good-living people, but on Sundays there were always so many things to do that they had got out of the habit of going to church. They had got out of the habit of other things, too, such as saying grace.

But when Andrew announced, " Teacher wants us to look at this picture and say, ' Thank you, God, for everything ' " perhaps some uncomfortable thoughts went through their minds. Perhaps they wondered how soon their little son would forget. But day after day the little boy looked at his picture and his parents bowed their heads while he said grace . . .

This all began many months ago. It is not for me to suggest how a miracle, even a little miracle works, but I do know that once Andrew's father used to drop him off at church and then drive home to carry on with his usual Sunday activities. Now you will see both father and mother in church every Sunday.

This isn't meant to be a sermon. It's just a simple tale of what happened since Andrew took home his picture of the harvest field.

TUESDAY—MAY 9.

DOES the future frighten you ? If it doesn't scare you at times, then you are a whole lot braver than I am. I like to think of the comment of a dear old friend who had the gift of putting his thoughts in a nutshell. " The best thing about the future," he once said, " is that it comes only one day at a time."

THE FRIENDSHIP BOOK

WE sometimes perform actions which have far-reaching results.

Canon Rawnsley of Keswick was an energetic and engaging man who wrote books about his beloved Lake District. He hated to see the beautiful countryside around him being spoiled in any way, and he campaigned for the formation of The National Trust. After much hard work he won his fight, and now many places of natural beauty are preserved for us all to share.

One day, a shy little lady called to see him. She knew that he had written books and she needed advice and lots of encouragement about the publication of a story she had written, very attractively illustrated by herself. When she showed it to Canon Rawnsley he found himself looking at four little rabbits, Flopsy, Mopsy, Cottontail and Peter! He gave Beatrix Potter the advice and encouragement she needed, not knowing that in so doing he was helping to give generations of children " The Tale of Peter Rabbit."

It is impossible to measure the results of an act of kindness.

EMILY DICKINSON, the American poetess who died in 1866, has a lovely verse which expresses her compassion for humanity:

> *If I can stop one heart from breaking,*
> *I shall not live in vain;*
> *If I can ease one life the aching,*
> *Or cool one pain,*
> *Or help one fainting robin*
> *Unto his nest again,*
> *I shall not live in vain.*

DREAM DAYS

All afternoon I've sat here —
My line has not been tight;
Who cares, on such a day as this,
If these fish never bite!

DAVID HOPE

FRIDAY—MAY 12.

WHEN the Rev. James Currie decided the time had come to leave his big Glasgow church and go to a country church, one of his new parishioners asked if he minded leaving his old congregation.

Mr Currie told him, truthfully, that he had been heart-broken, whereupon the questioner looked hurt. He seemed to think the reply was an insult to the people the new minister had come to.

But Mr Currie, who is a man of strong views, quickly corrected him. " You see, he should have been glad," he explained to me. " The time for a congregation to worry is when the new man is obviously glad to leave a charge. The chances then are that they are glad to get rid of him !"

SATURDAY—MAY 13.

JOYCE GRENFELL, famous for her monologues, served tea and biscuits to a party of journalists. They were there to ask about her book " Joyce Grenfell Requests the Pleasure " just before its publication.

They learned that she writes all her own monologues because she will not " say anything that she does not like to say," and that she also sings, paints and draws. She told them simply, " I believe we all have talent, but some of us work at it when the moment comes."

Fortunately Joyce Grenfell knew when the right moment had come. She worked hard, developed her talent and shares it with all of us.

SUNDAY—MAY 14.

BE thou exalted, Lord, in thine own strength : so will we sing and praise thy power.

THE FRIENDSHIP BOOK

MY neighbour, John, was standing at the top of the road, gazing into the distance. " See that steeple ?" he said. " It's St Margaret's."

I nodded agreement.

" Couldn't see it yesterday," he went on. " Now it looks as near as my finger."

" The air certainly is very clear today," I suggested.

" No, no," said John, taking off his glasses and holding them up. " It's these. New glasses ! I only got them yesterday. Now I'm seeing things I haven't seen properly for years. It's like a new world."

I congratulated the happy man and went off to collect the groceries the Lady of the House had asked me to get. And I couldn't help thinking, as I went along, that though new glasses can work wonders, perhaps you and I could see even finer horizons if each morning we looked into the day stretching ahead and made up our minds to find in it just one opportunity of helping someone in need or even just giving somebody a few words of cheer.

TUESDAY—MAY 16.

THE evangelist, D. L. Moody, drew great crowds in America and Britain by his eloquence. One night, after speaking to a crowded audience, he received his hat from the negro attendant in the side cloakroom.

" I could never speak like that, Massa Moody," enthused the attendant, " I have not the gift. But I knows hats, any shape and colour, an' I never makes a mistake in handing one back—no, sah."

Pride gleamed in his eyes. We feel that sometimes we are only cogs in the wheel of circumstance, but what use is a wheel without a cog ?

MASTER-STROKE

We cannot know the answer
Or begin to understand
How beauty is created
At one stroke of His hand.

DAVID HOPE

WEDNESDAY—MAY 17.

I AM sure many of my readers know Derek Tangye's books about his life as a flower-farmer in Cornwall. His favourite daffodil, he tells us in one of these books, is the beautiful *Joseph MacLeod*. This is how it got its name.

A member of the Dutch Resistance bred the bulb while Holland was under German occupation. He knew it would be a very long time before he could market his discovery, but he very much wished to give it a name.

Part of his duty, as a member of the Resistance, was to listen secretly to the news broadcasts from London. One night, when Germany was still sweeping all before her, he lifted up the floorboard under which his radio was hidden and tuned in to London. A voice was just announcing the British victory at El Alamein. The bulletin ended with the words: "That was the news and this was Joseph MacLeod reading it."

Something to celebrate at last! In honour of the occasion the Dutchman gave to his new daffodil the name of the man who had brought the good news — Joseph MacLeod.

THURSDAY—MAY 18.

THE Oath of Youth in Ancient Greece still has something to teach us:

" *I will not disgrace my sacred weapons, nor desert the comrade by my side. I will fight for things holy and things secular, whether I am alone or with others. I will hand on my Fatherland greater and better than I found it. I will hearken to the magistrates and obey the laws. I will not destroy or disobey the constitution. I will honour the temples and the religion of my fathers.*"

THE FRIENDSHIP BOOK

OFTEN when I am down in the dumps, or have suffered a disappointment, I dip into the works of Robert Louis Stevenson. The author of *Treasure Island* and other much-loved books, suffered almost all his life from poor health, but rarely does any suggestion of this creep into his writings. These words seem to me to sum up his whole way of looking at life :

" Even if the doctor does not give you a year, even if he hesitates about a month, make one brave push and see what can be accomplished in a week."

DO you put the milk in the cup before you pour in tea ?

Nowadays, it doesn't matter very much, but to a hostess of earlier days who wished to impress her friends it was very different.

At that time good china was more easily damaged than it is now. So, if a hostess poured tea in first, it was a sign that she was willing to risk spoiling the decoration on a cup or even cracking it. She could afford it — she had plenty more cups in the cupboard.

How hostesses must have welcomed the famous Worcester pottery ! Worcester Works were set up in 1751 by Dr Joseph Wall and his partners. By adding a new ingredient to the ware, Dr Wall was able to produce pieces that could stand up to hot water and yet be sold more cheaply than anything his rivals produced.

Dr Wall was an immensely busy man. Not only did he have his medical work, he was also a prolific painter. When asked how he managed to fit in all his activities, he simply said, " I make time."

SUNDAY—MAY 21.

JESUS saith unto him, Follow me. And he arose and followed him.

MONDAY—MAY 22.

I LIKE this story which Mr Sinclair Lewis, the famous American novelist, told against himself.

It was of an occasion on board a liner bound for Southampton. The novelist and a friend were pacing the deck when they came upon a woman reading.

Sinclair Lewis noticed her book was one he had written and, pulling up sharply, he whispered to his friend, " Look, she's reading one of my books ! That's fame ! Here am I, Sinclair Lewis, and there is an obviously intellectual woman absorbed in what I have written !"

Next moment the woman shut the book with a snap — and tossed it overboard !

TUESDAY—MAY 23.

THIS is the time of the year when we gardeners are watching eagerly for the first signs of growth in the seeds we planted so hopefully. There is a short prayer, going back I am told 500 years, which seems to me to sum up the feelings of every true gardener, even if he or she has no more than a window-box :

" The Holy Spirit of God which hath created all things for man and hath given them for our comfort, in Thy name, O Lord, we set, plant and graft, desiring that by Thy mighty power they may increase and multiply upon the earth, in bearing plenty of fruit, to the profit and comfort of all Thy faithful people, through Christ our Lord."

THE FRIENDSHIP BOOK

PETER MARSHALL, the Clydeside boy who became chaplain to the Senate in Washington, had a severe heart attack but he would not let it interfere with his work and continued his ministry with a courage that inspired others.

However, it proved beyond his physical strength, and one night he suffered such a severe attack that he had to be taken to hospital.

As he was carried to the waiting ambulance he said to his wife, as he had said so often, " See you in the morning, dear."

But this time it was not to be, and by morning he had died. Mrs Marshall never forgot those last words. For her they carried an eternal message of love and comfort. And when she wrote the biography of his life, that was the theme she chose to bring comfort to others.

I HAVE a great fondness for the poems of Henry Lawson. He was the voice of Australia, bringing to vivid life her people and her scenery. Here are some lines from a poem called " When There's Trouble on Your Mind " which seem to me to epitomise the meaning of friendship:

The main thing for the present is just only to be kind—
You can always hear the scandal but you don't know
*   what's behind.*
Take what friends can give in friendship and pass on
*   what you can get,*
And while jokes and kindly words can cheer, your life's
*   not wasted yet —*
Never fret !
While a friend's in need of cheering, life is full of
*   interest yet.*

THOMAS PALMER was an American naval officer who lived 200 years ago. As well as writing up the ship's log he also kept a log of his own life. This is how he saw it:

" First part of the voyage — pleasant, with fine breezes and fair winds. All sails set. Fell in with many vessels in want of provisions. Supplied them freely.

" Middle passage. Weather variable. Short of provisions. Hailed several of the vessels we had helped earlier. Made signals of distress, but they up sail and bore away.

" Latter part. Boisterous, with contrary winds. Current of adversity setting hard. Towards end of current, voyage slackened. With the quadrant of honesty made an observation. Corrected my course and made up my reckoning. After a passage of fifty years came into Mortality Road, with the calm, unruffled surface of the Ocean of Eternity in view."

OUR Queen's grandmother, Queen Mary, was once speaking to a party of children from a Dr. Barnado's Home on the eve of her departure to Australia. She told them, " Life is made up of loyalty: loyalty to your friends; loyalty to things beautiful and good; loyalty to the country in which you live; loyalty to your King; and, above all — for this holds all other loyalties together — loyalty to God."

SEEK ye the Lord while he may be found, call ye upon him while he is near.

MONDAY—MAY 29.

AT week-ends Bill Campbell of Liberton, Edinburgh, likes nothing better than escaping with his rod and line to the bank of some quiet river.

But that doesn't stop him telling the story of the angler who was refused admission through the pearly gates. " Sorry," said St Peter firmly, " but I'm afraid you've told too many lies to get in here."

" Have a heart, Peter," pleaded the new arrival. " After all, you were once a fisherman yourself !"

TUESDAY—MAY 30.

A MILLIONAIRE with surplus cash I'm sure I'll never be,
But with my dear ones by my side this will not bother me;
I'm sure it's true for most of us small families everywhere,
We've all the riches that we need if we have love to share.

WEDNESDAY—MAY 31.

" DON'T worry " is the easiest advice in the world to give. And just about the most useless, unless we have some clear idea about helping to remove the source of the worry.

But many a worried person could see daylight through his or her difficulties by examining them in this way:

There are three kinds of worries.

Those we have had.

Those we now have.

Those we may have.

Never bear more than one of these at a time.

COME AND BUY!

We're up very early erecting our stalls
When market day comes to the town,
And soon we're in business with bargains for all,
No rest till the sun has gone down ;
Our trade will still flourish, we venture to say,
When the new supermarkets have faded away.

DAVID HOPE

JUNE

THURSDAY—JUNE 1.

ONE of life's surest blessings is to have had a good mother. This letter from Lily Kelly, of Dumfries, echoes this in a moving way —

" My sisters and I were fostered when we were only babies. I am now nearly 20 and my sisters are older. And we are so glad to say we still have our foster mum. She's really great and very understanding. Even as children we always had the feeling that if it was in her power she would have got the moon for us.

" She's a wonder mum. After all, she's over 70, and she never married. Her path has not been all roses. In her earlier years she fostered a young lad who was crippled from the age of seven and died when he was 20. After that she just dedicated her life to bringing up other children. We're so glad she did.

" To us she is not a foster mother, but Mum in the truest, deepest sense of the word. Even if I were to write a book, I couldn't put into words all she's done."

Something tells me no book in the world will be as precious to Lily and her sisters' Mum as this simple salute from the daughters to whom she gave not just a home, but her whole heart.

FRIDAY—JUNE 2.

*M*Y *home is not a palace, it's neither rich nor grand,*
  But in the stakes of happiness I'm the richest in the land,
For I have friends a-plenty — I see them every day,
They help me and I help them along life's busy way.

SATURDAY—JUNE 3.

WHEN General Eisenhower was President of the United States, a local newspaper in Denver carried a letter from six-year-old Paul Haley, who had an incurable cancer. Paul wrote that he would love to see the President.

One Sunday morning not long afterwards, a large car stopped outside the Haley home, a big man got out, and knocked at the door. When Paul and his father opened it, there stood the President. " Paul," he said to the little boy, " I understand you want to see me. Glad to meet you." Then he shook hands with the six-year-old, took him out to see the Presidential car, shook hands again, and left.

A small incident? Yes, but what a lot it meant to a little boy who had nothing to hope for.

SUNDAY—JUNE 4.

SHEW me thy ways, O Lord; teach me thy paths.

MONDAY—JUNE 5.

MARY WILSON was asked about her future when her husband retired from his job as Premier. She said, " I'll make myself a cloak from the thread of everyday happenings and familiar things. It will serve to keep out the cold of advancing years far better than the cloth of gold of great events."

I was reminded of her words when I visited my friend Annie, now over 70. Her room was simple, with old furniture, and lots of books new and old. A fire was glowing in the grate, and her window looked out to hills and a river. The room was like Annie, it had a pleasant and peaceful outlook. It helped me to understand what Mary Wilson meant about simple everyday things and happenings.

TUESDAY—JUNE 6.

YOU wouldn't expect to find treasure while hanging out the washing, would you?

Mrs Florence Tweedle went into the garden of her home at Town End Farm, Wiggonby, Cumbria, with a basket of washing to hang on the line.

Bees buzzed among the sweet-scented wallflowers. The sun shone on the tulips and white lilies, and rose trees and blossom seemed to have burst overnight.

The birds were twittering and a robin sat on the clothes pole. A thrush in the apple tree seemed to be wondering if it was time to build her usual nest in the holly bush and somewhere above Florence's head, a skylark trilled, lost in the blue sky.

Suddenly, through the still air, she heard the sound of children's voices. She paused to listen and realised they came from the school nearby, where the children were singing their morning hymn — " All things bright and beautiful, all creatures great and small . . ." It was a perfect salute to the start of a beautiful day and so moving that Florence stood transfixed, her heart full with the glory of it all.

A magic moment, indeed — and all the gold in the world could not have bought it.

WEDNESDAY—JUNE 7.

WHEN things go wrong, and the outlook's bleak,
And you feel you can't get through,
Don't mope around, but go and seek
Someone worse off than you.
A cheery word, a happy smile,
A helpful little deed,
And you'll find that life is still worthwhile,
When you've helped a friend in need.

THE FRIENDSHIP BOOK

*B*RIGHT *the sunshine in the springtime,*
Bright the flowers and fields today,
But the shadows of my sadness
Darken all upon my way.
May the warmth that wakes the world
Light my soul with joy, I pray.

FRIDAY—JUNE 9.

IN Nottingham at the pipe band championships, the Gordon Highlanders had a regimental stall and some of the men were helping out, including Private Nigel Burnett.

During the afternoon, a middle-aged woman approached Nigel and began to speak to him about the Gordons. Nigel wondered why she turned away with tears in her eyes.

As usual, each band thrilled the listening crowd. But with one band, somehow it was different. The tune they played was unknown, but as its haunting sweetness drifted through the air, the 10,000 listeners fell silent.

It was then Nigel turned to find the same woman at his elbow, her eyes still bright with tears. " You asked how I know so much about the Gordons," she said. " Well, that's my son's tune. It's called after him — Piper Eddie Morrice."

It seems Eddie, a piper in the Gordons, was only 23 when he died. The pipe-major of his old band, Fergie Ferguson, composed the tune as a salute to him, and the crowd sensed it was no ordinary performance.

Only a few noticed the lonely figure standing beside a soldier, her heart bursting with sadness and pride, listening to the tribute her son would surely have treasured above all . . .

SATURDAY—JUNE 10.

SOME mornings I get young Neil down the road. He's at the denims and long hair stage and thinks I'm a bit of a fuddy-duddy. I suspect he sometimes says something outrageous just to see if I'll rise to the bait.

One day, he said, " Courtesy isn't dead, Mr Gay. Only last night I was at the pictures with my girl friend and I was most particular to ask if her seat was comfortable. She said it was, so I asked if she could see past the hat of the person in front. She said she could. I even asked her if the man behind had his feet against the seat and she told me he hadn't."

" Whatever next, Neil ?" I responded.

" Then I asked her if she'd change places with me, of course," he grinned.

SUNDAY—JUNE 11.

THE stone which the builders rejected is become the head of the corner.

MONDAY—JUNE 12.

MRS MACKAY, of Bruntsfield, Edinburgh, is a proud grannie now.

She has two daughters and a son, all with young families, and she gets on famously with them and is always welcome in their homes. A friend, envious of the happy relationship Mrs Mackay enjoys with her family, asked her how she did it.

Mrs Mackay smiled, " I just remember the three ages of a woman," she said. " From 20 to 30, she's a Muddle Ager. From 30-50, she's a Middle Ager. And from 50 on, she's a Meddle Ager!

" A successful grannie," she said, " has to watch out in the Meddle Ages . . ."

SUCCESS

I love the sunny, sparkling sea,
The golden, glistening sands;
But nothing's quite so wonderful
As standing on my hands.

DAVID HOPE

THE FRIENDSHIP BOOK

LAST week a friend asked his five-year-old son if he still wanted to be a fireman.

" No, I've changed my mind," said the wee boy. " I want to be God. He can do anything," My friend pointed out there were difficulties in being God. For one thing there isn't likely to be a vacancy.

" Well," responded the boy, " maybe I could get a job as His helper. He must need someone to help Him keep the world right. Why not me?"

Why not, indeed?

WEDNESDAY—JUNE 14.

ONE good turn deserves another, so the saying goes.

Some twenty odd years ago, I was sent some cases of grapes from South Africa to distribute as gifts where they would be appreciated. Of course, I was pleased to do so, and it was no bother to arrange for bunches of grapes to go to various hospitals along with a little card telling where they'd come from.

One bunch went to a patient down in the dumps after a big operation. The grapes, or perhaps it would be truer to say the knowledge someone some-where cared, helped her on her way. She put the little card aside. Now, 20 years later, she has passed on, and when her sister was going through her things, she came across the card. Remembering how the grapes had cheered her sister, she has arranged for ten bunches of grapes to go to others who may equally enjoy and be heartened by them.

Which is why I'm inclined to rewrite the old saying as — one good turn begets another. It may not happen right away, but it will eventually. Of that I am sure.

THE FRIENDSHIP BOOK

THE Rev. Walter F. Mayer, a Methodist minister about the turn of the century, never forgot a fellow student he knew at college. The young man was a very hard worker and one day Walter Mayer found what lay behind his friend's hard work and success.

Hung on the wall of his study was a plaque with these words : " Lost, sometime between sunrise and sunset, so many hours made of so many minutes. They are lost, and lost for ever."

As someone else once said, " Look after the minutes and the hours will look after themselves."

I EXPECT every Grandma forgets her glasses once in a while.

In a certain house in Toronto, a small boy was caught trying Grandma's glasses and his mother asked why. Here's what he said :

" I want to wear glasses like Grandma's — 'cause she can see much more than other people.

" She can see when folk are hungry and tired or sorry, and she can even see what'll make them feel better. She can see how to fix a lot of things to have fun with, and she can see what a feller meant to do, even if he didn't do it right. She can see when a feller is going to cry, and she can see how to get him smiling again.

" I asked her one day how she could see so good, and she said it was the way she learned to look at things as she got older. So when I get older, I want a pair of glasses just like Grandma's, so I can see as good as that, too."

Grandma may forget her glasses — but there's so much more she remembers . . .

THE FRIENDSHIP BOOK

HERE is a story of a man of vision. Percy Shaw lived near Halifax in Yorkshire. His parents were poor and he learned young to be resourceful.

One dark foggy night while driving home on an unlit hill road, he lost his bearings and was rather frightened. Suddenly, two pin-points of light pierced the darkness. It was a cat and it saved him from disaster. And that was how he got the idea of the " cats' eyes " which are now on roads all over the country.

A tribute was paid to him when the Queen, then Princess Elizabeth, visited Halifax, and saw an exhibition where the " cats' eyes " were on display.

" Oh, ' cats' eyes '! They have always intrigued me. I think that they are the most wonderful thing on the road." And she asked to meet Percy Shaw, their inventor.

Awareness and resourcefulness are wonderful things to have with you on the road of life.

SUNDAY—JUNE 18.

LO, I am with you always, even unto the end of the world.

MONDAY—JUNE 19.

I'M all for looking on the bright side.

And I've never heard the difference between an optimist and a pessimist better put than by a youngster who lives down the road. Despite the fact he's only 12, and though he smiled as he said it, I think there's a lot more in it than perhaps he realises yet:—

" The optimist," said Kenneth, " is the man who invented the aeroplane. The pessimist is the man who invented the parachute !"

THE FRIENDSHIP BOOK

AN American tourist was visiting one of Britain's quaint country villages, and got talking to an old man in the local pub.

"And have you lived here all your life, sir?" asked the American. "No, not yet, m'dear," came the sage reply.

CATHIE and Bill were as happy a family as you could meet in all Glasgow.

Then Bill was killed in a car crash, leaving Cathie and two children — a baby girl of 18 months, and Andrew, coming up five. How quiet the wee lad was after his Dad died, and sometimes Cathie heard him sobbing in his room when he thought she wasn't listening.

When Andrew started school, Cathie took him down the first day, but after that he said he'd go on his own. She worried a bit, but she noticed a new firmness in his step, a determined set to his chin. On the following Friday, she knew it would be all right — as soon as she saw the dustbin.

You see, every Friday morning as he left for work, Bill used to take the bin to the gate and leave it there for the dustmen, so Cathie wouldn't have to struggle out later with it. For months, of course, she'd been doing it herself, but when she went for it that morning, it wasn't to be seen. Puzzled, she went to the gate. There it was, just where Bill used to leave it.

How Andrew managed to move it 25 yards, she's no idea, but it brought tears to her eyes. When Andrew came home, he found his place set at the head of the table, where his father used to sit, and he understood.

After all, he's the man of the house now . . .

THE FRIENDSHIP BOOK

IN 1955, George Rainbird had the idea of publishing an illustrated Bible for Catholics, and journeyed to Rome to commission a notable scholar to write the necessary commentary to accompany it.

Father Dyson, a Principal Professor at the Gregorian College, readily consented to write the commentary, although he was in his middle 70's and not in the best of health. Four months later, the first part of the commentary arrived, written in his own handwriting in a sixpenny exercise book. George Rainbird at once sent the manuscript to an outside copyist — and it went missing.

Knowing what this would be likely to mean to Father Dyson (who had not kept a copy of his work), George Rainbird set off to Rome to break the news. At first, Father Dyson was shattered, but then, philosophically, he accepted the situation as the will of God.

And, without more ado, he sat down to do his work again, completing his task within the originally agreed period. A few weeks later the volume of over a thousand pages was printed and published.

MRS HILDA HOLMES, of Wythenshawe, was telling me about a telephone operator who used to get a call every day from a man who wanted to know the right time.

That was easy enough for, from her window, she could see the clock on the local factory tower. All she'd to do was glance out at it.

After several months, the man explained why he'd to make sure of the time every day. " You know the clock on the factory tower?" he asked. " Well, I've to see it's kept at the correct time!"

THE FRIENDSHIP BOOK

<u>SATURDAY—JUNE 24.</u>

YOU find many a filling in a sandwich — but Maureen, of Bolton, found something else.

Her father died in 1976. He was 69, and a compulsive gambler. When Maureen was young, she and her mother and the rest of the family had a pretty thin time of it, because her father would often arrive home with nothing in his wage packet — it had all been gambled away.

But Maureen loved him until the day he died, and she tells me one of the reasons is that one night when she was a little girl, he was getting ready to go out to the dog-racing, and making up sandwiches in the kitchen. She knew he didn't usually take sandwiches, so she asked about them.

" Well, dear," he said, " when I was there last night, I saw a man rooting in the bins for food." He smiled to her. " You know," he added, " hunger's a sharp thorn. I'm taking these to give him tonight."

Maureen never forgot that. It made her see her Dad in a new light. True, the neighbours looked down on him and tutted about his gambling. But it was *he* who took sandwiches to give to a tramp.

<u>SUNDAY—JUNE 25.</u>

WATCH therefore: for ye know not what hour your Lord doth come.

<u>MONDAY—JUNE 26.</u>

W HEN summer gardens smile, it's nice
To roam the avenues,
Enjoying other people's scents
And countless rainbow hues;
You too can see the flowers sweet,
Though there's no garden down your street.

SPOT THE WINNER

One little boy has broken the rules,
Another is very unsteady,
But one little girl, with eyes ahead,
Is looking a winner already!

DAVID HOPE

TUESDAY—JUNE 27.

DURING the long hot summer of 1976, the refrigerator in a mixed surgical ward at the Royal South Hampshire Hospital broke down. But they soon got a new one. Do you know how? Mrs Barney Rattan, a cleaner in the hospital, went straight along to a shop and ordered one. She paid for it with money she had saved up for her annual holiday.

When folk heard what Barney had done, many well-wishers sent her money so that she could have her holiday after all. But Barney handed it all over to the hospital. No wonder big-hearted Barney is so popular with patients and staff at the South Hampshire.

WEDNESDAY—JUNE 28.

AGGIE'S just become a pensioner, and I suppose to a wee lad of six or seven, she must seem very old indeed ! That's probably why, one day when she was out for a walk with her dog, a little boy ran up to her with his hand outstretched. " Here's a penny for you," he said. And, sure enough, in his grubby palm lay a bright new penny piece. Aggie was touched, but she hesitated. " I hope you're not giving me all the money you have," she said. " Yes," replied the wee lad, " but I don't need it — you take it."

Well, Aggie took it. And, as she did so, she says the look of joy on the boy's face brought a lump to her throat and made her feel very humble. Of course, that coin will never be spent, because it is too precious — all that a child possessed. Indeed, says Aggie, it's like the widow's mite in reverse.

So one small boy now knows how blessed it is to give. And Aggie will certainly tell you it's sometimes even more blessed to receive.

THURSDAY—JUNE 29.

OLIVER WENDELL HOLMES once remarked, " To be seventy years young is sometimes far more cheerful and hopeful than to be forty years old."

FRIDAY—JUNE 30.

I DON'T suppose you'll know the name of Donald Tippett.

Years ago, Donald was a minister in New York. One day, two young tearaways came to see him on some pretext or other, and he received them warmly. What he didn't know was that they were planning a robbery, and their visit to him, a minister chosen at random, was purely to set up an alibi. While they were there, he had to take a phone call in another room. The two young men thought he'd seen through their story and was reporting them to the police. So they burst into his room, set upon him with brass knuckledusters and beat him up, badly injuring his eye.

That might have been the end of the story, but it wasn't. For when they were arrested, Donald went into the witness-box; not to give evidence against them, but to plead for them ! He managed to persuade the judge to lighten their sentences. He went to see them in jail. He helped them to decide what they'd do once they were released, and he enabled one to enrol at college, helping him through his studies until he qualified as a doctor.

Remarkable, isn't it, that the young man who caused the minister's eye to be permanently injured is now a gifted eye specialist who helps the blind to see again ?

And all because Donald Tippett had it in his heart to forgive.

JULY

SATURDAY—JULY 1.

TWO years ago Mrs Johanna Stirrat, of 2 Springbank Road, Ayr, broke her spine in an accident. Up till then she'd had a busy life bringing up a family and managing a hairdressing business. Now she was housebound, lonely and depressed, as one weary day followed another.

Then one morning the phone rang. Slowly and painfully Mrs Stirrat dragged herself over to it— only to find the caller had dialled the wrong number.

Instead of exploding with anger, she accepted the apology with good grace, for she guessed she was speaking to an elderly lady who was upset and flustered at her mistake. And, to her surprise, the old lady asked her not to hang up. " I'm so lonely," she said. "And you sound such a nice person, I feel I'd like to talk to you — would you mind ?"

Touched, Mrs Stirrat didn't hang up. She found the old lady didn't live far from her, though in all the years they'd been in the district, they'd never met. Their chat that day was the first of many. For now the stranger who dialled the wrong number is one of her dearest friends and, despite the difference in their ages, they have spent many happy hours together.

All because Mrs Stirrat gave the right answer to a wrong number !

SUNDAY—JULY 2.

BLESSED is he that cometh in the name of the Lord.

MONDAY—JULY 3.

ONE morning, Mrs Routledge, of Stoney Rigg, Haltwhistle, was in the park with five friends when a young mother appeared with her two small girls, one scarcely a year old, the other not yet three.

The old ladies smiled at the family, and the young woman smiled back. Then she bent and whispered something to the elder of her children. Eyes shining, the little girl began to pick some clover, and when she had gathered a bunch, her mother said, " Now, dear, give each of the old ladies a flower." Obediently, the child went up to Mrs Routledge and her friends, and shyly presented each with a piece of clover, saying she was sorry, but she couldn't find any daisies !

Needless to say, they were all deeply touched. Indeed, Mrs Routledge told the young woman that teaching her children to give love and flowers to old ladies showed how good a mother she was. For it is never too early for a child to learn the joy of bringing happiness to others, in little un-expected ways.

TUESDAY—JULY 4.

MY friend Mac Paterson has a job that takes him all over the country.

A week or two ago he found himself in a little Highland village and called in at the only shop for a newspaper.

" Certainly," said the smiling old body who was serving behind the counter. " Would you be wanting yesterday's or today's paper ?"

" Today's, please," said Mac.

" In that case," she replied, " you'll have to come back tomorrow."

It could only happen in the Highlands !

THE FRIENDSHIP BOOK

TO have a good memory's an asset, no doubt,
But some folk, I fancy, are cursed
With the unhappy knack (and I pity them all)
Of remembering only the worst.
I don't want to boast, but I'm going to declare
That I haven't met anyone yet
More expert than I in the very rare art
Of knowing what things to forget!

THURSDAY—JULY 6.

AFTER 27 years of happy marriage, Mrs Emily Brought, of Glasgow, lost her husband. It was all so sudden, she just couldn't believe he was gone.

Even at the funeral, Emily was unable to shed a tear. Everyone told her she'd feel better if she had a good cry. But it was no use. She simply couldn't admit to herself that her husband was dead.

Then, on the following Sunday, Emily went into the bathroom to run her bath. Just as she was about to turn on the tap, she suddenly saw a big spider in the bath — and spiders terrify the life out of her. Instinctively she shouted, " Jim !" — just as she had done all the other times there were any creepy crawlies to be got rid of.

And that's when she suddenly realised she'd have to do it herself. For Jim wasn't there any more. Jim was dead. There and then, Emily sank to her knees on the bathroom tiles, buried her face in her hands, and wept her heart out.

The comfort of friends. The help and kindness of neighbours. The support of those closest to her. Emily had all these — but it took a spider in the bath to give her the courage to go on alone.

H

FRIDAY—JULY 7.

A LITTLE word when passing by,
A little, kindly word —
But how it comforted and cheered
The weary one who heard.
A little smile of welcome home,
A little quiet prayer,
These little things are big, because
They rid our souls of care.

SATURDAY—JULY 8.

CHARLIE CASSIDY was a church officer at Queen's Park West, Glasgow. He was a keen gardener and when he found the soil round the church was poor he was determined to do something about it. He barrowed load after load of rich top-soil to the church surrounds. Then he landscaped it and nurtured it. It was, at last, perfect, and Charlie set to with bulbs—daffodils, tulips, crocuses, and shrubs and bushes too. When his friends complimented him on how neat it was, Charlie said, " Wait till spring."

Well, spring came, but sadly, Charlie had died just as the first of his bulbs were pushing through the soil. The garden was a mass of spring colour as daffodils, tulips and shrubs unfolded in the sunshine. And Charlie's friends, the Brownie Pack, had been keeping an eye on it for him so there was not a weed or sweetie paper to be seen.

Charlie couldn't have wished for a finer memorial than his garden.

SUNDAY—JULY 9.

MANY that are first shall be last; and the last shall be first.

THE FRIENDSHIP BOOK

AN old man with his crony,
Two sweethearts, hand in hand,
Two scholars walking home from school —
These make you understand
That having someone by your side
To walk a mile or two,
Or just to chat, is something that
Makes life worthwhile for you.

TUESDAY—JULY 11.

WINSTON CHURCHILL had a gift of immediate compassion for people who were suffering. When he was making a quick visit to a South Country town just after a fearful bombing, he was very deeply impressed by the sight of a little home and shop, all exposed by the walls being blown down. With tears in his eyes he declared : " We've got to do something about that damage *now*."

And he did. That day the seed was sown which was to grow into the War Damage Commission. It paid out thousands of pounds and enabled people like the owner of that little shop to rebuild, not only their homes, but their lives.

WEDNESDAY—JULY 12.

A TEACHER told a class of boys to write an essay on " Mother " for their homework. The following day, on going through their work, he found two essays written by two brothers to be exactly alike. He called one of them to him.

" John," he said, " how is it that you've written the same as your brother wrote ?"

" Well, sir," came the prompt reply, " we have the same mother !"

THURSDAY—JULY 13.

I'D a letter from a lady who lives in Ulster Terrace, Edinburgh.

But not at No. 13 — dear me, no! In fact, she once made all sorts of excuses to her husband for not buying a house at No. 13 — the garden wasn't right, it faced the wrong way, it was too far from the shops, and so on. Truth is, she just wasn't happy at the thought of living in a house with the number 13! In the end, a friend of theirs bought it instead, and has lived very happily in it ever since.

But the odd thing is her husband is Ukrainian — and for Ukrainians 13 is a lucky number. Many Ukrainian families in this country live at No. 13, for they believe it will bring them good fortune.

In the same way, she's always pleased to see a black cat cross her path while to her husband a black cat means bad luck!

Maybe believing a thing strongly enough helps to make it come true. If you believe a black cat to be lucky, then you stride out more happily and hopefully after meeting one — and it is the hope and the happiness that bring you good fortune, not the cat.

In a word — optimism. Believe in the best, keep looking for it, and you may be surprised how often you find it!

FRIDAY—JULY 14.

W HEN joy abounds for other folk,
Yet all is grief for you,
Then secret loneliness is worst,
And anguish deepens, too.
But smile with them, though sharp your pain;
'T will help you find true joy again.

THE FRIENDSHIP BOOK

SATURDAY—JULY 15.

I'VE been speaking to a friend of mine who was once
on a cruise aboard the *S.S. Uganda*.

When I asked the highlight of his trip, he
told me not about the midnight sun on the clear
blue sea in the Norwegian fiords, but about
Mrs Wilson of Wishaw and the handicapped
children.

Along with three friends, and with the help of
the shipping line, Mrs Wilson organised a trip
for seven children, aged from eight to twelve,
all handicapped by spina bifida. From dawn to
dusk these ladies worked to give the youngsters
the holiday of a lifetime. And the way the boys'
eyes shone was all the testimony needed of how
well they had succeeded.

When going along a companionway late one
night, my friend passed an open door. Inside, he
saw the four ladies down on their knees cleaning
the youngsters' shoes—they're always scuffing their
toes so, explained Mrs Wilson.

Amidst all the grandeur of a wonderful cruise
that little cameo of service is the memory most
abiding for my friend.

Hats off to Mrs Wilson and her noble friends!

SUNDAY—JULY 16.

WHERE two or three are gathered together in
my name, there am I in the midst of them.

MONDAY—JULY 17.

MR PHILLIPS BROOKS, the wise and gentle
giant who was Bishop of Massachusetts, once
said: " It is very easy to find reasons why *other
people* should be patient."

TUESDAY—JULY 18.

WE all have a grumble now and again—I know I do—and here are a few lines which may apply to you—and me !

We grumble at the cold day, we grumble at the hot;
We grumble when it's raining, we grumble when
it's not.
We grumble at the labour that every day renews;
We grumble at the leisure which we don't know
how to use.
We grumble life's too serious, we grumble it's a joke;
We grumble at the cares of wealth, we grumble
that we're broke.
But what's the use of grumbling, all the way along?
The road seems so much shorter if we take it with
a song!

WEDNESDAY—JULY 19.

A YOUNG lad called Freddy joined the local brass band. He became a professional musician, and eventually one of the leading players in the finest orchestra in Britain.

The strain began to tell on Freddy, however, and he took to the bottle. After trying to stop drinking time after time, he joined Alcoholics Anonymous, and was soon on the road to recovery.

In 1972 he fell ill and entered hospital. There he had time to think and when he came out of hospital, cured, he was determined to help others who had problems like himself. And he did. He wrote a book called *The Alcoholic Problem Explained*, which has been acclaimed as one of the best books available on the subject. Not only had Freddy won his own battle, he is helping others to fight theirs.

THE FRIENDSHIP BOOK

I PASS on this tongue-in-cheek story from George Bruce, of Stonehaven, because I know pipers have a sense of humour !

George tells me that a Scot was brought into a California hospital suffering from an unidentifiable disease which left him in a deep coma. It looked like the end of the road, until one of the doctors had an idea. He scoured Los Angeles till he found a brother Scot, a piper, and got him to come to the hospital, pipes and all.

The piper stood at the foot of his fellow-countryman's sick-bed and struck up a lively reel. Inside a minute the patient's eyes flickered, soon his head came off the pillow, he smiled, spoke, and from that moment never looked back.

But, George tells me, such was the effect of the pipes on the other patients in the ward that the hospital had to bring in 15 extra staff to nurse them through their shock !

I TOOK these lines from some verses by the Canadian poet Edna Jaques.

Tell yourself you're happy
  And you'll find your heart aglow,
And reaching out for all it's worth
  To try to make it so.
Just say a dozen times a day,
  " I'm happy as a lark,"
And everyone who speaks to you
  Will catch that happy spark.
Think happy thoughts, dream happy dreams,
  Say happy words like these,
And if you don't believe it — well —
  Still try it, won't you, please?

MAGIC HOURS

They may land bigger catches
In days unguessed-at still,
But none completely matches
That first exciting thrill.

Each prologue has its sequel,
  Each bud expands and flowers,
But what in life can equal
  Those magic childhood hours?

DAVID HOPE

SATURDAY—JULY 22.

AMERICAN missionaries Jay and Angeline Tucker ran a Bible school at Andudu in the Congo for two and a half years. Their most remarkable African student was a middle-aged blind man, Eliya. He was so eager to learn that he rapidly outpaced his fellow-students. His memory was amazing and he never forgot anything, so much so that the missionaries were astonished by his knowledge.

Eventually Eliya went out into the bush in the Betongwe area, where he preached for many years until he was almost 80. He memorised vast portions of the Bible, and was often heard to correct a reading mistake; he would listen and then say something like, " Just a minute. Are you sure you haven't left out a word ?" The missionaries never remembered his being wrong.

A remarkable achievement for a simple man, of whom it was said, " Without ever having seen the Bible, I'm sure he will continue to spread its word until the day he dies."

SUNDAY—JULY 23.

AND thou shalt love the Lord thy God with all thine heart, and with all thy soul, and with all thy might.

MONDAY—JULY 24.

ARE you lonely and fed-up?
  Just make a cup of tea.
Nothing like it to dispel
Self-pity, you'll agree.
TWO cups cost but little more,
Take them with you — go next door!

THE FRIENDSHIP BOOK

TUESDAY—JULY 25.

JUST a budgie, a wee bundle of blue, but what a lot he meant to lonely Mrs Mackay. When her husband died years ago, she brought home Billy the budgie. From the day she got him he was a cheery companion, and Mrs Mackay looked on him as a friend.

Nothing robbed the hours of loneliness as Billy did. He never forgot to say, " Good morning," and chattered away happily. Then Bill became strangely quiet, he folded his blue wings and sat silent.

Soon after, Mrs Mackay buried him under the apple tree in her garden. She wept over the little grave. And she thanked God for all the power of a little bird to comfort and bless, all the happy companionship they had shared for so long.

You may, of course, think the death of a budgie something of no moment. But if you do, may God forgive you for being unable to understand what it can mean to have nothing but a little bird between you and loneliness.

WEDNESDAY—JULY 26.

I DON'T think you'll find Salada tea on the shelves of our shops or supermarkets.

In a way, that's a pity. Not because it's good tea, which I'm told it is, but because on each packet there's stapled a small, eight-sided tag no bigger than a 5p piece, with a thought or saying. Some of them well worth remembering.

A friend in America sends me a few of these tags now and again, and as I was cleaning out a drawer in my desk, I found one hidden beneath some papers. On it, I found these words:

You can break even the strongest habit by dropping it.

> *THE pain of small remembered things,*
>   *What bitter anguish there —*
> *A garden spade against the wall,*
>   *His silent, empty chair;*
> *The way he closed the door, his laugh —*
>   *All break your heart anew,*
> *Yet memories bring sweetness —*
>   *Yes, and strength and comfort, too.*

FRIDAY—JULY 28.

MAY I tell you about Private Campbell's proudest medal?

He didn't win it serving as a soldier in Germany, but when, still a boy, more than ten years ago, he fell seriously ill with kidney trouble and was taken to the children's ward in Leith Hospital, Edinburgh.

John was only nine. He was in a lot of pain and for some time he was near death. But there was one light in the darkness - a nurse whose name he never knew. He called her " the lady with the lamp " because he'd been hearing about Florence Nightingale at school, and because she was always on duty at night.

Small, with dark hair and a friendly smile, she would sit by his bed cheering him when things were bad and it seemed almost too much to bear. And one day, when she came in, she pinned a home-made medal on his pyjama jacket with the words, " For bravery shown whilst receiving injections."

Well, after four months, John left hospital and will tell you it was that unknown nurse, and her medal, who gave him the will to live. I hope that perhaps she may read this salute from a soldier who has who has never forgotten her.

SATURDAY—JULY 29.

WHEN the late Bishop George Ingle was appointed Bishop of Fulham at the age of 55, he wrote a letter to himself which he gave to his bank manager to be posted on his seventieth birthday.

It read —
" Dear George,
Many happy returns of the day. You have always said that there should be compulsory retirement at the age of 70 for bishops. Today you are 70, and you are saying to yourself, ' Of course, I am an exception to the rule !'

I write to say that you are not."

Bishop Ingle retired !

SUNDAY—JULY 30.

INASMUCH as ye have done it unto one of the least of these my brethren, ye have done it unto me.

MONDAY—JULY 31.

ARTHUR TENNYSON, the brother of Alfred Tennyson, Poet Laureate, became blind as the result of cataract. However, this did not sour his outlook.

He remarked, " God has sent me to His night school. "

His other senses remained as keen as ever. To a friend who met him strolling along the lanes near Freshwater Bay one spring morning, he exclaimed in evident delight how excited he was because it was spring.

And in that spirit he continued to live until he died at the marvellous age of 85.

AUGUST

TUESDAY—AUGUST 1.

MILDRED MURDOCH, of Riverside, California, is an old and wise friend of ours.

She is a minister's widow, and, in the years when she was helping her husband, she learned to see through the false front so many people hide behind and to come face to face with the real person.

Often she found the richest and most successful people were by no means the happiest and, in her latest letter, this thought is expressed in a telling way. Writes Mildred —

The only suitable gift for the man who has everything is sympathy.

WEDNESDAY—AUGUST 2.

MY friend Mary Atherton used to say a prayer for her shoulder regularly. Not that it was stiff or sore or gave trouble in any way. No, Mary was in the Salvation Army and spent much of her life helping people in trouble, many of them in the hospital in her home town of Windsor, Ontario.

Often they had no one else, and it was Mary's shoulder they leant on, or wept on, or clung to. People who had lost hope. People in despair. Those who could see no way out of the darkness — men and women, young and old. And that is why Mary asked God to make her shoulder strong enough, comforting enough and brave enough. " You know," she once said to me, " so often they just need someone to talk to."

I think we should all say a prayer tonight for shoulders everywhere — especially the ones that, like Mary's, give new strength to those in need.

THE FRIENDSHIP BOOK

" **M**AMMA, I've got a tummy-ache," complained
six-year-old Helen.

" That's because your stomach's empty," said her
mother. " You'd feel better if you had something in
it. You didn't take your lunch."

Next afternoon the vicar called, and during
conversation he mentioned he had rather a bad
headache.

" That's because it's empty," piped up Helen.
" You'd feel better if you had something in it !"

FRIDAY—AUGUST 4.

SOME of my letters in 1975, and I daresay yours,
carried an unusual stamp.

Half of the stamp is occupied by a design of
someone in a wheelchair, and the stamp was on sale
for a month. It raised £57,000 for cancer research,
handicapped children, the blind and disabled, old
people, research into mental illnesses, and other
causes.

A good idea thought up by Tom Major, the caretaker of a block of flats in Hove, near Brighton.

Tom used to work with the Post Office as a mes-
senger, and after seeing a TV programme about
the handicapped, began making a collection on pay
day among his workmates. He'd such a splendid
response, he began to devise other ways of raising
money for charity — and one day, at his work in the
Post Office, the idea came to him.

All that was some years ago. He had many battles
to fight before his brainwave was accepted. But
others came to his aid and on January 22, 1975,
victory was his — the first charity stamp was issued.

I raise my hat to Tom the caretaker — the little
man who had the courage to fight until he won.

SATURDAY—AUGUST 5.

JOHN WESLEY, the preacher and founder of the Methodist Church, wrote the following lines and called them his Rules of Conduct:

Do all the good that you can
By all the means that you can
In all the ways that you can
At all times you can
To all people you can
As long as ever you can.

SUNDAY—AUGUST 6.

FOR the Son of man is come to save that which was lost.

MONDAY—AUGUST 7.

NOT long ago I'd a letter from someone who says she is the luckiest woman in the world.

What kind of person is she?

Famous, clever, rich, successful? Here is her letter:

" Dear Francis, I'm the luckiest woman in the world. I've a nice council house and a good husband who thinks, bless him, that he's got a good wife. He has a very ordinary job, and no ambitions to climb any higher. Our two teenage children will never set the heather on fire academically, but they've happy natures and we get along well, all things considered. We're all healthy and we can afford to go to the seaside for a holiday this year, which we're all looking forward to very much."

Well, now, do you think she's got a right to believe she's the luckiest woman in the world? I do. For she possesses the most precious gift of all — contentment.

RIVER DAYS

Up the river, down the river,
We could drift and dream for ever,
Till the call we can't ignore,
— Hunger brings us back to shore!

DAVID HOPE

TUESDAY—AUGUST 8.

MISS FLORENCE TUDOR of Glasgow told me a story about Sir Harry Lauder I am delighted to pass on. She says — " I was a young singer auditioning for variety. It was terrible. The orchestra made no attempt to help me. I got more and more flustered. Then, as tears came, Sir Harry stepped on stage and came over to me. I couldn't believe my eyes.

" After a sharp rebuke to the orchestra, he patted my shoulder and asked did I know *The Crookit Bawbee*. We sang it together and I felt wonderful. Even more so when Sir Harry said we'd sing the song again at the performance.

" Well, we brought the house down with our duet. What a difference his kindness made at the start of my career in the theatre."

Yes, Sir Harry was a proper gentleman.

WEDNESDAY—AUGUST 9.

WANTED says your paper,
　　Wanted for a crime;
But there are more than criminals
　　Wanted all the time.
Wanted for the nursery,
　　Wanted for the school,
Wanted every hour of life,
　　To work the Golden Rule.
Wanted in the sick room,
　　To mend the weak and faint;
Wanted down in Slumland,
　　To be a helpful saint.
Wanted in this dull world,
　　To be a ray of sun;
Wanted up in heaven,
　　When our life is done.

THE FRIENDSHIP BOOK

WHEN the Two Thousand Guineas horse race was televised for the first time, the TV cameras pinpointed jockey Frank Barlow standing beside his horse. The commentator remarked that " Barlow is resting his horse on this hot day — he's taking the weight off the horse's back for as long as possible."

When the horses had arrived at the starting post they were three minutes too early; so he had decided to dismount for his horse's sake.

No other jockey bothered to dismount — and in the event Barlow won easily on a horse which was reckoned to be least likely to win this century.

Sometimes a little thoughtful deed seems so trifling that it's hardly worth doing. Frank Barlow showed just how important a small kindly act can be.

REPORTER John Hargreaves' car coughed, spluttered and died near a road bridge. Let me tell you what happened then.

First, an angry motorist coming in the opposite direction flashed him to get out of the way. So he pushed his car until it was just off the road. Next, a church-going acquaintance saw his plight and passed on laughing. Then a man came up and told him to " shift it or else " as he was on private land.

Finally, a night-shift worker at a nearby mill arrived and helped John to push his car on to the mill car park.

John Hargreaves had never seen the man before and hasn't seen him since, but he now understands, as never before, the old, old story of the Good Samaritan.

SATURDAY—AUGUST 12.

WHY?

"Why do they bother to land on Mars?"
I heard a man ask. "Why do they climb Everest?"
another asked. "What good will it do?" And
another: "Why do people train so hard and so long
for events like the Olympic Games?"

Let me tell you about young Ian, who lives not
far from us. He's lucky, for his house has a garden
with a swing, a chute and a sand-pit, and paved
paths where he can ride his tricycle. Plenty to keep
him busy and occupied, you'd imagine.

But his mother was telling the Lady of the
House the other day that the garden gate has only
to be open for a minute, and Ian is away through it,
turning his back on the safe, easy and familiar, and
crossing the road in search of fresh interests, and in
pursuit of the unknown.

Why? Don't ask me. All I know is that youth —
and the young in heart — must always be thus,
seeking new lands to conquer, striving after something new and better.

Life's like that, and I'm glad. Aren't you?

SUNDAY—AUGUST 13.

FOR what is a man profited, if he shall gain the
whole world, and lose his own soul?

MONDAY—AUGUST 14.

*Y*OU *feel depressed? A little blue?*
  Don't sit alone and sigh;
Cheer, if you can, some troubled soul,
  It may be hard — but try!
And as you ease another's pain,
You'll find you, too, will smile again.

BEST OF ALL

Seek out a dappled place
If you would rest;
A bright, sun-dappled view
Is the world's best.

DAVID HOPE

THE FRIENDSHIP BOOK

HERE'S a smile from Harold Richmond, of Green Island, New Zealand.

It's about two nuns who went shopping in their new red mini-car. While one went into a store, the other decided to park the car. The first nun, on her return from the shop, couldn't find her friend, and decided to ask a passing minister if he could help.

" Excuse me," she said, " but have you seen a nun in a red mini ?"

The minister glanced at all the young women passing to and fro in their short skirts, and shook his head. " No, I haven't," he said sadly. " But nothing would surprise me these days !"

WHEN Rosalind Hay, of Wallsend, was a child, she and a friend were given a bag with two oranges inside. Rosalind's eyes popped when her friend reached in and brought out the first orange — it was big and round, with a bright orange skin. Really, it was the finest orange Rosalind had ever seen. But when she drew hers out of the bag — oh, the disappointment ! It was much smaller. Its skin was dull. There were a few black patches on it.

But, bravely, she peeled it. It didn't look too bad. She took a bite — and what d'you think ? It was quite the sweetest, juciest orange she'd ever tasted ! And her friend's ? Inside that proud, bright skin, it was sour, dry, stringy and tasteless.

Says Rosalind, " Through the years I've found people to be a lot like those oranges. Some *look* nicely dressed, pleasant and kind, but underneath they can be cynical, dishonest and cruel. While folk who are shabby and plain may turn out to be just like my orange — the nicest and best ones to know."

THE FRIENDSHIP BOOK

THURSDAY—AUGUST 17.

YOUNG Andrew, aged ten, was just leaving by the back door as I arrived home the other day.

Having sampled the scones the Lady of the House had made for *my* tea, he was now about to go off to see what his mother had made for *his*! But he paused long enough to throw a challenge at me.

" Mr Gay," he called, " what d'you call a big bully who's wearing ten balaclavas ?"

I was beaten before I started, and Andrew knew it. " You can call him anything you like," he grinned, " because he won't hear a word you say !" And off he sped.

Oh, to be young again !

FRIDAY—AUGUST 18.

HERE'S a wee smile passed on to me by Sister Paul of the Sacred Heart Convent in Carlisle.

A young man went into his local library and asked if they had a copy of " Harmony in Marriage."

The young assistant thought for a moment, then asked doubtfully — " Is that fiction ?"

SATURDAY—AUGUST 19.

I CAME on the following poem the other day. It's by Karle Wilson Baker, and it holds a rather lovely wish:

Let me grow lovely, growing old —
So many fine things do;
Laces and ivory and gold
And silks need not be new,
And there is healing in old trees,
Old streets a glamour hold;
Why may not I, as well as these,
Grow lovely, growing old ?

OVER THE HILLS . . .

There are places far from cities
Where the spirit finds release,
Where the mountains, moors and meadows
Speak eternally of peace.

They are havens of contentment
  Far removed from care and fret.
They are Edens, when we find them,
  That we never shall forget.

DAVID HOPE

SUNDAY—AUGUST 20.

A PROPHET is not without honour, save in his own country, and in his own house.

MONDAY—AUGUST 21.

NOW for a tale of two buckets . . .

"How dismal you look!" said one bucket to his companion as they were being taken to the well.

"No wonder," said the other. "It's all so useless. No matter how full they make us, we always come back empty."

"Dear me! How strange to look at it in that way!" said the first bucket. "How I enjoy the thought that, however empty we come, we always go away full."

He had the right idea, hadn't he?

TUESDAY—AUGUST 22.

HERE'S a word of advice from Jim Fullerton, of Dundee. He came across these words in America last year, and liked them so much he brought them home.

There are only two things to worry about.
You are either sick, or you are well.
If you're well, there's nothing to worry about.
If you're sick, there are only two things to worry about.
You'll either get well or you'll die.
If you get well, there's nothing to worry about.
If you die, there are only two things to worry about.
You'll either go to heaven, or you won't.
If you go to heaven, there's nothing to worry about.
But if you don't, you'll be so busy shaking hands with friends, you won't have time to worry!

THE FRIENDSHIP BOOK

I'M told this took place in Aberdeen.

But with children's shoes costing what they do nowadays, I'm sure it could have happened anywhere !

It seems young Ian had been out shopping with his mother for a new pair of shoes. When they arrived home, Ian proudly showed his father his new shoes, and Dad went pale when he heard the cost.

Next day, as they set out for church, Dad laid a hand on Ian's shoulder. " Are these your new shoes you're wearing ?" he asked. Ian nodded.

" Well," warned Dad, " be sure and take big steps !"

NOBODY ever called Hector MacLean a softie.

Kindly, gentle and understanding, but you don't rise to be an inspector in the Glasgow Police without strength and determination, and Hector had these in plenty. The wrong-doer feared him, and the law-abiding slept easier in their beds when they knew Hector was on the beat.

He retired years ago, and spent much of his time painting. His home in Hillhead was filled with pictures. And when he died a card with these words upon it was found on his easel :

> Reckon it isn't the job we do,
> But the hope and faith to carry us through
> That count at the evening fall of dew,
> As wearily home we plod.
> And it's never the learning we display,
> But the smile and the help we give away
> That figure a deal at the end of the day,
> When we square accounts with God.

HARRY MUDD has learned a lot in his many busy years as Director of the Great House Experimental Husbandry Farm since it began in 1951.

He knows that all good farmers are attached to their animals, and have a sensitive regard for them. He says: " A stockman learns to appreciate the animals and understand their little ways, and treat them as individuals — not a collective herd."

He told me a surprising fact — that two men can have the same kind of stock, the same conditions, and feed them the same food, yet the one who treats his cows as individuals can get two hundred gallons of milk a year more from an animal.

Animals, like people, respond to love and care.

SATURDAY—AUGUST 26.

PISISTRATUS, the Grecian general of the sixth century B.C., was walking through some of his fields when he met several people who were begging for money.

" If you want *beasts* to plough your land," he said, " I will lend you some; if you want *land*, I will give you some; if you want *seed*, to sow your land, I will give you some; but I will encourage none in idleness."

By this principle, in a very short time, he had ensured that there was not a beggar to be found in his dominions.

SUNDAY—AUGUST 27.

COME unto me, all ye that labour and are heavy laden, and I will give you rest.

THE FRIENDSHIP BOOK

FATHER HEALY was an Irish priest who not only had a twinkle in his eyes, but a shrewd way with uppity people.

Once, I'm told, a young woman came to him and told him she wanted to confess to the sin of vanity. "And why is that?" asked Father Healy. The young lady fluttered her eyelids and smiled. "Well, Father," she said, "every day I look in the mirror and tell myself how beautiful I am."

"There, there, child," said the old priest comfortingly. "That's not a sin — it's a mistake!"

ONE Saturday in August, 1976, the train from Blair Atholl to Perth was late.

Someone travelling by that train missed a connection to Arbroath because of it. It could have been downright infuriating. But it wasn't — as you'll see.

On the platform were Scouts with their leaders going home from summer camp. As time passed, and no sign of any train, they whiled away their wait by playing games.

Then a young Scout leader climbed the steps of the iron bridge that crosses the railway from one platform to the other. Standing there, he began to sing "The Holy City" in a beautiful tenor voice. A hush fell over the crowded platform as the words of the old song rang out, broken only when the throng joined in with the chorus. The very hills seeming to resound to the young man's voice.

And when the train finally drew in, there was no anger, no annoyance — just simple gratitude from everyone there that they'd been privileged to share in those unforgettable and heart-lifting moments.

WEDNESDAY—AUGUST 30.

WHEREVER junior football is played in Scotland everybody knows Willie Blaney. Willie has devoted his life to the game and his home club, Yoker Athletic. He is assistant secretary to the Scottish Junior Football Association. He has also been its president. Countless numbers of young men have found happiness, sport and friendship because of the work Willie and others like him do so unassumingly.

But there's another side to Willie's life. He saved a man's life. The man was out of work, estranged from his family and heading to the bottom through drink, when someone told him — " Go to Willie Blaney, he'll help you." And he did. Willie pulled him through a misery that non-alcoholics can scarcely imagine. Now the man is back with his family, in a good job, and hasn't touched a drop for years.

Well done, Willie !

THURSDAY—AUGUST 31.

DURING the Second World War, the Chinese stokers on a ship sent to bring Canadian troops across to Europe suddenly deserted. As no troop-carrying ship dare be held up for even one unnecessary hour in wartime, volunteer stokers were called for.

A selection of volunteers stripped and sweated and shovelled in the unaccustomed heat of Puerto Rico for the best part of a week with cruelly blistered hands. One of these volunteers earned, through this spell, a certificate showing him to be a qualified stoker. The certificate is one of which H.R.H. Prince Philip, then still a midshipman barely out of his teens, is extremely proud.

SEPTEMBER

WHEN the Rev. Samuel Chadwick had his first vacation from the ministerial training college at Didsbury, Manchester, he said to his father: "You have not had a holiday for years. Now you are going away for a fortnight." His father protested that it was impossible. He could not leave his work in the cotton mill for a whole fortnight.

But his son insisted. And he took his father's place as an operative in the mill to enable him to go. "Honour thy father . . ."

WHEN you visit the sleepy little village of Cavendish in Suffolk, with its brightly-painted thatched cottages, church and sloping green, all seems sunshine and peace. There is a house there, too—once the home of Sue Ryder.

During World War II, the founder of the Sue Ryder Foundation met heroes and heroines of Europe's Resistance Movements and saw what terrible hardships they endured. After the war she turned her own home in this little haven of tranquillity into a refuge for concentration camp victims, and worked for them and other sick, homeless, destitute people. It is still the headquarters of the Foundation.

There is an old hourglass at the church in Cavendish, reminding worshippers and visitors that the hours of life are passing. Sue Ryder has certainly reminded us, by her compassion for those who suffer, that it is possible to fill each hour with purpose, effort and sacrifice.

COME IN !

Lattice windows beneath the thatch
  Nestling among the trees,
An old-world garden of flowers to match,
  A lure for the honey bees;
Houses like this were never planned,
They simply GREW with their roots in the land.

DAVID HOPE

THE FRIENDSHIP BOOK

SUNDAY—SEPTEMBER 3.

HE that findeth his life shall lose it: and he that loseth his life for my sake shall find it.

MONDAY—SEPTEMBER 4.

THE Lady of the House and I came in quite late the other night, after visiting our new neighbours, John and Elizabeth.

She was very thoughtful as we set out the breakfast things for morning. I was wondering what was on her mind when she said suddenly:

" Do you know what it is I specially like about Elizabeth?"

" Well," I said, " she's kind and friendly and—"

" No, it's not just that," answered the Lady of the House. " We've other friends who are these things, but there's something *special* about Elizabeth. It's the way her face lights up when she meets you. There's a smile in her eyes as well as on her lips, and you *know*, you just *know* she's pleased to see you."

Wasn't that a lovely compliment? And it's one that I know to be true.

TUESDAY—SEPTEMBER 5.

MANY years ago, Stanford Chaparral wrote the the following lines:

> "*I'd rather be a Could Be*
> *If I couldn't be an Are;*
> *For a Could Be is a May Be*
> *With a chance of touching par.*
> *I'd rather be a Has Been*
> *Than a Might Have Been by far;*
> *For a Might Have Been has never been,*
> *But a Has was once an Are!*"

K

THE FRIENDSHIP BOOK

JAMES CASH PENNEY was an American merchant who established the famous Golden Rule Stores, founded in partnership with men he trained himself in his store in Wyoming. After his retirement he established the James C. Penney Foundation to aid religious, scientific and educational projects—including a Memorial Home near Green Cove Springs. He lived well into his nineties, and was able to say, " I thank God for my difficulties. They have taught and disciplined me. They have made me strong. Without difficulty I would have been weak."

More than a thousand Golden Rule Stores in the U.S.A. bear witness to his industry and perseverance.

THERE'S more than one way of getting what we want !

Little Debbie is the last of her brothers and sisters still at home. The other night she was allowed to sit up to eat with the guests at her first grown-up party.

" But remember," Mother warned, " you're not to speak till you're spoken to. And you mustn't ask for anything."

Well, little Debbie was as good as gold till the sweet course came along. Then somehow she was passed over. She sat disconsolately, trying to catch her mother's eyes as the grown-ups ate their ice-cream and meringue. But the busy hostess had other things on her mind.

At last Debbie could stand it no longer. In a small, sad voice she asked, " Does anybody here want a clean plate?"

THE FRIENDSHIP BOOK

FRIDAY—SEPTEMBER 8.

A CERTAIN professor on entering his classroom always bowed deeply to his scholars. One day a friend of the professor's accompanied him to his class, and after seeing him bow to the scholars, asked him, " Why do you do that ?"

The professor replied : " It is not just those boys I bow to, but to the men of the future they will become."

SATURDAY—SEPTEMBER 9.

VOLVIC is a little town in the mountains of Central France. Kirriemuir is a little town in Scotland, one thousand miles away. But the two towns have made a bond of friendship and become twin towns.

So, to Volvic travelled sixty men, women and children of Kirriemuir, to be treated as honoured guests for six days and to be shown the wonders of the district.

What impressed many of the visitors was a very simple thing, if anything so important can be simple — the water. Volvic's water is so pure that it is bottled and sent all over the world. You see, Volvic is on the site of ancient volcanoes and these now form a gigantic underground filter. When a shower of rain falls in the mountains, it runs into this filter and three years — yes, three years! — later, this water runs through the taps in the houses of Volvic. A most wonderful example of the workings of nature, so slow yet so sure.

SUNDAY—SEPTEMBER 10.

OUT of the mouth of babes and sucklings hast thou ordained strength.

THE FRIENDSHIP BOOK

MONDAY—SEPTEMBER 11.

HIGH up in Edinburgh Castle is Queen Margaret's Chapel, visited every year by thousands of people. Margaret was the queen of King Malcolm, and for her good deeds she was revered as a saint by ordinary people.

In the days before the royal court came to Edinburgh, Malcolm and Margaret lived in Dunfermline, across the Firth of Forth. Malcolm noticed that each day Margaret disappeared into the forest. He was puzzled, then suspicious. Ashamed of himself, but desperate to know the truth, he followed her one day.

He went along a little path deep into the forest till on a bush he saw his queen's cloak. Behind the bush was the mouth of a cave. He crept inside. In the darkness ahead he saw his wife kneeling at an altar of natural stone.

Sick with shame, he would have turned back. But it was too late. She had seen him and turned to answer his unasked question :

" My lord wonders why I come here? The court is busy and there is nowhere I can be alone. I come here to pray for our country."

For the next twenty years Malcolm was to rule well and wisely over Scotland, upheld by the devotion of his wife, who, by deed and example, never ceased spreading true Christianity among her people.

TUESDAY—SEPTEMBER 12.

MUM found little Jenny washing the new kitten with soap and water.

" I don't think Mother pussy would like her kitten washed that way," said Mother. " Well, I really can't lick it," came the reply.

THE FRIENDSHIP BOOK

WEDNESDAY—SEPTEMBER 13.

THE other day I went to visit an old lady who is blind. We sat and chatted in her bright little room, and then it dawned on me that her light had been burning when I arrived. A waste of money, surely?

So I asked her about it, casually. " Why do you put the light on when you're sitting here by yourself?"

" Well," she said with a little smile, " it's not for me, it's for the neighbours. When I used to leave the light off they worried about me and kept coming in to see if everything was all right ; so now I leave it on and they know that everything's fine."

When I left I looked back at the bright window shining reassuringly ; a thoughtful gesture from one who spends her life in the dark.

THURSDAY—SEPTEMBER 14.

WHEN Andrew Carnegie was a boy in Pittsburgh, U.S.A., a great man of the city made his private library of books available to the town's working boys. Andrew at once applied to be allowed to use it but was refused because he was not an apprentice. Conscious of the principle at stake, he wrote to the local newspaper about the limitation, with the result that the library was thrown open to working boys whether apprentices or not.

As the twig is bent, so does the tree grow, and Andrew Carnegie developed a constant concern to overcome poverty and ignorance through the spreading of knowledge. He donated public library buildings throughout the English-speaking world ; and Dunfermline, his home town in Scotland, was one of the earliest recipients.

THROUGH THE AGES

These noble walls were raised to God
Nine hundred years ago,
And still these towers crown the banks
And still the waters flow.
Such sight and sound together brings
The message of eternal things.

DAVID HOPE

FRIDAY—SEPTEMBER 15.

IT'S hard to climb an uphill road
When rough the slope and steep,
Some folk turn back, or weary grow,
Or simply go to sleep !
So let's salute the gallant few
Who gaze upon the splendid view.

SATURDAY—SEPTEMBER 16.

WONDERFUL things are done by people who know what they want to do, and work hard to achieve their goal.

I have been reading about two sisters who did this, Elizabeth and Millicent Garrett, who lived last century. Elizabeth became a doctor, and Millicent the wife of a blind Member of Parliament.

Elizabeth was England's first woman doctor. She had fought hard for her own education, and she defended the rights of the women medical students who followed her. As a wife and mother, too, she overcame the same difficulties which confront the working mother of today.

Her sister, Millicent, was the wife of Henry Fawcett the blind Postmaster-General. She worked for women's rights and campaigned strongly for Parliamentary votes for women. She was created a Dame of the Order of the British Empire for her services to the nation.

These sisters knew that the true measure of life is usefulness, and that dedicated work faithfully done lives on in others.

SUNDAY—SEPTEMBER 17.

O LORD our Lord, how excellent is thy name in all the earth !

THE FRIENDSHIP BOOK

BILL and Donald were at school together in the North of England. Work took them different ways and they were not to meet again till forty years after they had sat side by side in the same classroom.

Schoolday memories flew thick and fast. Many of these centred round a master called Charles Friend. He was one of those rare teachers who can make others share their own enthusiasm and keep discipline without even raising the voice.

" He once made me feel ashamed of myself," said Donald.

" I can guess the time you mean," said Bill. " It was near Christmas. We'd finished work. He had to leave the classroom and he told us to read whatever we wished. . ."

Donald nodded. " Then, when he came back he found some of us playing cards. He didn't even raise his voice, but boy did he make us work for the rest of that period !"

" Yes," said Bill. " And we felt so rotten that we had let him down."

It was Bill himself who told me this story. I think he was glad to confide it to somebody. He had once betrayed a trust and he remembered. Perhaps that far-away memory had, in a strange way, helped to make him the man he is today.

WHAT if the summer sky is blue,
If winter's in your heart?
How can you keep on day by day,
How CAN you play your part?
If faith and courage have not gone
You'll find you can keep plodding on!

THE FRIENDSHIP BOOK

JAMES HOGG, the " Ettrick Shepherd " was a poet of great gifts, a man much admired by Sir Walter Scott. Hogg came from the humblest of backgrounds. At the age of seven he got a job looking after cows and for this his wage for the half-year was a pair of shoes and a ewe lamb.

He wished that, when he died, he might be remembered by " a bit monument in some quiet place." Today, we can see this monument by lovely St Mary's Loch, in the heart of the Scottish Borders. It bears the words: " He taught the wandering winds to sing."

He was given another epitaph, too, this one from Tibbie Shiel, a woman in whose inn near the loch Hogg and his friends had spent many a happy evening. Tibbie knew little about poetry but much about men and women.

She said, in her own homely way: " He was a sensible man, for all the nonsense he wrote." James Hogg would have thought that praise indeed!

DAME LILIAN BARKER, former Governor of the Borstal Institution for Girls at Aylesbury, seldom did "the expected thing." And she was always ready to see the funny side of any situation.

One girl recollected how she had made up a highly dramatic tale to impress the Governor — and all Miss Barker said was " Really?" in such a kindly, gentle way that the whole tale suddenly seemed silly. The girl laughed — and so did Miss Barker.

Towards the end of her career Dame Lilian said, " I have laughed more people into being good than if I had preached to them for a hundred years."

FRIDAY—SEPTEMBER 22.

A NEIGHBOUR was telling me he had been out walking with his little grandson when they met a man known to be a bit of a grumbler. This time was no exception. The youngster listened to him with wide eyes, and afterwards, to excuse the man to him, my friend told him the man was suffering from sunstroke.

As they returned home his grandson suddenly said solemnly, " Grandpa, I hope you never suffer from a sunset."

Perhaps with the simplicity of a child he had spoken more truly than he realised. So many may take a dim view of life because they look always on the dark side—the sunset rather than the sunrise.

SATURDAY—SEPTEMBER 23.

HILAIRE BELLOC, the famous writer, was holidaying in Spain with a friend, and one night they camped in the Pyrenees. Towards dawn a wild storm struck their little tent and blew it clean away. Terrified, his friend asked, " Is this the end of the world?"

" Oh, no," replied Hilaire Belloc calmly. " This is how dawn comes in the Pyrenees."

Nearly every step in the progress of civilisation has been preceded by some storm of conflict. It is the wound on the oyster that grows the pearl. The pressure of the earth forms the gold.

Do we not sometimes say to console ourselves or others, " The darkest hour is before the dawn "?

SUNDAY—SEPTEMBER 24.

I WILL bless the Lord, who hath given me counsel.

THE FRIENDSHIP BOOK

IN his book about his father, Doctor W. E. Sangster, the great Methodist minister, Paul Sangster tells us that the doctor had once thought of writing a book about all the unknown saints who live in our midst; the ones who go unsung . . .

When Nell Johnson died there were nearly 300 people at her funeral. Mrs Johnson was one of the last of London's flower-sellers. She lost her husband when she was 29, and was left with eight children. For years she cleaned at her local Town Hall before setting off to sell her roses. " She was a lovely lady and she helped more people than you have ever known," said one man.

Nell's life was like a flower — it poured out a rich perfume of love and kindness. She was just one more of Doctor Sangster's saints.

HOW much are you worth?

A friend who hates hearing about people being worth so much in terms of money says, " I don't think a person is worth anything in that way. Whatever we possess has nothing to do with what we are worth."

One of the most remarkable people I have ever met is Nurse Alida Silver, who, for many years, worked in Africa with Dr Albert Schweitzer. Small, white-haired, frail, she seemed to radiate kindness, gentleness and strength. I was told that Nurse Silver carried everything she possessed in the world in a small Gladstone bag !

So little Nurse Silver, who has comforted and healed and blessed for a lifetime, is worth only a few bits and pieces in a Gladstone bag? I think not— and I repeat, how much are YOU really worth?

GATEWAYS

Life is full of gateways,
A place to take the view,
To leave behind our failures
And face the road anew.

DAVID HOPE

WILL MUDIE, of 87 Waverley Drive, Glenrothes, is a retired blacksmith.

After his wife died of cancer, Will found himself thinking back over the long road they'd walked together, with all its memories, and he began writing poems about the things that have meant most to him — friendship, his grandchildren, his garden, the countryside, his boyhood.

His friends liked them — so Will had them made up into little booklets to sell and raise money for research into cancer. He got a collecting can and a card from the cancer research people. And on the anniversary of his wife's death, he set out round the doors in Glenrothes.

A neighbour shook her head. " You'll soon be disheartened, Will," she said. But in fact, Will tells me it was the most rewarding summer of his life. For his booklets sold so well he had to have more printed, and he was able to send £200 to cancer funds.

In a way, Will's happiest memories are of helping in the fight against the illness that claimed his wife, and I know this has made these memories doubly precious to him.

MANY years ago the following unsigned verse appeared on the children's page of a weekly paper :

Why need I sigh or strive for wealth?
  It is enough for me
That heaven hath sent me strength and health,
  A spirit glad and free;
Grateful these blessings to receive,
  I sing my hymns at morn and eve.

THE FRIENDSHIP BOOK

SO you feel there is only darkness ahead? Then read this.

A young Glasgow woman wakened on her first wedding anniversary morning, but what should have been a happy day was the saddest of her life, for her husband John was not there to share it with her. Five months after their marriage he had been killed in an accident on his way to work.

How bitter and bereft she felt! John had everything to live for. Only the day before his death, they'd learned their first baby was on the way, and it seemed their joy was complete.

People told her time would heal the wound, but her pain and loneliness grew worse as the months passed. On the day of her first anniversary the sun was shining as bright and clear as on her wedding day and she was overwhelmed with sadness.

That very night, her baby was born — a little boy. And as he was placed in her arms all her bitterness suddenly vanished, to be replaced by a joy she thought she'd never know again. Looking down at him as she cradled him, she knew she'd found her reason for going on. It was almost as if in some strange way John had come back to her.

Of course, there will always be some sadness. It could not be otherwise, but the life she thought was not worth living is now filled with promise.

FRIEND, bitterness is like a rust
That comes when loved ones part,
To tarnish golden memories
And eat into the heart.
Though easy to feel bitter then,
Be brave, and smile—and live again!

OCTOBER

HAPPY is the man that findeth wisdom, and the man that getteth understanding.

I WONDER if the Queen Mother remembers Nix?

Nix was a young soldier, just 17, from Hull who was injured in the 1914-18 war. He was sent to convalesce at Glamis Castle, the Scottish home of the Earl of Strathmore.

One ward maid there stole Nix's heart. She was only 16, but her sweetness and kindness captivated him, and all the other soldiers, too. Her name was Elizabeth and she was the Earl's daughter.

When he was well enough to go home, Nix promised to write to Elizabeth, and she to him. He sent her postcards, and she wrote back with news of herself and of his comrades who were still there, enclosing a photograph. Of course, Nix's family teased him and pulled his leg when the letters with the Scottish postmark arrived. But all he'd say was, " She's beautiful — she'd make a lovely Queen."

Well, Nix went back to the battlefield, and two years later he was killed in action. Only one photograph was left of him—sitting between Elizabeth and her mother, the Countess. His sisters also found three letters from Elizabeth, which they still treasure.

Though he was never to know it, Elizabeth did become a Queen — and the charm and sweetness of our Queen Mother, which won Nix's heart at Glamis sixty years ago, is still winning hearts today wherever she goes.

AFTER the war between Argentina and Chile in 1900, the guns of the frontier fortresses lay silent and useless. Then they were taken to the arsenal in Buenos Aires and melted down. Out of them was cast a great bronze figure of Jesus. The right hand was stretched out in blessing; the left held a cross.

The statue was to be erected on a mountain top 13,000 feet high. To get there, it had to be taken by train and then transported on gun carriages drawn by mules. For the final steep rise to the top of the mountain, it was dragged with ropes by soldiers and sailors. On March 13, 1904, it was at last erected and unveiled, and there it still stands.

Beneath it is written the words: " These mountains themselves shall fall and crumble to dust before the people of Chile and the Argentine Republic forget their solemn covenant sworn at the feet of Christ."

On the other side is inscribed the text: " He is our peace who hath made both one."

A LITTLE group of people were talking about acts of heroism. A young man turned to an old woman. She looked so ordinary, so serene, no-one would have guessed that, for her, life had been a series of tragic events. " And what kind of heroism have you practised?" he asked with an obvious air of thinking that he did not believe that there could be any heroism in a life like hers.

" I ?" she said, quietly. " I practise the heroism of going on."

You don't get any medals for her kind of courage. But today I salute all heroes and heroines who simply carry on, despite all adversities.

THE FRIENDSHIP BOOK

WHAT lies in front we cannot see;
If happiness for you and me,
Let us be glad indeed.
But if troubles wait for us ahead,
God grant us strength that road to tread
Till brighter days succeed.

THE Lady of the House was intrigued when I came home one evening and told her the story of the great sowing-bee.

Especially when I pointed out that in this case "sowing" is spelt with an "o" not an "e"!

I heard about it from Nora and Jack Morrison, who live in Vancouver, Canada. It seems a farmer out there died of cancer, still in his forties, leaving a wife and five children, the youngest only six. Of course, there were problems, not the least of which was the thousands of acres of wheat waiting to be planted. It had to be done. The family's livelihood depended on it. The question was — how?

That's when the sowing-bee took place. Not a get-together of ladies with their knitting, mending and embroidery—but 23 weatherbeaten farmers, each manning a massive tractor. All roared up early one day, seed drills hitched on behind them. Off they sped to every corner of the farmland. And there, back and forth, they toiled until sundown, when every last square yard had been sown with wheat. Then, raising their hats, the farmers chugged off home again.

Can you do anything finer than light a candle in another's darkness—whether it's sowing a thousand acres of wheat, or simply offering a friendly cup of tea?

RELEASE

When I tire of rooms and walls
Then give to me, I pray,
The glory of an English wood
Upon a summer's day.

DAVID HOPE

THE FRIENDSHIP BOOK

THE sun through the window,
A card through the post,
A call from a neighbour
To share tea and toast.
The hours slip by
In a curious way,
Till you find you have spent
A most wonderful day.

SUNDAY—OCTOBER 8.

HE that seeth me, seeth him that sent me.

MONDAY—OCTOBER 9.

THERE are many cancer sufferers living today who have cause to be grateful to the Reverend Brian Hession. A victim himself, he had been told at one time that he had only a few days to live, but he insisted upon undergoing a major operation and survived for over seven years.

In this time he did all he could to help fellow-sufferers by bringing the subject of cancer into the open, and by the example of his courage he inspired countless others in their fight. In his book, *Determined To Live*, he wrote, " Do not imagine for one moment that being a Christian means that you have not got to face the problems that come to human beings. It *does* mean that it gives you a greater power and strength to face these things— the knowledge that underneath are His everlasting arms to support you."

He faced *his* illness with courage, and through his organisation, " Cancer Anonymous," he enabled countless others to do the same.

His work lives on after him.

TUESDAY—OCTOBER 10.

IT had been one of those days. Some things had gone right, but quite a lot hadn't, and by the end of the afternoon George was feeling really fed up. He was glad to be on his way home.

As soon as he opened the door he noticed that his wife looked a bit depressed. Perhaps she, too, had had one of those days—she was certainly looking tired. To cheer her up he said, " You're looking very pretty this evening, darling."

" Really?" she exclaimed, and, do you know, she suddenly did !

George and his wife might have spent that evening bickering and grumbling at one another. Instead, they spent it in warm companionship. And isn't that what marriage is all about?

WEDNESDAY—OCTOBER 11.

IN a nursing magazine there once appeared the following definitions of the word " home "—

Home — A world of strife shut out, a world of love shut in.

Home — The place where the small are great, and the great are small.

Home — The father's kingdom, the mother's world and the children's paradise.

Home — The place where we grumble the most and are treated the best.

Home — the centre of our affection round which our hearts' best wishes twine.

Home — The place where our stomachs get three square meals a day, and our hearts a thousand.

Home — The only place on earth where the faults and failings of human nature are hidden under the sweet mantle of charity.

Truly, there's no place like it.

THE FRIENDSHIP BOOK

I SAW her the other evening on my way home. She's only four, and she was sitting on the doorstep of her home, pretending to feed her doll with wee coloured sweeties. She was lost in a world of her own, and I smiled to myself as I thought of a man who lived many years ago in Stockport.

He was in business making sweets. One day he thought to himself — why not try producing little sweets for little children? Instead of only three or four in every ounce, there would be a dozen or two.

So he made a simple batch, some of icing, some of jelly, and all gaily coloured. Then he put a handful in a paper bag and took them home to try out on his own little girl. She was delighted. She ran and brought her doll and began pretending to feed them to it. " Look, Daddy!" she cried. " They're my dolly's own sweets!" And that, as perhaps you've already guessed, is how they found the name by which they're still known today — dolly mixtures!

The firm has been selling dolly mixtures ever since. I'm told 3000 tons are bought every year now, bringing delight to countless children, and helping them to create that same wonderland which a small girl found in the first bag of dolly mixtures ever made.

Y OU do not need to stride the earth
Or win the public gaze
To spread a little happiness
In simple, secret ways.
A kindly word, a helping hand,
Or just a friendly smile,
All help to smooth another's path
And brighten every mile.

THE FRIENDSHIP BOOK

THE class of five-year-olds were on their best behaviour for the inspector's visit. They were answering his questions well. Then it came to Tommy's turn. The inspector looked him in the eye.

"What do five and one make?" No reply. "Well," he repeated, "if I gave you five rabbits yesterday and one today, how many would you have?"

"Seven," said Tommy. The inspector frowned. "How do you make that out?" he asked.

"Because I've got one at home already," said Tommy innocently.

I CAME not to judge the world, but to save the world.

MRS ANDERSON received an urgent summons to return to her native Australia where her widowed mother was seriously ill. She was lucky enough to find, at the last minute, a housekeeper to look after her husband and three young children, but she was distressed at the thought of leaving the children, perhaps for some time, in the hands of a complete stranger.

She left a note for the housekeeper which read, "Please just do the best you can—I know there won't be time for everything. I shan't care if there's dust on the mantelpiece and scuffs on the lino, if the carpet needs hoovering and the windows need cleaning—but please, *please*, leave plenty of time for loving the children."

I think Mrs Anderson had her priorities right, don't you?

THE FRIENDSHIP BOOK

DAME FLORA ROBSON has always been admired in the theatre, not just for her work but for her kindness and modesty, too. Some years ago she was making a film which had a number of child actors in it.

During the last day's filming one small boy asked Dame Flora for her autograph. " Only if you give me yours," she replied. The boy thought she was joking, but she wasn't. She insisted on getting his autograph in exchange for hers. They exchanged signatures, and one small boy went home very happy—Flora Robson had treated him as a fellow actor, and he was proud of it !

IT'S not too late to plot and plan,
Do all the secret good you can,
Take young and old folk by surprise,
And scatter stardust in their eyes.
For you won't know the joy of living
Until you share the thrill of giving.

YOU can believe it if you like.

The heel of a girl chorister's shoe got caught in a grating during a processional hymn. With great presence of mind she slipped off the shoe and walked on without it. A chivalrous male behind her tried to free the shoe and give it to her. But it was stuck fast. So he picked up the whole grating, with the shoe firmly fixed to it, and carried it along behind the girl.

The officiating clergyman promptly fell down the hole.

THE FRIENDSHIP BOOK

STAGE fright can be paralysing as even David Livingstone, the famous African missionary and explorer, found. While attending the college of the London Missionary Society in London, he was sent, as was the custom with the students, to preach in a local church.

So overcome was he that, after ascending the pulpit, he had to come down again without having said a word. And this was the adventurer who was not afraid to face a lion!

Shy? Nervous? Tongue-tied? If you have been any of these things, you've been in good company.

SATURDAY—OCTOBER 21.

FROM 1941 till 1946, Queen Mary spent all her spare time weaving a tapestry. So big was it that it required four panels to display its beauty. When it was finished, she determined to offer it for sale to help the country. Eventually it was bought by Canada and exhibited in Ottawa.

Of course, it attracted many visitors. One day, a schoolmistress brought her class. They gazed in breathless admiration until the silence was broken by one boy: " Gee, it just shows you what you can do if you only keep agoin'."

The story was related to the mayor of Ottawa who passed it on to Queen Mary. I'm told she was delighted. For of course the youngster was quite right. Her tapestry did show what can be accomplished if we only " keep agoin'."

SUNDAY—OCTOBER 22.

SEARCH me, O God, and know my heart: try me, and know my thoughts.

THE FRIENDSHIP BOOK

JANE, who's nearly five, just wouldn't go to sleep. She'd been sent to bed three times, and three times she'd come downstairs again, to the room where her mother and father and grandparents were chatting. Finally, Grandpa rose. " I'll see what I can do," he said with quiet confidence and, hand in hand, the two went off up the stair.

Ten minutes later, the sitting room door opened silently. Jane tip-toed in, her finger to her lips.

" Sshh," she whispered. " I told Grandpa a story, and he's fast asleep!"

NOT long ago John and Georgina Brown celebrated their diamond wedding anniversary.

On the day before, John talked to me about the lessons he'd learned during those years. But, with respect, I didn't quite agree with one thing.

It was this. " I reckon if a husband and wife quarrel today," said John, " they should make it up tomorrow." Well, there's nothing wrong with that. But I'd go further. I'd say — if you quarrel today, you should make it up *today*. You see, time and again, I've known tomorrow to be too late. The young wife who made up her mind to say " Sorry " to her husband next day — only to find he'd left her and wasn't coming back. The husband, too proud to say sorry, who came home the following day and found a farewell note on the table. The sweethearts who parted in anger because neither would ask forgiveness. For them, there was to be no happy tomorrow.

" Let not the sun go down upon your wrath . . ." Sadly, the world is full of people who wish, with all their heart, that they hadn't.

THANKSGIVING

Another harvest safely in
And as we've done for centuries,
We deck the church with golden sheaves
And offer up our thanks and praise.

DAVID HOPE

THE FRIENDSHIP BOOK

I'M not passing any opinion.

But I'm sure you will find this experience as intriguing as I do. I heard about it from Mrs Jessie Barlow, of Montford Terrace, Rothesay, and it concerns a friend of hers whom she calls Mary.

Mary was a confirmed atheist, and could not accept there might be life after death. Her husband, on the other hand, was convinced there is an after-life. One evening, after discussing immortality, Mary was as unconvinced as ever. " Well," said George, " if I die first I'll send you one beautiful rose." Mary just laughed.

Within two years George was dead, although quite young, and one evening the following summer Mary was leaning over her front gate, calling her dog. Suddenly an old man came round the corner, a complete stranger, and handed her the most beautiful rose she had ever seen. Mary was thunder-struck. " Why me?" she asked. He didn't answer —he merely smiled and went on his way. She never saw him again.

Coincidence? I leave you to make up your own mind about that. But I am told that afterwards Mary's arguments against life after death never carried quite the same conviction . . .

SOME thoughts on marriage:

Every man is a worse man in proportion as he is unfit for the married state. (Samuel Johnson).

What a number of marriages seem to be breaking up! How loose the manners of young people have grown! (Written in a letter 300 years ago.)

A bachelor life is just one undarned thing after another. (Grateful husband!)

THE FRIENDSHIP BOOK

AS the Lady of the House will tell you, even the best husbands slip up now and again . . .

I heard about one man who forgot his wife's birthday for the umpteenth time. There was no card from him in the morning post. No best wishes over the breakfast table. No surprise parcel when he came home in the evening. Oh, it was plain he just hadn't a clue, and, hurt and somewhat affronted, she tackled him about it.

Deeply repentant, he apologised. " But, darling," he added, with a twinkle in his eye, " how *can* you expect me to remember your birthday when you never look a day older . . .?"

I don't know what you think, but I'd say he deserved to be forgiven !

CHARITY, like honesty, is its own reward.

But not always, as this story from a friend shows. It seems a sweet old lady, who always had an eye for the poor and needy, spied a sad old man standing on the pavement in a city street.

As she passed, she slipped £1 into his hand and, with a smile, whispered, " Chin up !"

Next day, as she passed the same street corner, the same old man shuffled up to her, this time wreathed in smiles.

" You sure know how to pick a winner," he said gratefully, handing her a £5 note. " ' Chin up ' came in first !"

I WILL lift up mine eyes unto the hills, from whence cometh my help.

THE FRIENDSHIP BOOK

I'D like to tell you about a bus shelter in far-away Perth, Australia.

I learned of it from Mrs Anne Roberts, who lives in Albany there. Some time ago a woman, who was recovering from an illness, was allowed out for a walk from her house. She couldn't go far and sat on the seat in the nearby shelter for a rest. As she was sunning herself, a visitor came out of the hospital across the road and joined her. When they got into conversation the visitor poured out her worries. Then, remarking how much better she felt for having got things off her chest, she jumped on the bus and waved good-bye.

Now the convalescent woman walks to the shelter each day and sits there for a spell. Often she's able to bring comfort to other worried hospital visitors, simply by listening and chatting to them.

Next time you're standing in a bus queue, smile to your neighbour. You never know how much it may mean to a stranger.

WHEN Michelangelo was preparing to sculpt the figure *David*, he first studied the character of the brave young shepherd boy.

The artist began by asking himself: " When did David achieve greatness? Was it when he killed Goliath? Or when he *decided* to do it?"

He concluded that it was the decision and not the slaying that made David a giant in his own right.

Look back on your own life. Haven't your greatest struggles taken place in your heart and mind? And isn't it there that your finest victories have been won?

NOVEMBER

Wednesday—November 1.

MARGARET E. SANGSTER, who died in 1912, penned the following lines entitled " The Duty of Friendship " :

Comfort one another
For the way is often dreary
And the feet are often weary,
And the heart is very sad.
There is heavy burden-bearing,
When it seems that none are caring,
And we half-forget that ever we were glad.

Comfort one another
With the hand-clasp close and tender,
With the sweetness love can render
And the looks of friendly eyes.
Do not wait with words unspoken,
While life's daily break is broken—
Gentle speech is oft like manna from the skies.

Thursday—November 2.

I WAS preparing to set light to a bonfire of garden rubbish one week-end when a tousled head, wearing a wide grin and a few dirty smudges, appeared over the wall.

" Hello," said Andrew, who's nine, and a Cub Scout. " D'you know the best way to light a fire with two sticks ?"

" Rub them together ?" I suggested.

" No," grinned Andrew. " Make sure one of them is a match !"

And down he ducked before I'd time to wave my hoe at him !

THE FRIENDSHIP BOOK

HANK was a cowboy. He worked on a ranch in Texas, lived in a cabin, and his only possessions were the clothes he stood in, his boots, his lariat, his saddle and his horse.

One day he found himself in one of the biggest stores in Dallas. He walked around for a long time, gazing in bewilderment at the variety of goods on display. He ventured into every department — the hardware, radio, toys, millinery, food, footwear, men's outfitting, soft furnishings and many others — and at last an assistant stepped forward. " Anything I can get you, sir ?" she asked.

Hank smiled. " Thanks a lot," he said, " But I reckon there's nothing here I'm needing."

Yes, you're rich if there's nothing you need !

TWO travellers were approaching the statue of a knight in shining armour from different directions.

" What a lovely gold shield," commented one, while the other said, " You mean a silver shield." As they argued with growing anger, a local inhabitant pointed out, " You are both right and both wrong. Half of the shield is gold and the other half silver, and it depends which side you see it from."

There are two sides to every argument, and we should always make sure we take a close look at the other side as well as our own.

BUT thou, O Lord, shalt endure for ever; and thy remembrance unto all generations.

THE FRIENDSHIP BOOK

THERE'S someone old and lonely
Who lives along the way,
You'd like to go and visit
But you'd not know what to say?
My friend, you needn't worry;
If good-will you have to spare,
You'll do the job that's needed
By simply being there.

LENNY was an inmate of the Spitalfields Crypt for alcoholics and drop-outs in London's East End.

Years of drinking and living rough had taken their toll, but there was one thing he treasured and would not part with — an old leather Bible.

One afternoon Princess Alexandra dropped in. She'd cut the ribbon when the Crypt was opened and now, five years later, she wanted to see how things were going. She had a chat with all concerned, including Lenny.

" Look, dearie," he said, " I'd like to remember this day. How about giving me an autograph ?"

In no way offended by his " matey " approach, she found a pen in her handbag. But what could she sign it on ? Lenny had an inspiration — the front page of his precious Bible.

A few months later the Warden of the Crypt was to leave. He had seen Lenny through many rough spells, and Lenny wanted to express his gratitude. But how could he ? He was broke, as usual. Then he remembered that he still had his old Bible. He shuffled up to the Warden, and presented his friend with his dearest possession.

God bless you, Lenny !

THE FRIENDSHIP BOOK

YOU are a happy teenager. Just left school and looking forward to teacher training college. Then, out of the blue, it's found you've multiple sclerosis.

That is what happened to April Nye, of Dover. It seemed her dream of working with children would never come true. However, she was given a job as an unqualified teacher. She loved her work, and her pupils loved her. Then it was decided all unqualified teachers would have to go — April among them.

For two years she grew slowly more helpless. But one day she told her parents she wanted to live on her own. A girl who could not stand unaided, let alone walk! How on earth would she manage?

April still can't walk without help, but she looks after herself in her own house, cooks and cleans, though even washing a teacup is a triumph for her. She works tirelessly for the old and ill, writes and produces musical shows and concerts, and works two days a week in a hospital for handicapped boys, bringing to it the special understanding of one who really knows what a handicap means.

Nearly twelve years ago, in effect, April was told she was finished. She could have believed it. Instead, she made up her mind to prove the doubters wrong. And how splendidly she has succeeded!

IN old China they used to say :
If there is righteousness in the heart, there will be beauty in the character ; if there is beauty in the character, there will be harmony in the home ; if there is harmony in the home, there will be order in the nation ; if there is order in the nation, there will be peace in the world.

M

FRIDAY—NOVEMBER 10.

WILLIAM GRAHAM lived in Kilwinning, where he was an elder of the Abbey Kirk for over 30 years. He wrote these lines and carried them in his head all his days. They are a creed any man might be proud to follow —

To live as gently as I can; to be, no matter where,
a man;
To take what comes of good or ill; to cling to faith
or honour still;
To do my best, and let that stand as record of my
brain and hand.
And then, should failure come to me, still work and
hope for victory;
To live undaunted, unafraid, of any step that I
have made;
To be without pretence or sham, exactly what men
think I am.

SATURDAY—NOVEMBER 11.

I WAS preparing to travel south on business and the Lady of the House was helping me by looking up the train timetable. As she did so, she began to smile. " What's the joke ?" I queried.

" Just something Rose said once," she replied, referring to a friend. It seems Rose and her husband had to go somewhere by train, and he suggested the 10.10 a.m. But Rose shook her head.

" Nobody ever travels by *that* train," she declared. " It's always far too crowded !"

Only a woman could have said it !

SUNDAY—NOVEMBER 12.

IT is better to trust in the Lord than to put confidence in man.

MONDAY—NOVEMBER 13.

THE association of ideas in young children often makes me smile. There was the small boy, for instance, who was taken to church for the first time and was warned by his parent to be very quiet as the preacher was about to pray.

The child stared at the pulpit and then whispered back, "He can't be, Dad. He hasn't got his pyjamas on!"

TUESDAY—NOVEMBER 14.

THE secret of contentment, they say, is to live a day at a time. But is that really possible?

For none of us can really live just for the moment. What we did yesterday affects today, and what we plan for tomorrow depends on what we think today. It's like a stream ever flowing.

Time and purpose go together. And all the time we are building up our character. Thoughts and actions far distant will be shaped by what we do today.

WEDNESDAY—NOVEMBER 15.

THE letter bore no name and address. It came from overseas and across the flap were these words:

Dear Letter, go on your way o'er mountain, plain or sea;
God bless all who speed your flight to where I wish you be.
And bless all those beneath the roof where I bid you rest;
But bless even more the one to whom this letter is addressed.

It is not poetry; it is not even good verse. But doesn't it warm the heart to get a message like that?

THURSDAY—NOVEMBER 16.

HE was the happiest man in town. A wealthy businessman? No, his job, six days a week, was to wash dirty motor cars.

What a pride he took in that job! He washed them with such thoroughness and such pride that you could run your hand along the inside of the mudguard on the wing and withdraw it spotless.

Someone said that what the world needs, and what God needs, is not so much people who can do extraordinary things, as people who can do ordinary things extraordinarily well. A bus conductor or conductress can collect fares in a way that lights up the whole day for passengers. A shop assistant can serve customers in a way that makes this world a better place for everyone who enters the shop.

And you and me? What can we do? Let's make a fresh start today.

FRIDAY—NOVEMBER 17.

FROM Mrs D. Hunt of Warlingham, Suffolk, I I received this poem with a lovely thought—not just for the old, but the young as well. She calls it "A Virtue":

I've passed my three-score years and ten,
And soon I'll reach four-score;
Now I must learn to realise
There can't be many more.
And so, I ask myself at times,
What virtue I would treasure
If I could have my life again
To give more people pleasure;
Of all the traits I call to mind
Please grant me, I implore,
To learn the art of being kind
To more, and more, and more.

THE FRIENDSHIP BOOK

ON my desk as I write is a little black diary. Its cover is torn and worn, and many of its pages are loose. And yet I handle it with reverence and wonder. It was sent to me by John Kavanagh, of St Mary's Road, Eccles, who tells me he used to work with the man who wrote it, Alf Ryder.

Alf, a pensioner now, was taken prisoner at Dunkirk, and spent five years in a p.o.w. camp. When the hours seemed long he would take out his diary and just write down his thoughts in verse. Some were of his wife. Others of his longing to be home. But one of the finest is called, simply, *Courage*. In a way, its message is as true today as it was more than 30 years ago :

It's easy to be nice, boys, when everything's OK, it's easy to be cheerful when you're having your own way; but can you hold your head up and take it on the chin, when your heart is nearly breaking and you feel like giving in?

It was easy back in Britain among the friends and folks, but now you miss the friendly hand, the joys, the songs and jokes; the road ahead is stony and unless you're strong in mind, you'll find it isn't long before you're lagging far behind.

You know there is a saying that sunshine follows rain, and soon enough you'll realise that joy will follow pain. Let courage be your password, make fortitude your guide, and you will triumph in the end whatever may betide.

When John told old Alf he'd like to send his book to me, Alf said, " But who would want to read that?" I think Alf would be surprised . . .

BE still, and know that I am God.

PARTNERS

A man is proud, with such good friends,
The land to turn and till;
Their strength—aye, and their beauty, too,
Are fit match for his skill.

DAVID HOPE

THE FRIENDSHIP BOOK

A READER saw a young man singing to his baby daughter, and wrote to tell me about it.

It happened not in their home, or while they were out for a walk in the park — but in church, where the child had been brought to be christened. After the ceremony, the custom in that church is for the father to stand near the font with his baby in his arms, facing the congregation while they sing the blessing.

The child, then, had been baptised. The organ sounded a chord. The congregation began to sing. And so, I'm told, did that young man. He stood before the congregation with his baby girl in his arms, she looking up at him, and he looking down at her, as he sang —

" *The Lord bless thee and keep thee; the Lord make his face to shine upon thee, and be gracious unto thee; the Lord lift up his countenance upon thee, and give thee peace.*"

What a moving moment it was for the congregation, and what a perfect prayer for a father to offer for his child, asking that the little life, begun only a few short weeks earlier, might be blessed: filled with grace and sunshine; kept in safety and surrounded with joy and peace.

May it be so for little Kathleen.

A. J. GOSSIP used to love to tell a story about Mungo Park, the great explorer. He had been journeying for days and miles in the wilds of China, in the most desolate surroundings. Then quite suddenly he saw on the ground at his feet a little blue flower. Mungo Park looked up at the sky and then said gently, " God has been here!"

THE FRIENDSHIP BOOK

ASK my friend Tom to help you
And he'll give a little grin.
And no matter how he's burdened
Tom will say, " I'll fit it in."

THURSDAY—NOVEMBER 23.

DICK WALSH is a bus driver. On the face of it, that's an everyday, ordinary job that many people might think isn't much fun. Especially in wintry weather, when there are icy roads, blizzards and sometimes fog to contend with.

Yet lots of people envy Dick Walsh, who drives the bus on the Dunoon to Toward run. For Dick always seems so happy in his work. He has so many friends, and his bus is such a cheery place.

Of course, Dick has *made* his bus the friendliest in Scotland. For example, he'll take a detour to drop a pensioner off at her gate. If one of his regulars isn't at the stop in the morning, then Dick will wait till he turns up. When an old body who's a bit shaky on her legs, or a housewife laden with parcels and messages is ready to get off the bus, Dick will be out of his seat as soon as he has pulled up, giving her a hand. And it's the same when he stops to pick them up. What's more, mothers know they don't need to worry about the children if Dick's driving, for when he sets them down at their stop, he'll keep an eye on them to see they're safely on their way before he goes off again.

All this doesn't mean Dick believes driving a bus is the best job in the world. What he *does* believe is that your job — any job — is worth doing as well as you are able. That's why he's happy. That's why he's liked by everyone. And that's why his is the friendliest bus in Scotland.

THE FRIENDSHIP BOOK

THE Rev. Dr Harry Whitley told how, when he was minister at Port Glasgow, he received an excited telephone call one Christmas Eve from the local Roman Catholic priest. " Come quickly. Something dreadful has happened."

The minister went to the chapel immediately and was met by the priest, who told him, " The Baby Jesus has disappeared from the crib."

Just then a little girl came in, wheeling a pram in which lay the missing child doll. As she gently replaced it in the cradle, she looked up with the thrill of delight in her eyes : " I just thought that Baby Jesus would like a walk in my pram." And then off she went, completely unaware of the consternation she had caused, or the large lumps in the throats of the two clergymen !

AS many will remember, George VI had an impediment in his speech. He often found difficulty in framing his words.

One day he was seeing over a certain film studio. By an unfortunate coincidence, the engineer showing him round had exactly the same kind of impediment. In his nervousness the engineer found he was becoming worse and worse.

King George put his hand on the man's shoulder. " It's all right, friend," he said. " I know what it's like."

From that moment, the two got on famously.

FOR thy mercy is great unto the heavens, and thy truth unto the clouds.

MONDAY—NOVEMBER 27.

YOU'RE too old for fairy tales? Well, here's one with a difference:

A fairy visited this world in order to find out what kind of people were really happy. She came to a large house where very rich people lived. They had horses and carriages, flowers, pictures, music, and all kinds of luxuries. And yet they were not *happy*. In fact, the fairy found only one happy person in the whole great household — and he was the servant boy who cleaned the boots, carried in the coals, and did all sorts of odd jobs, singing away the whole of the time from morning to night.

His wise mother had taught him that to be of use to others was the best and highest thing that any one could do — and in so doing, she had given him a priceless gift — contentment.

TUESDAY—NOVEMBER 28.

A TWELVE-Page magazine called *The Road* came into the house the other day. It seems that Peggy Harding of Avon, who suffers from ill-health, began some time ago to edit and circulate *The Road* amongst other housebound people.

It's full of messages, little poems and other items sent in to Peggy by readers scattered all over the country. Peggy calls her readers " the Fellowship of the Road," and she tells me that they belong to all religions and that amongst their aims is " to link sufferers together through prayer and correspondence," and " to bring spiritual comfort and inspiration."

Amongst their other aims, I rather liked one which could mean a lot to a lonely person living on his or her own: " to try to remember their birthday !"

THE FRIENDSHIP BOOK

WHAT a wonderful thing is friendship! High or low, rich or poor, we all need good friends. Pitt, the great Prime Minister, had a friend called Dundas, of whom he once said, " Dundas is no orator, Dundas is not even a speaker, but Dundas will go out with you in any kind of weather."

You could depend on him hail, rain or shine.

THINK of it. You're a fit young man in your 30's, always on the go. Suddenly you are robbed of the power of your legs, and told you'll never walk again.

That, precisely, is what happened to Elliot Patterson. A tyre of his car burst on the A1. He crashed, and lay trapped for three hours with a broken back.

How do you cope with that? Elliot must have had his moments of despair. But, if he did, he kept them to himself, and from the start he made up his mind that life was still for living.

He took up archery, and the following year he won the Scottish archery title. He began playing basketball—from his wheelchair. He'd been a naval diving expert for 15 years—so he took charge of the Sea Cadets, calling his orders to the boys in their boat from his wheelchair on the quayside, and proudly watched them win two regattas. He has even been commissioned as an officer in the Royal Naval Reserve—the only wheelchair officer in any of the services.

You can let misfortune or tragedy overwhelm you, and face it with a chip on your shoulder. Or, like Elliot, you can take a deep breath, put the past behind you, and make the best of it.

Can you doubt which way is the finest?

DECEMBER

MRS BROWN of Edinburgh keeps a very special scrapbook. And it's all because she's been so lucky. She's middle-aged, with two lively youngsters and a good husband. Her parents live nearby and they all get on well. In fact, Mrs Brown knows how lucky she is — and sometimes wonders just how long it can last. Some day, she feels, she may not be so lucky. And as she's never been tested, she doesn't know how she'll stand up to misfortune.

That's why she keeps what she calls her Book of Courage. Every time she reads of people who have known sorrow and hardship but who have continued to face life even when their hearts were breaking, she cuts out their story and pastes it in her book.

If and when her own turn comes, she hopes she'll be able to turn the pages of her Book of Courage and perhaps find strength from its stories. And if ever she gets too sorry for herself, she'll pick up her book and take courage from it.

THE children of a Hebridean island school were presenting a nativity play. Little David, who was playing the innkeeper, was most upset at having to turn Joseph away. In his own home—as in all the island — the door was never shut to anyone.

On the night of the play, as he said his piece, his heart swelled with genuine compassion for Mary and Joseph. " There is no room at the inn. You must go away," he dutifully intoned. Then, quietly, he added, " But come back later and have a cup of tea."

THE FRIENDSHIP BOOK

THE earth is the Lord's, and the fulness thereof; the world, and they that dwell therein.

CECIL BEATON took many official photographs of Royalty. He was an artist of the camera who made every photograph look as if it was the only one on its subject that could possibly have been taken. But things did not always go smoothly.

One day, not long after the death of King George VI, he was called on to photograph the present Queen Mother. Everything seemed to go wrong, including the jamming of his camera shutter. Some lesser people might have showed signs of impatience, but that was not her way. In a book of reminiscences, Cecil Beaton writes:

" Her smile and warmth of sympathy made it seem as if the sun had come out." He goes on, " She manages to disperse anxiety and care, even makes it seem impossible that people should ever behave badly or that things could go wrong. She will always say just the one thing that puts people at ease and makes them feel a glow of happiness."

Isn't that a wonderful way to be thought of?

THE clock shrills out its warning,
*   It's a bitter winter morning*
And you feel you've got a cold
*   And life is rotten;*
But there's breakfasts to prepare
So you stagger down the stair
And by the time you've made the tea
*   Your cold's forgotten!*

WEDNESDAY—DECEMBER 6.

FOUR short lines that sum up friendship:
Each season brings its colours bright,
For constant hope and cheer,
But friendship weaves the brightest hues
In all we hold most dear.

THURSDAY—DECEMBER 7.

BEFORE moving to their present home, Mr and Mrs Christie lived near Manchester, where a housing development and a new road were being built.

One night, Mrs Christie was anxiously waiting for her husband to come home from work, as there was a thick fog. He was late in arriving, and afterwards he told her that as he walked along beside the new houses, he had heard a voice calling for help. He had made his way through the rubble towards the voice, and found a man hopelessly lost in the fog. He'd wandered into an empty house that had been newly built and had no idea where he was.

Mr Christie told the man to take his arm, guided him back through the building site to the road, and asked where he lived. Then he had led him through the night safely to his gate. The stranger couldn't thank him enough. " But I've no idea how on earth you were able to see your way through that fog," he added. Mr Christie smiled, and said goodnight.

What that stranger will never know—unless he happens to read this—is that the man who guided him home on that fearful night is totally blind. To him, of course, the fog meant nothing—his way was as clear as if the sun had been shining.

Sometimes a handicap can be a blessing, if you know what I mean . . .

FRIDAY—DECEMBER 8.

MAE McEWAN of Troon calls this "My Selfish Prayer." I don't really think the title is appropriate, but I do agree with the sentiments she expresses:

> *In this busy world, I pray,*
> *Grant me, please, O Lord, each day,*
> *Just some moments to be free,*
> *To sit alone and just be me.*
> *Let me express my thoughts in rhyme,*
> *It's not a lot I ask, just time,*
> *I ask you, Lord, to let me be*
> *A little while, each day, just me.*

SATURDAY—DECEMBER 9.

DURING the last war, Tom Davidson and his big brother were evacuated from their home in a city tenement to a big house in the country. Grubby and dusty from their journey, they were met by a large woman of commanding presence, who marched them straight upstairs to the bathroom, all tiled and shining with chromium, where a bath full of piping hot water was awaiting them. It was the first real bathroom—and the first real bath—they'd ever seen.

" Now," she said firmly, " off with your clothes and in you get."

As she strode off to fetch some towels, Tom's big brother—seven years old, and wise in the ways of the world—dug him in the ribs. " Don't take off a thing," he whispered urgently. " I think she's going to drown us !"

SUNDAY—DECEMBER 10.

LEAD me, O Lord, in thy righteousness.

THE FRIENDSHIP BOOK

MONDAY—DECEMBER 11.

> *I REMEMBER vanished faces*
> *When Christmas time comes round,*
> *But I don't feel sad or lonely*
> *For an inner peace I've found.*
> *There's pleasure in the children*
> *As I watch them at their play,*
> *For it's all part of the pattern*
> *Of a world new-made today.*

TUESDAY—DECEMBER 12.

WHO is the most important person in a school?
It would be hard to argue if you answered
" the headmaster." But I'm sure many headmasters
might say there could be another answer.

I'm thinking of Charlie Stronach, head janitor at
Mackie Academy, Stonehaven. A janitor's isn't an
easy job. You're always on call and the hours are
many. You're there to open the school long before
teachers or children start to straggle in. You're often
back at night for badminton or evening classes. Lost
gym shoes, bandages for bleeding knees, fixing the
central heating, maybe even feeding the school
guinea pigs at holidays, the list is endless.

Charlie met every problem with a smile and
nothing was ever too much bother. To Charlie,
Mackie Academy was *his* school, with his teachers,
his pupils and his cleaners. And his devotion to
making life pleasanter for everyone in it was bound-
less. When he passed away quite suddenly, there
wasn't a dry eye in the school. I know this from a
woman who is proud to call herself one of Charlie's
cleaners.

Jannies are usually in the background till something goes wrong, but our schools would be poorer
places without them.

SUCH BEAUTY

All year Nature's magic
Has prepared the way for this,
Through spring and summer weather
To autumn's golden bliss.

DAVID HOPE

WEDNESDAY—DECEMBER 13.

HAVE you ever stood in a pulpit?
    If so, there's just a chance you might have stumbled on the secret hidden in almost every one in the land ! Before I tell you what it is, here's a story about Professor William Barclay the Scottish churchman and writer.

Like me, you may have marvelled at his phenomenal knowledge and his amazing memory. But did you know that the first time he stood in a pulpit, he had one of the most unnerving experiences that can befall any minister?

He forgot the Lord's Prayer ! It wasn't that he didn't know it well enough. The fact is, he knew it too well—and felt he didn't need the words before him. All was fine for the first few lines—then, disaster. His mind went blank !

That's why, to this day, he never enters a pulpit without a copy of the Lord's Prayer, just in case. And that, too, is the secret most pulpits hold.

"Drying up" is something every minister dreads—so much so, almost every one hides a copy of the Lord's Prayer somewhere—pasted inside the big Bible, or pinned on the book-rest.

As Professsor Barclay so wisely says, "Don't take familiar things too much for granted !"

THURSDAY—DECEMBER 14.

MOIRA, aged four, was taken to see the doctor. "Put your tongue out, dear," he said kindly, "and we'll see what it looks like." Shyly, Moira poked the tip of her tongue between her lips.

The doctor smiled. "That won't do," he said heartily. "Put it right out !"

Tears welled up into Moira's eyes. "I can't," she wailed. "It's joined on to me at the back !"

THE FRIENDSHIP BOOK

JOHN and Alec, two brothers, were regular visitors
to the Church of Scotland Eventide Home at
Belmont, near Dundee. They came to see their
mother who was a resident there. As time went by,
they noticed that no visitor ever came to see Mrs
MacFarlane who, had spent most of her life
in Derbyshire and had lost touch with all her old
friends.

So one of the men went over and had a few words
with Mrs MacFarlane, leaving the other with their
mother. Lonely Mrs MacFarlane was so grateful
that it soon became part of their visit that each one of
them should sit in turn and talk to her.

Eventually, Mrs MacFarlane passed on. Among
the handful of people at her funeral were the two
men, with their wives, come to pay their last respects
to a woman who had no claim on them — except the
claim that the solitary and lonely should have on
all men and women who have love and compassion
in their hearts.

SATURDAY—DECEMBER 16.

YOU cannot see the light for clouds
That dark around you loom,
You cannot feel life's warmth—no sun
Can penetrate the gloom.
Yet, trusting, venture bravely on,
Even though all hope seems vain,
For, come what may, joy will one day
Lift up your heart again.

SUNDAY—DECEMBER 17.

LEAD me in thy truth, and teach me: for thou
are the God of my salvation . . .

THE FRIENDSHIP BOOK

MONDAY—DECEMBER 18.

TOM CURR, a councillor in Edinburgh, gave his time and talent to a great many charitable causes. But his chief dedication was to the local company of the Boys' Brigade in Leith. He illustrated his talks to them with cartoons and told jokes to lighten the mood of his address.

Occasionally he spoke on radio and, one night, at the weekly parade of the company, a boy came up to him and said, " Mr Curr, I heard you on the wireless this week." " Did you?" said Mr Curr, rather pleased. " Did you recognise my voice?" The boy shook his head. " No, but I recognised all your stories."

Tom Curr, a humble man, used to take great pleasure in telling this tale against himself.

TUESDAY—DECEMBER 19.

THE other evening, the Lady of the House and I dropped in on old Mrs Jones. She had spent all her early life in the country and was over the moon because she had just found a little account book kept by her father when he was in charge of a small farm.

She read out some of the figures and it was like a glimpse of another age. They all worked so hard — and were paid so little for it.

" I suppose it *was* hard work," agreed Mrs Jones. " But we were all very happy together. I remember working alongside a friend, Mrs Robertson. Every now and then she would look back and say, ' Well, that's another row I won't have to do again.' "

Of course, we're all much better off now, and a good thing too. But we shouldn't forget brave souls like Mrs Roberston and all the hard work they did, so cheerfully and uncomplainingly, and for such small rewards.

REWARD

A farmer's year of care
Scents the evening air;
Beneath the sinking sun
Rests his harvest safely won.

DAVID HOPE

WEDNESDAY—DECEMBER 20.

THE following pieces of advice from the boss appear on a notice in a factory in Canada:

You owe so much to yourself you cannot afford to owe anybody else.

Dishonesty is never an accident. Good men, like good women, never see temptation when they meet it.

Don't do anything here which hurts your self-respect.

Don't tell me what I'd like to hear, but what I ought to hear. I don't want a valet to my vanity.

THURSDAY—DECEMBER 21.

GOING into hospital is an ordeal at any time, but to be suddenly whisked away at three o'clock on a winter's morning is a real test of fortitude. That is what happened to my friend Alec. He knew it was a marvellous new hospital he was going to, and that he would be in the hands of experts, but still, he was a very worried man as the ambulance drove out of the darkness into the light of the reception area.

Alec is now making a fine recovery from a heart attack and it was while I was sitting by his bedside at visiting hour that he told me about the ambulance man who had brought him in.

" He just took charge of cheering me up," said Alec. " Mind you, I can hardly remember a thing he said. But he made a whole lot of little jokes. and it took my mind right off my worries. What a difference he made!"

I'm sure you know exactly what Alec meant. However wonderful a hospital, nothing can replace the small human touches that bring reassurance and comfort.

FRIDAY—DECEMBER 22.

MRS ELIZABETH FRY, the great reformer, once issued half a dozen rules for the guidance of life:

1. Never lose any time. I do not think that lost which is spent in amusement or recreation every day, but always be in the habit of being employed.
2. Never err the least in truth.
3. Never say an ill thing of a person when thou canst say a good thing of him. Not only speak charitable, but feel so.
4. Never be irritable or unkind to anybody.
5. Never indulge thyself in luxuries that are not necessary.
6. Do all things with consideration, and when thy path to act right is most difficult, put confidence in that Power alone which is able to assist thee, and exert thine own powers as far as they go.

SATURDAY—DECEMBER 23.

ROSIE ROWE sells hundreds of pounds worth of Christmas cards and seasonal gifts on behalf of the mentally handicapped. In fact, her sales are well over £500 every year.

You're impressed? But there's more to the story than that. For Rosie has been a hospital patient herself for the last thirty years and since she was six years old she has been confined to a wheelchair.

She never feels the least bit sorry for herself. She knows there are too many in greater need — and she is happy to do what she can for them.

SUNDAY—DECEMBER 24.

AND they came with haste and they found Mary and Joseph, and the babe lying in a manger.

MONDAY—DECEMBER 25.

YOU can know someone for a long, long time and still not know them, if you get my meaning. I am thinking of a relative of the Lady of the House, who sometimes comes to see us.

Rachel has just enough money to get by, and seems to be quite contented living on her own. Her husband was an official in a far-away part of what used to be the British Empire, but he died several years ago. She rarely spoke of him, and she sometimes gave the impression of being, well, just a little unfeeling.

So we thought until one day the talk turned to buying presents for Christmas. Suddenly she burst out: " Christmas is the one day in the year I can't stand. You don't know how horrible it is to waken up in the morning with no one there to say ' Happy Christmas !' "

If we have our way Rachel won't spend this Christmas alone. Perhaps you, too, have somebody like Rachel for whom Christmas is a time of sadness rather than of joy.

TUESDAY—DECEMBER 26.

EVERY year Mrs Miller makes 29 Christmas puddings. She calls them her " specials." And she gives them all away. She lives in Forfar in Scotland, and she has been delighting her friends this way for years.

Twenty-nine Christmas puddings . . . That's pretty good going for a Senior Citizen, isn't it? And a very senior Senior Citizen she is, too, for Mrs Miller is 86!

Do you wonder that her " specials " have a place of honour on every Christmas dinner table they grace.

WINTER FUN

We built a fine snow castle,
   Its walls were thick and high.
We thought that it was strong enough
   All weathers to defy.
But came a warm and sunny day—
Our castle melted quite away.

DAVID HOPE

WEDNESDAY—DECEMBER 27.

MRS ELIZABETH GOZNEY of Berkhamsted
sent me this " recipe for living " :
Take kindly thoughts with more to spare,
Add tact and patience—mix with care;
A dash of faith, and hope—a smile
To make it all seem so worthwhile,
And weigh upon the scales of life
The joy that cancels out the strife;
Resulting recipe is such—
It costs so little—it means so much!

THURSDAY—DECEMBER 28.

EVER heard of a " Grudge Day "?
When Mrs Scott, of Dumfries, was a girl at
school in Galloway, they had a Grudge Day every
year. First, the boys were sent out to rake up all
the autumn leaves that had fallen around the school,
and gather them into a pile in the playground. Then
pupils and teachers alike wrote down all the grudges
they held against anyone else, and the lists were
collected.

That afternoon, just before four o'clock, everyone
marched outside to form a circle around the mound
of leaves. The lists of grudges were placed on top and
then, before the assembled school, the headmaster
stepped forward and set light to the bonfire. The
leaves, dry as tinder, blazed furiously — and with
them, every grudge went up in flames. " At that
moment," says Mrs Scott, " friendships were
restored, arguments forgotten, wrongs forgiven,
quarrels patched up, all without a single word being
spoken."

I don't know who first thought of holding a
" Grudge Day," but don't you agree it was rather
a fine idea?

THE FRIENDSHIP BOOK

EDWARD EVERETT HALE, a Lord Chief Justice of England, once gave some wise advice to a friend who was anxious to stay among " cultivated people " and enjoy " good society." He counselled him, " Make good society *where you are.*"

It was the rule he followed himself. Wherever he went, the company was always good. His genuine interest in everybody, his sympathy, his quick, witty mind, his way of seeing the best in every happening, gathered people around as to a magnet. Where he was, there was always good conversation. He was at home among all classes because he did not recognise any.

IT is not always easy to choose the appropriate message for a greeting card. George Lansbury, respected for his principles as well as his politics, chose well when he picked these lines by an American author for his personal Christmas card:

Let me live in a house by the side of a road
   Where the race of men go by;
The men who are good and the men who are bad,
   As good and as bad as I.

I would not sit in the scorner's seat
   Or hurl the cynic's ban;
Let me live in a house by the side of a road
   And be a friend to man.

LET integrity and uprightness preserve me; for I wait on thee.

Where the Photographs were taken

PERFECT — *St John's, Woking, Surrey.*

COME OUT — *Eildon Hills, Roxburghshire.*

LUNCHTIME — *Haddenham, Buckinghamshire.*

MASTER-STROKE — *Elgol, Skye.*

COME AND BUY — *Evesham, Worcestershire.*

RIVER DAYS — *St Clement, Cornwall.*

BEST OF ALL — *Sissinghurst, Kent.*

OVER THE HILLS — *Loch Shiel, Argyll / Inverness-shire.*

COME IN — *Selworthy, Somerset.*

THROUGH THE AGES — *Durham Cathedral.*

GATEWAYS — *Lychgate, Stoke Poges, Buckinghamshire.*

RELEASE — *Mickleham Woods, Surrey.*

THANKSGIVING — *Hambleden, Buckinghamshire.*

SUCH BEAUTY — *River Tay, near Dunkeld, Perthshire.*

REWARD — *near Newtonmore, Inverness-shire.*

Printed and Published by D. C. Thomson & Co., Ltd.
185 Fleet Street, London EC4A 2HS.
© D. C. Thomson & Co., Ltd., 1977.

COIN COLLECTOR'S PRICE GUIDE

REVISED EDITION

Robert Obojski

Sterling Publishing Co., Inc.
New York

ACKNOWLEDGMENTS

In compiling the values of coins for this volume, careful study has been devoted to published authorities, as well as prices quoted in recent dealer advertisements and auction sales.

In particular, the book owes a great deal to the cordial cooperation of Burton Hobson, Chairman and CEO of Sterling, Joseph H. Rose, past President of Harmer Rooke Numismatists, Ltd., and Lou Pascale, of MTB Banking Corporation, who assisted in the pricing for this new edition. We also wish to acknowledge the assistance given us by André Girard and Michael Francis of the Royal Canadian Mint at Ottawa, especially in regard to providing photos of new issues. We also shouldn't fail to mention John Woodside, Sterling's Editorial Director, who played a key role in seeing the last several editions of *Coin Collector's Price Guide* through the presses. Producing *Coin Collector's Price Guide* has taken a team effort.

The magnificent enlarged photographs which appear on pages 8–16 were made by DeVere Baker of the American Numismatic Society. The coins illustrating the various conditions were selected by the Capitol Coin Company.

We must also thank Q. David Bowers, Chairman of Bowers & Merena Galleries, Inc., Wolfeboro, New Hampshire, for supplying us with information on his sale of the "Louis E. Eliasberg, Sr. Collection of United States Coins" staged this past May 20–21, 1996 at New York City. Many records for rarities were broken at this historic auction, which grossed nearly $12.5 million. A number of those record prices are cited in this catalog. We've also cited a number of prices attained for Canadian coins at Bowers & Merena Galleries sale of the "Norweb Canada Collection" staged at Baltimore on November 15, 1996.   —*Robert Obojski*

10   9   8   7   6   5   4   3   2   1

Published by Sterling Publishing Co., Inc.
387 Park Avenue South, New York, N.Y. 10016
© 1997 by Sterling Publishing Co., Inc.
Originally published as *Coin Collector's Handbook*
Distributed in Canada by Sterling Publishing
$^{c}/o$ Canadian Manda Group, One Atlantic Avenue, Suite 105
Toronto, Ontario, Canada M6K 3E7
Distributed in Great Britain and Europe by Cassell PLC
Wellington House, 125 Strand, London WC2R 0BB, England
Distributed in Australia by Capricorn Link (Australia) Pty Ltd.
P.O. Box 6651, Baulkham Hills, Business Centre, NSW 2153, Australia

Sterling ISBN 0-8069-3192-2

CONTENTS

COIN COLLECTOR'S PRICE GUIDE
UPDATED EDITION

The *Coin Collector's Price Guide* covers all United States and Canadian coins, from the historic U.S. Continental issues of 1776 through to the commemorative issues from the mid-to-the-late 1990s, and Canadian commemoratives issued up to the mid-to-the-late 1990s.

Complete with the latest up-to-the-minute retail value—based on auction records, sales catalogs, market reports, and dealer consultations—this comprehensive guide provides valuations for as many as seven different conditions (from "Good" to "Uncirculated" and "Proof") and pictures every major variety, making identification easy. It also specifies individual dates and mint marks (plus recognized collectors' varieties within these groups) and mintage figures for all issues and every major variety.

A Note About Commemoratives . . .

In recent years both the United States and Canada have greatly accelerated their commemorative coin issuance programs. In the 1980s the U.S. has produced five major commemorative coin sets: a one dollar silver and ten dollars gold in 1983–84 to honor the 1984 Los Angeles Summer Olympics; a fifty cents silver, one dollar silver and five dollars gold in 1986 for the Statue of Liberty Centennial; a one dollar silver and five dollars gold in 1987 for the Constitution Bicentennial; a one dollar silver and five dollars gold in 1988 for the Seoul Olympics and a fifty cents silver, one dollar silver and five dollars gold in 1989 for the Bicentennial of the American Congress. All these 1980s commemoratives have become highly popular with collectors throughout the world.

The United States Mint continued its ambitious commemorative program into the early and mid-1990s, with the coins treating a wide variety of topics, including the "Mount Rushmore Golden Anniversary," the "Korean War Memorial," the "United Nations Service Organization Golden Anniversary," the "Barcelona Summer Olympics," the "World Cup Soccer Tournament" and the 1996 "Atlanta Summer Olympics."

Canada turned out silver and gold sets to commemorate both the 1976 Montreal Summer Olympics and the 1988 Calgary Winter Olympics, and since 1977 has struck $100 gold commemoratives on an annual basis. Since 1969 Canada has also released a commemorative silver dollar annually.

In 1992 Canada came forth with an ambitious set of 13 coins (one a $1 value and the others 25¢ denominations), marking the 125th anniversary of Confederation. One of Canada's most attractive recent commemoratives is the 1994 "Anne of Green Gables" $200 gold coin.

Note: All values listed are in American dollars. Values in Canadian currency are slightly higher.

1

HOW TO
DETERMINE A COIN'S
CONDITION

Have you ever noticed how people react to the condition of coins? They take a childlike pleasure in a bright, clear, shiny, sharply outlined coin. Even if it's only a penny, they find something festive and cheerful about a coin when it's brand-new—just put into circulation.

On the other hand, a worn, faded, tired-looking coin, even if it's worth fifty times the value of a shiny penny, evokes no emotional reaction at all. We part with it readily, whereas disposing of the shiny new penny costs us something of a pang.

Well, the man who feels that slight tinge of regret is really akin to the coin collector, who loves coins for their own sake. The physical state of coins—*their condition*—is tremendously important to the collector. A coin in splendid condition is a desirable coin—a miniature work of art. It is likely to be worth considerably more than its face value. But a worn, faded coin is depressingly close to an anonymous metal disc, totally lacking in distinctive character.

COIN CONDITIONS

During the mid-1970s, the American Numismatic Association completed a standard grading system for coins based on a numerical scale from 1 to 70. The scale was originally devised by Dr. William H. Sheldon, a noted numismatist, for his book *Penny Whimsy* (1958), and it has now been adapted for use with the entire United States and Canadian series, thus providing uniform grading terminology. The Sheldon scale can also be easily utilized for grading most world coin issues.

According to Sheldon, the term "uncirculated," interchangeable with "mint state" (MS), refers to a coin which has never been circulated. A coin as bright as the time it was minted, or with a very light natural toning, can be described as "brilliant uncirculated." A coin which has natural toning can be described as "toned uncirculated." Except in the instance of copper coins, the presence or absence of light toning does not affect an uncirculated coin's grade. Indeed, as Sheldon emphasizes, among silver coins attractive natural toning often results in the coin bringing a premium. Moreover, because uncirculated coins may have slight imperfections, there are several subdivisions in that category within the Sheldon scale.

Here, in generalized terms, are the accepted standards for each condition:

Perfect Uncirculated (MS-70)—In perfect new condition. This is the finest quality available. Such a coin under four-power magnification shows no bag marks, lines, or other evidence of handling or contact with other coins. A brilliant coin can be described as "MS-70 brilliant," or "perfect brilliant uncirculated." An MS-70 brilliant is extremely rare, and many veteran dealers and collectors claim they've never seen one. In Europe, the absolutely perfect coin is usually referred to as FDC (Fleur de Coin).

Choice Uncirculated (MS-65)—This refers to an above-average uncirculated coin which may be brilliant or toned (and described accordingly), and which has very few bag marks. The MS-67 or MS-63 rating indicates a slightly higher or lower grade of preservation. In trying to pinpoint grades more exactly, numismatists now often use MS-67+ and MS-64 designations.

Uncirculated (MS-60)—This is called "typical uncirculated" without any other adjectives. This designation refers to a coin which has a moderate number of bag marks on its surface. Also evident may be a few minor edge nicks and marks, although not of a serious nature. A coin may be either brilliant or toned. A true uncirculated coin has no trace of wear.

Choice About Circulated (AU-55)—Only a small trace of wear is evident on the highest points of the coin. Most of the mint lustre remains.

About Uncirculated (AU-50)—Traces of wear are visible on many of the high points of the design. Only half of the mint lustre is still present.

Choice Extremely Fine (EF-45)—Light overall wear shows on all the highest points. All design details are clear and sharp. Mint lustre remains only in the protected areas of the coin's surface, such as between the star points and in the letter spaces.

Extremely Fine (EF-40)—The design is lightly and evenly worn overall, but all features are quite sharp and well defined. Small traces of lustre may show.

Choice Very Fine (VF-30)—Light even wear is visible on the surface, with wear being more evident on the highest points. All lettering and major features remain sharp.

Very Fine (VF-20)—The design exhibits moderate wear on all high points. All major details are clear.

Fine (F-12)—A moderate to considerably worn coin, but still a collectible specimen. The basic outline still must be very clear. All lettering, including the word "LIBERTY" (on coins with this feature on the shield or headband), is visible, but with some weaknesses.

Very Good (VG-8)—A much worn but not altogether unattractive coin. Specimens in this condition should be free of major gouges or other mutilations, but may be somewhat scratched from use.

Good (G-4)—A heavily worn coin. The major designs are visible but faint in many areas. The date and mint mark must be legible to qualify the coin for this rating.

About Good (AG-3)—A barely minimum-condition coin that is very heavily worn, with portions of the date, lettering and legends worn smooth. The date may be barely readable.

Poor—Coins in poor condition are usually highly undesirable and considered uncollectible. They may be bent, corroded, or completely worn down.

As in the case of coins struck for circulation, proof coins can also be graded according to the Sheldon scale. Utilizing this numbering system, the American Numismatic Association places proofs into four major categories:

Perfect Proof (Proof-70)—A coin with no handling marks, hairlines, or other defects. There must not be a single flaw. The Proof-70 may be brilliant or have natural toning.

Choice Proof (Proof-65)—This refers to a proof coin which may have a few very fine hairlines, generally from friction-type cleaning or drying after rubbing or dipping. To the unaided eye, it appears to be virtually perfect, but five-power magnification reveals some minute lines.

Proof (Proof-60)—This designation refers to a proof with a number of handling marks and hairlines which are visible to the naked eye. The Intermediate Grade, Proof-63, is widely used.

Impaired Proofs—If a proof has been excessively cleaned, has numerous marks, scratches, dents, or other flaws, it is categorized as an "impaired proof." If the coin shows extensive wear, then it is assigned one of the lesser grades: Proof-55, Proof-45, etc. It isn't logical to label a slightly worn proof as AU (about uncirculated) for it was never uncirculated to begin with—thus, the term "impaired proof" is appropriate.

U.S. COINAGE ACT OF 1965

Through the provisions of the U.S. Coinage Act of 1965, the composition of dimes, quarters and half dollars was modified to eliminate or reduce the silver content of these coins. The new "clad" or "sandwich" dimes and quarters are composed of an outer layer of copper-nickel (75 percent copper and 25 percent nickel) bonded to an inner core of pure copper.

The clad half dollar struck from 1965 through 1970 consists of an outer layer of 80 percent silver bonded to an inner core of 21 percent silver, with a total silver content of 40 percent. Due to sharply rising prices, however, all silver was removed from the Kennedy half dollars struck for circulation from 1971 on. They are now copper-nickel clad types—identical in metallic content to the current dimes and quarters. Copper also has risen in value resulting in periodic shortages of one-cent pieces. These coins also are now being struck on different planchets—copper-plated zinc. These coins weigh 19 percent less than the copper cents and the value of the metal is far below the coins' face value.

Slabbed Coins

In recent years an effective system of certifying the grading of coins is by "slabbing" them. Coins are assigned a particular grade—say, MS65—placed in a hard, transparent plastic container and sealed. This process is popularly known as slabbing. A panel indicating the coin's grade, certification number, and grading service is also inserted. As long as the seal remains unbroken, the grades are accepted.

Now look at these coins (in their exact size) side by side and notice the variation.

Proof sets

Proof coins are specially prepared with the finest workmanship and materials that modern technique can devise. They are the choicest of all our coins, as far as condition is concerned. This makes them highly desirable coins, as far as most collectors are concerned.

The subject of coin condition is far from academic. As you will see in

UNCIRCULATED (MS-60)

All the details are sharply outlined:
the shield
the eagle's eye
the eagle's neck
the eagle's feathers
the lettering on the inscription
the dots between "United" and "Quarter" and between
"America" and "Dollar"

the eagle's claws
the arrows
the leaves
the dots in the border
the lettering on the ribbon

this chapter, condition is one of the crucial factors that determine a coin's value and suitability for investment.

In order to describe in detail just how these generalized terms apply to an actual coin, let's examine greatly enlarged photographs of the reverses of eight Liberty Head ("Barber") Quarters.

EXTREMELY FINE (EF-40)

All the details are still distinct.

Note, however, that there are slight scratches on the shield, and that the feathers are slightly faded toward the sides.

There is no proof coin in these photographs, for the high luster of a proof does not show up well in a photo. In evaluating the various conditions, we shall consider 11 features of the reverse of these coins.

VERY FINE (VF-20)

The eagle's eye and neck are distinct, and so are the arrows, the leaves, the dots and lettering on the inscription.

The shield is fairly distinct, but there are some nicks on it, and there are traces of fading toward the sides.

The feathers are considerably faded toward the sides, and the outside dots are beginning to grow fuzzy.

The claws are still fairly distinct, and so is the lettering on the ribbon, although *unum* is a little faded.

FINE (F-12)

The shield and the eagle's eye are fairly distinct. However, there are some nicks and scratches on the shield and the fading toward the edges is getting more pronounced.

The neck is considerably faded, and the feathers are badly faded toward the sides.

The arrows, the leaves, and the lettering on the inscription are still distinct, and the dots in the inscription can be clearly seen.

The dots in the border have become fuzzier than in the previous condition.

The lettering on the ribbon is faded somewhat and several letters are unreadable.

The claws are no longer as distinct as they were previously.

(Note the "D" mint mark under the eagle.)

VERY GOOD (VG-8)

The eagle's eye, the leaves, the dots and the lettering on the inscription are still distinct.

The lines on the shield are completely gone, and the details on the neck have almost disappeared.

Little of the detail on the feathers is left, and the claws seem to merge with the arrows and leaves.

The arrows have grown fuzzy, and the dots in the border are no longer distinct.

The lettering on the ribbon is badly faded and is becoming more unreadable.

GOOD (G-4)

The shield is completely faded; all detail is gone on the neck.

The leaves, the inscription dots, and the inscription lettering are still distinct.

The eye is rather faint, the feathers are almost completely faded, and the claws are no longer sharply outlined.

The arrows are becoming fuzzy, and the dots in the border are considerably faded.

Most of the lettering on the ribbon is unreadable.

ABOUT GOOD (AG-3)

General comment: badly scratched and blotched.
The leaves are still distinct—the only good feature.
One of the inscription dots is clear, the other faded.
The inscription lettering is decidedly weaker than previously; the ribbon lettering is completely unreadable.
The claws are no longer sharply outlined, and the remaining features are completely rubbed off.

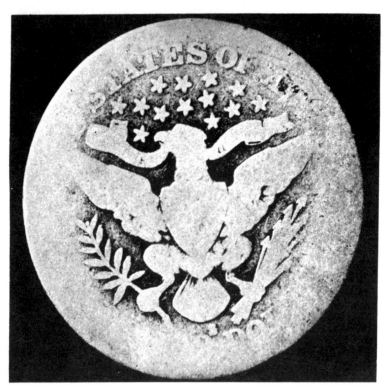

POOR

The leaves are still fairly distinct, but all the other details are completely or almost completely rubbed off.

2

CATALOG OF
UNITED STATES COINS

EARLY AMERICAN COINS

Among the coins which appeared before the first regular Mint issues of 1793, there is a great deal of variation, and considerable confusion or obscurity about their origin or the authority for issuing them.

CONTINENTAL DOLLAR

YEAR		GOOD	FINE
1776	Pewter; "CURENCY"	$1400.00	$2750.00
1776	Silver; "CURRENCY" (very rare)		
1776	Brass; "CURENCY" (rare)		
1776	Pewter; "CURRENCY"	1100.00	2500.00
1776	Pewter; E G FECIT	1100.00	2500.00
1776	Silver; E G FECIT (very rare)		

NOVA CONSTELLATIO COPPERS (CENTS)

1783	Pointed rays; "CONSTELLATIO"	30.00	100.00
1783	Blunt rays; "CONSTELATIO"	27.50	100.00
1785	Blunt rays; "CONSTELATIO"	35.00	115.00
1785	Pointed rays; "CONSTELLATIO"	25.00	85.00

BAR CENT

no date (about 1785)	250.00	500.00

Top left: the Continental Dollar, first issued in 1776. *Top right:* the Bar Cent, supposedly designed from Revolutionary soldiers' buttons, with 13 bars for the 13 states. *Bottom:* Nova Constellatio Cent, with 13 stars for the 13 states.

Most of the coins in this group were issued before the United States Mint began operating. President Washington on April 2, 1792 signed the bill authorizing the establishment of the Mint.

WASHINGTON PIECES

YEAR		GOOD	FINE	UNC.
1783	1 cent: draped bust on obverse; wreath on reverse	$25.00	$40.00	$250.00
1783	1 cent: draped bust on obverse; female figure on reverse	25.00	35.00	200.00
1783	1 cent: military bust on obverse; female figure on reverse	35.00	50.00	275.00
1783	1 cent: military busts on obverse and reverse ("double head cent"); no date	30.00	65.00	300.00
1791	1 cent: large eagle on reverse	65.00	150.00	850.00
1791	1 cent: small eagle on reverse	65.00	150.00	900.00
1791	"Liverpool" halfpenny	300.00	750.00	2500.00
1793	1 halfpenny; ship on reverse	75.00	125.00	500.00
1792	eagle cent, copper (rare)			
1792	eagle cent, silver (very rare)			
1792	eagle cent, gold (outstanding rarity)			
1792	1 cent: "WASHINGTON—PRESIDENT"	2000.00	5500.00	
1792	1 cent: "WASHINGTON—BORN VIRGINIA"	1500.00	2350.00	
1792	half dollar, silver (rare)	2250.00	4500.00	
1792	half dollar, copper	800.00	1750.00	
1792	half dollar: large eagle on reverse (outstanding rarity)			
1795	1 cent: grate reverse	65.00	125.00	275.00
1795	1 cent: no date, LIBERTY AND SECURITY	75.00	150.00	500.00
1795	1 cent: date on reverse (rare)			
1795	halfpenny; lettered edge	25.00	275.00	1000.00

FUGIO CENTS

1787	1 cent ("STATES UNITED")	50.00	125.00	600.00
1787	1 cent ("UNITED STATES")	75.00	150.00	750.00
1787	1 cent: blunt rays	80.00	175.00	1000.00
1787	1 cent ("UNITED" above, "STATES" below); rare			

There are some other varieties, generally quite rare.

EARLY MINT ISSUES

1792	half disme, silver	1300.00	3750.00	
1792	half disme, copper (outstanding rarity)			
1792	disme, silver (outstanding rarity)			
1792	disme, copper			
1792	1 cent; silver center (rare)			
1792	1 cent; no silver center (rare)			
1792	BIRCH cent (rare)			
1792	1 cent: without BIRCH (very rare)			

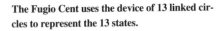

The Fugio Cent uses the device of 13 linked circles to represent the 13 states.

One of the many interesting Washington pieces issued by patriotic Americans as a tribute to an outstanding hero.

STATE COINAGE

Connecticut

		GOOD TO VERY GOOD
1785–88	1 cent: laureate bust; seated figure of Liberty	$65.00

Massachusetts

1787–88	1 cent: Indian with bow and arrow; eagle	55.00
1787–88	1/2 cent	75.00

New Jersey

1786–88	1 cent: horse's head and plow; shield	50.00

New York

1787	1 cent: laureate bust; seated figure of Liberty	125.00

Vermont

1785–86	1 cent: hillside and plow; eye	125.00
1786–88	1 cent: laureate bust; seated figure of Liberty	100.00

U.S. MINT ISSUES

The following tables give a comprehensive listing of all the regular issues of the United States Mint. You will note that the values depend on various types of condition, as described on pages 4–16.

The column on the extreme left of the tables gives the quantity of coins issued in a given year. Sometimes a total figure includes several varieties lumped together. In other cases the Mint reports have broken down the quantities that apply to each variety in a given year.

Wherever it seemed essential, individual varieties issued in the same year have been listed separately and carefully described in order to distinguish them from other varieties issued in the same year.

Note also that mint marks play an important part in determining valuation. In most cases—but not all—the *quantity* issued by each Mint will give you the clue to the *variations in value* between the coins of the different Mints.

Half Cents

HALF CENTS—LIBERTY CAP TYPE

QUANTITY	YEAR	ABOUT GOOD	VERY GOOD	FINE	VERY FINE
35,334	1793	$600.00	$1500.00	$2750.00	$6500.00
81,600	1794	100.00	425.00	550.00	2000.00

1795

QUANTITY	YEAR	ABOUT GOOD	VERY GOOD	FINE	VERY FINE
25,600	1795 lettered edge, pole	75.00	200.00	450.00	1100.00
	1795 lettered edge, 1,795	200.00	450.00	1100.00	
	1795 plain edge, 1,795	75.00	200.00	450.00	1100.00
	1795 plain edge, no pole	75.00	200.00	450.00	1100.00
115,480	1796	1200.00	3750.00	7000.00	12,500.00

The 1796 "no pole" half cent sold for $506,000 at the May 1996 Eliasberg sale, the record price for a U.S. copper coin.

QUANTITY	YEAR	ABOUT GOOD	VERY GOOD	FINE	VERY FINE
	1797 lettered edge	150.00	500.00	750.00	2750.00
107,048	1797 plain edge	70.00	200.00	350.00	900.00
	1797 1 over 1	70.00	200.00	300.00	900.00

HALF CENTS—DRAPED BUST TYPE

QUANTITY	YEAR	ABOUT GOOD	VERY GOOD	FINE	VERY FINE
211,530	1800	15.00	40.00	60.00	125.00
14,366	1802 over 1800	85.00	250.00	500.00	1300.00
97,900	1803	20.00	30.00	60.00	200.00
1,055,312	1804 plain 4, stems	17.50	30.00	40.00	75.00
	1804 plain 4, no stems	17.50	30.00	40.00	75.00
	1804 crosslet 4, stems	17.50	30.00	40.00	75.00
	1804 crosslet 4, no stems	17.50	30.00	35.00	75.00
	1804 spiked chin	20.00	30.00	40.00	75.00
814,464	1805 small 5, stems	50.00	150.00	400.00	1250.00
	1805 large 5, stems	20.00	30.00	50.00	150.00
	1805 small 5, no stems	20.00	30.00	50.00	150.00
356,000	1806 small 6, stems	30.00	60.00	150.00	300.00
	1806 small 6, no stems	20.00	30.00	50.00	125.00
	1806 large 6, stems	20.00	30.00	40.00	100.00
476,000	1807	20.00	30.00	40.00	125.00
400,000	1808 over 7	40.00	100.00	175.00	600.00
	1808	20.00	30.00	50.00	125.00

HALF CENTS—TURBAN HEAD TYPE

QUANTITY	YEAR	GOOD TO VERY GOOD	FINE	VERY FINE	EXT. FINE	UNC.
1,154,572	1809	$27.50	$45.00	$75.00	$125.00	$500.00
	1809 over 6	27.50	45.00	65.00	110.00	450.00
215,00	1810	32.50	65.00	125.00	250.00	850.00
63,140	1811	110.00	350.00	1000.00	1500.00	3500.00
63,000	1825	35.00	55.00	100.00	175.00	600.00
234,00	1826	27.50	40.00	75.00	165.00	400.00
606,000	1828 12 stars	27.50	50.00	100.00	350.00	750.00
	1828 13 stars	25.00	40.00	80.00	135.00	375.00
487,000	1829	25.00	40.00	65.00	135.00	325.00
154,000	1832	25.00	40.00	65.00	135.00	350.00
120,000	1833	25.00	40.00	65.00	135.00	350.00
141,000	1834	25.00	40.00	65.00	135.00	350.00
398,000	1835	25.00	40.00	65.00	135.00	350.00

CATALOG OF UNITED STATES COINS **21**

HALF CENTS—BRAIDED HAIR TYPE

QUANTITY	YEAR	GOOD TO VERY GOOD	FINE	VERY FINE	EXT. FINE	UNC.
39,864	1849 large date	32.50	55.00	85.00	200.00	400.00
39,812	1850	32.50	55.00	85.00	200.00	400.00
147,672	1851	25.00	45.00	65.00	150.00	275.00
129,694	1853	25.00	45.00	65.00	150.00	275.00
55,358	1854	32.50	50.00	70.00	200.00	275.00
56,500	1855	32.50	50.00	70.00	200.00	275.00
40,430	1856	32.50	50.00	70.00	200.00	275.00
35,180	1857	32.50	55.00	85.00	175.00	325.00

Large Cents

LARGE CENTS—CHAIN TYPE

QUANTITY	YEAR	ABOUT GOOD	VERY GOOD	FINE	VERY FINE
112,212 (all varieties)	1793 chain; AMERI	$800.00	$3500.00	$4500.00	$10,000.00
	1793 chain; AMERICA	700.00	2250.00	3750.00	8500.00
	1793 chain; period after date	700.00	2250.00	3750.00	8000.00

LARGE CENTS—WREATH TYPE

112,212	1793 wreath; vines and bars	375.00	1100.00	1650.00	4250.00
	1793 wreath; lettered edge	375.00	1100.00	1650.00	4500.00

LARGE CENTS—LIBERTY CAP TYPE

QUANTITY	YEAR	ABOUT GOOD	VERY GOOD	FINE	VERY FINE
112,212	1793 Liberty Cap	550.00	1300.00	2500.00	6000.00
918,521	1794	50.00	100.00	175.00	650.00
	1795 lettered edge	75.00	150.00	275.00	800.00
82,000	1795 plain edge	50.00	100.00	250.00	550.00
	*1796 Liberty Cap	50.00	150.00	275.00	650.00

*This coin is included in quantity for 1796 cents of draped bust type.

LARGE CENTS—DRAPED BUST TYPE

974,700	1796 draped bust	$50.00	$100.00	$225.00	$750.00
	1796 "LIHERTY" variety	65.00	150.00	325.00	900.00
897,510	1797	30.00	65.00	175.00	325.00
	1797 no stems on wreath	50.00	125.00	275.00	650.00
	1797 crudely milled	35.00	75.00	250.00	450.00
	* 1797 with 1796 reverse	30.00	85.00	225.00	450.00
979,700	1798 over 97	30.00	75.00	225.00	500.00
	1798	20.00	35.00	150.00	300.00
	1798 with 1796 reverse	35.00	75.00	200.00	675.00
904,585	1799 over 98	325.00	1100.00	2750.00	8000.00
	1799	3000.00	1200.00	3000.00	7500.00
2,822,175	1800 over 1798	18.50	32.50	85.00	325.00
1800 over 179	1800 over 179	17.50	37.50	75.00	275.00
1800 perfect date	1800 perfect date	16.50	32.50	75.00	250.00
1,362,837	1801	17.50	35.00	85.00	250.00
	** 1801 three-error variety	35.00	85.00	225.00	800.00
	1801 fraction 1/000	20.00	45.00	150.00	375.00
	1801 1/100 over 1/000	25.00	45.00	135.00	425.00
3,435,100	1802	12.50	37.50	80.00	300.00
	1802 no stems on wreath	15.00	32.50	85.00	250.00
	1802 fraction 1/000	15.00	35.00	100.00	350.00
2,471,353					
	*** 1803 small date	10.00	25.00	85.00	250.00
	1803 small date, no stems	17.50	50.00	100.00	275.00
	1803 1/100 over 1/000	20.00	55.00	115.00	325.00
	1803 large date, fraction	35.00	100.00	215.00	500.00
	1803 large date, small fraction	325.00	2000.00	2500.00	7500.00
756,838	1804	250.00	800.00	1250.00	2500.00

LARGE CENTS—DRAPED BUST TYPE (continued)

QUANTITY	YEAR	ABOUT GOOD	VERY GOOD	FINE	VERY FINE
941,116	1805		30.00	85.00	275.00
348,000	1806	22.50	55.00	135.00	350.00
727,221	1807 over 6	15.00	32.50	85.00	275.00
	1807	12.50	25.00	85.00	250.00
	1807 comet variety	20.00	45.00	135.00	300.00

*1796 reverse has only one leaf at the tip of the right branch. The later reverses show two leaves at the tip of this branch.
**Three-error variety—fraction 1/000, no stem on the right branch and lINITED in legend.
***The small dates have blunt "1"s; the large dates have pointed "1"s.

LARGE CENTS—TURBAN HEAD TYPE

1,109,000	1808 13 stars	$16.50	$50.00	$125.00	$325.00
	1808 12 stars	17.50	60.00	125.00	350.00
222,867	1809	45.00	135.00	275.00	750.00
1,458,500	1810 over 9	17.50	50.00	100.00	375.00
	1810	15.00	50.00	100.00	375.00
218,025	1811 over 10	55.00	85.00	200.00	600.00
	1811	45.00	80.00	175.00	550.00
1,075,500	1812	15.00	40.00	85.00	325.00
418,000	1813	25.00	60.00	135.00	425.00
357,830	1814	20.00	40.00	100.00	350.00

LARGE CENTS—CORONET TYPE

QUANTITY	YEAR	GOOD TO VERY GOOD	FINE	VERY FINE	EXT. FINE	UNC.
2,820,982	1816	$10.00	$20.00	$40.00	$90.00	$400.00
3,948,400	1817 13 stars	9.00	15.00	32.50	85.00	350.00
	1817 15 stars	15.00	30.00	60.00	150.00	1100.00
3,167,000	1818	9.00	15.00	37.50	120.00	315.00
2,671,000	1819 over 18	13.50	30.00	45.00	150.00	550.00
	1819	9.00	16.50	35.00	100.00	400.00
4,407,550	1820 over 19	12.50	22.50	40.00	110.00	425.00
	1820	9.00	15.00	30.00	85.00	375.00
389,000	1821	22.50	55.00	150.00	400.00	2750.00
2,072,339	1822	9.00	16.50	37.50	120.00	800.00
855,730	1823 over 22	35.00	85.00	200.00	650.00	3500.00
	1823 normal date	40.00	135.00	325.00	1000.00	5000.00

QUANTITY	YEAR	GOOD TO VERY GOOD	FINE	VERY FINE	EXT. FINE	UNC.
1,262,000	1824 over 22	20.00	55.00	125.00	450.00	3850.00
	1824	9.00	25.00	55.00	275.00	2000.00
1,461,100	1825	9.00	20.00	50.00	200.00	1000.00
1,517,425	1826 over 25	25.00	50.00	125.00	300.00	1500.00
	1826	10.00	20.00	50.00	125.00	550.00
2,357,732	1827	10.00	15.00	42.50	100.00	425.00
2,260,624	*1828 large date	9.00	13.50	42.50	100.00	500.00
	**1828 small date	15.00	25.00	50.00	155.00	700.00
1,414,500	1829	9.00	15.00	42.50	85.00	475.00
1,711,500	1830 large letters	9.00	15.00	25.00	120.00	375.00
	1830 small letters	25.00	60.00	125.00	325.00	800.00
3,359,260	1831	9.00	17.50	30.00	80.00	400.00
2,362,000	1832	9.00	17.50	30.00	60.00	400.00
2,739,000	1833	9.00	17.50	30.00	60.00	400.00
1,755,100	1834	9.50	18.50	32.50	65.00	400.00
3,878,400	1835 head of 1834	8.50	17.50	32.50	60.00	375.00
	1835 head of 1836	8.50	17.50	32.50	65.00	375.00
2,111,000	1836	8.50	16.50	32.50	60.00	375.00
5,558,300	1837 plain hair cord	8.50	15.00	30.00	60.00	375.00
	1837 beaded hair cord	8.50	15.00	30.00	60.00	375.00
6,370,200	1838	8.50	15.00	27.50	60.00	350.00

*The "8"s of the 1828 large date have rounded centers.
**The "8"s of the 1828 small date have oval centers and a heavy crossbar.

LARGE CENTS—BRAIDED HAIR TYPE

QUANTITY	YEAR	GOOD TO VERY GOOD	FINE	VERY FINE	EXT. FINE	UNC.
3,128,661	1839 ove 36	$200.00	$600.00	$1100.00	$2750.00	Rare
	1839 type of 38	12.50	25.00	50.00	100.00	375.00
	1839 silly head	16.50	30.00	50.00	100.00	650.00
	1839 booby head	12.50	25.00	50.00	85.00	600.00
	1839 type of 1840	10.00	25.00	45.00	85.00	375.00
2,462,700	1840	8.00	10.00	20.00	60.00	325.00
1,597,367	1841	8.00	10.00	20.00	75.00	325.00
2,383,390	1842	8.00	10.00	20.00	55.00	300.00
2,428,320	1843 type of 1842	8.00	10.00	20.00	60.00	300.00
	1843 obverse of 1842 and reverse of 1844	20.00	40.00	60.00	90.00	400.00
	1843 type of 1844	8.00	12.50	30.00	60.00	375.00
2,397,752	1844	7.50	10.00	15.00	50.00	300.00

LARGE CENTS—BRAIDED HAIR TYPE (continued)

QUANTITY	YEAR	GOOD TO VERY GOOD	FINE	VERY FINE	EXT. FINE	UNC.
3,894,804	1845	7.50	10.00	15.00	45.00	275.00
4,120,000	1846 tall date	7.50	10.00	17.50	50.00	300.00
	1846 small date	7.50	10.00	12.50	50.00	275.00
6,183,669	1847	7.50	10.00	12.50	50.00	275.00
6,415,799	1848	7.50	10.00	12.50	50.00	275.00
4,178,500	1849	7.50	10.00	12.50	50.00	300.00
4,426,844	1850	7.50	10.00	12.50	50.00	275.00
9,889,707	1851	7.50	10.00	12.50	50.00	275.00
5,063,094	1852	7.50	10.00	12.50	50.00	275.00
6,641,131	1853	7.50	10.00	12.50	50.00	275.00
4,236,156	1854	7.50	10.00	12.50	50.00	275.00
1,574,829	1855	7.50	10.00	12.50	50.00	275.00
2,690,463	1856	7.50	10.00	12.50	50.00	275.00
333,456	1857	35.00	50.00	65.00	125.00	425.00

Flying Eagle Cents

In 1857 the Mint discontinued the issue of half cents and large cents because there was little use for them outside large cities, and it was therefore expensive to issue them. The half cents were never resumed, but cents continued to be issued, though in reduced size.

The 1856 Flying Eagle cent is probably the best-known American pattern coin. About 1,000 of these pieces dated 1856 were struck, even though the legislation authorizing the small cent was not enacted until February 21, 1857.

The 1856 issue totalled only about 1,000 pieces. Since they appeared before the 1857 authorizing law, many authorities consider them patterns rather than real issues.

QUANTITY	YEAR	GOOD	VERY GOOD	FINE	VERY FINE	EXT. FINE	UNC.	PROOF
1,000	* 1856 rare	$1750.00	$2500.00	$3250.00	$3850.00	$5000.00	$6500.00	$7500.00

FLYING EAGLE CENTS

QUANTITY	YEAR	GOOD	VERY GOOD	FINE	VERY FINE	EXT. FINE	UNC.	PROOF
17,450,000	1857	10.00	12.50	15.00	30.00	80.00	550.00	4000.00
24,600,000	1858 large letters	10.00	12.50	15.00	30.00	70.00	500.00	3500.00
	1858 small letters	10.00	12.50	15.00	30.00	80.00	500.00	3500.00

*Collectors are cautioned to examine any 1856 Flying Eagle cent very carefully. Altered date 1858's are frequently seen. On a genuine 1856 the center of the "o" in "of" is crude and nearly square. On the 1858 it is rounded. The figure "5" slants to the right on a genuine 1856 and the vertical stroke of the "5" points to the center of the ball just below. On an 1858 this vertical bar points to the left outside the ball. On the altered 1858, the lower half of the "6" is too thick. Some coins are crudely altered and the poor workmanship is obvious, but others are very cleverly done and the alteration can be detected only by careful examination with a magnifying glass.

Indian Head Cents

The Flying Eagle was discontinued in 1859 in favor of the Indian Head design. The first issues from 1859 through part of 1864 were struck on thick, copper-nickel planchets. The later coins were struck on thinner bronze planchets. About 100 pattern Indian Heads dated 1858 of the later-adopted design were made. These were made as specimens of the proposed new coinage and are not actual regularly issued coins. The 1859 Indian Head shows a laurel wreath on the reverse. In 1860 an oak wreath with a small shield was adopted.

1858 Indian Head cent; this was not regularly used until 1859 but about 100 pieces were dated 1858 using the later-adopted design.

QUANTITY	YEAR	PROOF
100	1858	$2000.00

INDIAN HEAD CENTS
(White Copper-Nickel, thick)

QUANTITY	YEAR	GOOD	VERY GOOD	FINE	VERY FINE	EXT. FINE	UNC.	PROOF
36,400,000	1859	$4.50	$6.50	$10.00	$22.50	$55.00	$325.00	$1250.00
20,566,000	1860	3.50	5.00	8.00	12.50	25.00	150.00	1200.00
10,100,000	1861	7.50	12.50	17.50	25.00	35.00	225.00	1100.00
28,075,000	1862	3.25	5.00	6.50	9.00	17.50	125.00	875.00
49,840,000	1863	3.00	4.00	5.50	9.00	16.50	125.00	875.00
13,740,000	1864	5.00	7.50	15.00	20.00	30.00	200.00	1200.00

INDIAN HEAD CENTS
(Bronze)

QUANTITY	YEAR	GOOD	VERY GOOD	FINE	VERY FINE	EXT. FINE	UNC.	PROOF
39,233,714	1864	$2.75	$4.50	$8.00	$16.50	$27.50	$85.00	$1000.00
	1864 L on ribbon							
	rare	12.50	25.00	45.00	65.00	90.00	350.00	12,500.00
35,429,286	1865	2.50	3.50	7.50	15.00	25.00	75.00	600.00
9,826,500	1866	15.00	20.00	30.00	45.00	70.00	175.00	600.00
9,821,000	1867	15.00	20.00	30.00	45.00	70.00	175.00	600.00
10,266,500	1868	15.00	20.00	30.00	45.00	70.00	175.00	600.00
	1869							
	over 68	70.00	100.00	200.00	300.00	450.00	900.00	
6,420,000	1869	20.00	35.00	60.00	85.00	125.00	350.00	750.00
5,275,000	1870	17.50	30.00	50.00	65.00	90.00	250.00	600.00
3,929,500	1871	22.50	35.00	65.00	80.00	115.00	275.00	700.00
4,042,000	1872	25.00	40.00	70.00	95.00	135.00	350.00	
11,676,500	1873	5.00	8.50	16.50	25.00	50.00	135.00	
14,187,500	1874	5.00	8.50	16.50	25.00	50.00	135.00	700.00
13,528,000	1875	5.00	8.50	16.50	25.00	50.00	120.00	400.00
7,944,000	1876	8.50	12.00	25.00	32.50	50.00	140.00	400.00
852,500	1877	200.00	225.00	300.00	500.00	700.00	1500.00	2800.00
5,799,955	1878	8.00	12.50	30.00	45.00	60.00	135.00	400.00
16,231,200	1879	2.00	3.50	7.50	15.00	20.00	60.00	400.00
38,964,955	1880	1.25	2.00	3.25	5.25	10.00	45.00	350.00
39,211,575	1881	1.25	2.00	3.25	5.25	10.00	45.00	350.00
38,581,100	1882	1.25	2.00	3.25	5.25	10.00	45.00	350.00
45,598,109	1883	1.25	2.00	3.25	5.25	10.00	45.00	350.00
23,261,742	1884	1.75	3.00	6.00	10.00	15.00	55.00	350.00
11,765,384	1885	3.25	6.00	9.00	15.00	25.00	75.00	350.00
17,654,290	1886	2.00	3.00	7.50	9.00	18.50	65.00	350.00
45,226,483	1887	1.00	1.25	2.00	3.50	10.00	45.00	350.00
37,494,414	1888	1.00	1.25	2.00	3.50	10.00	45.00	275.00
48,869,361	1889	1.00	1.25	2.00	3.50	10.00	45.00	275.00
57,182,854	1890	1.00	1.25	2.00	3.50	10.00	45.00	275.00
47,072,350	1891	1.00	1.25	2.00	3.50	10.00	45.00	275.00
37,649,832	1892	1.00	1.25	2.00	3.50	10.00	45.00	275.00
46,642,195	1893	1.00	1.25	2.00	3.50	10.00	45.00	250.00
16,752,132	1894	1.65	5.00	7.00	11.00	16.50	55.00	250.00
38,343,636	1895	.75	1.00	1.50	3.00	8.00	40.00	250.00
39,057,293	1896	.75	1.00	1.50	3.00	8.00	40.00	250.00
50,466,330	1897	.75	1.00	1.50	3.00	8.00	40.00	225.00
49,823,079	1898	.75	1.00	1.50	3.00	8.00	40.00	225.00
53,600,031	1899	.75	1.00	1.50	3.00	8.00	40.00	225.00
66,833,764	1900	.70	.85	1.35	2.50	7.50	40.00	225.00
79,611,143	1901	.70	.85	1.35	2.50	7.50	37.50	225.00
87,376,722	1902	.70	.85	1.35	2.50	7.50	37.50	225.00
85,094,493	1903	.70	.85	1.35	2.50	7.50	37.50	225.00
61,328,015	1904	.70	.85	1.35	2.50	7.50	37.50	225.00
80,719,163	1905	.70	.85	1.35	2.50	7.50	37.50	225.00
96,022,255	1906	.70	.85	1.35	2.50	7.50	37.50	225.00
108,138,618	1907	.70	.85	1.35	2.50	7.50	37.50	225.00
32,327,987	1908	.75	.90	1.50	3.00	7.50	40.00	225.00
1,115,000	1908 S	18.00	20.00	25.00	30.00	45.00	150.00	
14,370,645	1909	1.10	1.50	1.75	3.50	8.00	50.00	225.00
309,000	1909 S	85.00	120.00	125.00	150.00	200.00	400.00	

The "S" mint mark on the 1908 and 1909 issues is at the bottom of the reverse under the wreath.

Lincoln Head Cents

These coins have been issued in bronze since 1909. In 1943 the content was steel, and in 1944–1945 it was copper salvaged from shell cases. All years are quite inexpensive to obtain. The only notable rarity is the 1909 S issue with the initials VDB—standing for Victor D. Brenner, the designer of the coin. This variety was issued in rather a small quantity before the initials were withdrawn.

LINCOLN HEAD CENTS

The mint mark is on the obverse under the date.

QUANTITY	YEAR	GOOD	VERY GOOD	FINE	VERY FINE	EXT. FINE	UNC.
27,995,000	1909 VDB	$2.00	$2.25	$2.75	$3.25	$3.75	$17.50
484,000	1909 S VDB	200.00	275.00	325.00	375.00	450.00	650.00
72,702,618	1909 plain	.40	.45	.65	1.00	2.00	12.50
1,825,000	1909 S plain	30.00	35.00	37.50	50.00	75.00	135.00
146,801,218	1910	.15	.30	.50	.80	1.75	12.50
6,045,000	1910 S	6.00	6.50	7.50	9.00	15.00	65.00
101,177,787	1911	.15	.30	.65	1.25	4.50	15.00
4,026,000	1911 S	10.00	11.00	12.50	16.50	25.00	100.00
12,672,000	1911 D	3.00	3.75	6.00	10.00	20.00	80.00
68,153,060	1912	.20	.40	1.65	3.75	6.00	27.50
4,431,000	1912 S	9.00	10.00	12.50	16.00	25.00	90.00
10,411,000	1912 D	2.75	4.00	5.50	12.50	27.50	90.00
76,532,352	1913	.20	.35	1.25	3.75	6.50	22.50
6,101,000	1913 S	5.50	6.00	7.50	11.00	17.50	85.00
15,804,000	1913 D	1.25	1.75	3.00	6.75	17.50	85.00
75,238,432	1914	.20	.35	2.00	4.00	8.50	50.00
4,137,000	1914 S	7.50	8.50	11.00	15.00	27.50	125.00
1,193,000	1914 D	60.00	75.00	100.00	150.00	400.00	1200.00
29,092,120	1915	.75	1.40	5.00	10.00	22.50	100.00
4,833,000	1915 S	6.00	6.50	7.50	11.00	18.50	80.00
22,050,000	1915 D	.75	1.00	1.25	5.00	9.50	37.50
131,833,677	1916	.15	.20	.35	.75	3.00	12.50
22,510,000	1916 S	.50	.80	1.25	2.50	6.00	45.00
35,956,000	1916 D	.20	.35	1.00	2.75	6.50	37.50
196,429,785	1917	.15	.20	.35	.75	2.00	12.00
32,620,000	1917 S	.20	.40	.65	2.50	5.25	50.00
55,120,000	1917 D	.20	.30	.65	2.75	6.50	50.00
288,104,634	1918	.15	.20	.35	.75	4.00	13.00
34,680,000	1918 S	.20	.30	.50	2.25	4.50	40.00
47,830,000	1918 D	.20	.30	.60	2.25	5.00	40.00
392,021,000	1919	.15	.20	.30	.60	1.75	10.00
139,760,000	1919 S	.20	.30	.40	1.25	2.50	20.00
57,154,000	1919 D	.20	.30	.65	2.75	5.00	30.00
310,165,000	1920	.15	.20	.30	.65	1.75	10.00
46,220,000	1920 S	.15	.20	.50	1.50	4.00	37.50
49,280,000	1920 D	.15	.20	.55	1.50	4.00	42.50
39,157,000	1921	.20	.25	.50	1.00	4.50	35.00
15,274,000	1921 S	.60	.75	1.00	2.50	15.00	125.00
	1922	150.00	175.00	300.00	450.00	1200.00	3750.00
7,160,000	1922 D	6.00	6.50	7.50	9.00	17.50	75.00

LINCOLN HEAD CENTS (continued)

QUANTITY	YEAR	GOOD	VERY GOOD	FINE	VERY FINE	EXT. FINE	UNC.
74,700,000	1923	.15	.20	.35	.70	2.00	10.00
8,700,000	1923 S	1.50	1.75	2.25	4.50	16.00	300.00
75,178,000	1924	.15	.20	.35	.60	3.25	22.50
11,696,000	1924 S	.50	.75	1.25	2.50	6.00	120.00
2,520,000	1924 D	10.00	11.00	15.00	17.50	40.00	275.00
139,949,000	1925	.15	.20	.35	.60	2.50	10.00
26,380,000	1925 S	.15	.25	.40	1.00	4.00	55.00
22,580,000	1925 D	.25	.35	.55	1.10	4.00	50.00
157,088,000	1926	.15	.20	.35	.60	2.50	9.00
4,550,000	1926 S	3.00	3.50	4.00	5.00	12.50	175.00
28,020,000	1926 D	.20	.30	.50	1.00	3.00	40.00
144,440,000	1927	.15	.20	.30	.90	2.50	9.00
14,276,000	1927 S	.30	.40	.75	1.75	4.00	60.00
27,170,000	1927 D	.20	.30	.50	.75	2.00	27.50
134,116,000	1928	.15	.20	.30	.40	3.00	9.00
17,266,000	1928 S	.25	.80	.35	.90	2.75	45.00
31,170,000	1928 D	.20	.25	.30	.60	1.50	22.50
185,262,000	1929	.15	.20	.30	.50	1.25	8.00
50,148,000	1929 S	.15	.20	.30	.50	1.25	10.00
41,730,000	1929 D	.15	.20	.30	.50	1.25	12.50
157,415,000	1930	.10	.15	.20	.35	1.00	8.00
24,286,000	1930 S	.10	.15	.20	.50	1.50	9.00
40,100,000	1930 D	.10	.15	.20	.45	1.00	10.00
19,396,000	1931	.20	.25	.30	.55	1.50	17.50
866,000	1931 S	27.50	32.50	40.00	40.00	35.00	75.00
4,480,000	1931 D	2.75	3.25	3.50	4.00	7.00	55.00
9,962,000	1932	1.00	1.25	1.50	2.00	2.75	18.50
10,500,000	1932 D	.65	.75	1.25	2.00	2.50	16.50
14,360,000	1933	.50	.60	.70	.90	2.50	18.50
6,200,000	1933 D	1.75	2.00	2.25	2.50	4.00	25.00

QUANTITY	YEAR	UNC.	QUANTITY	YEAR	UNC.
219,080,000	1934	$4.00	181,770,000	1945 S copper	.75
28,446,000	1934 D	22.50	226,268,000	1945 D copper	.85
245,388,000	1935	1.75	991,655,000	1946	.35
38,702,000	1935 S	7.50	198,100,000	1946 S	.75
47,000,000	1935 D	3.50	315,690,000	1946 D	.35
309,637,569	1936	2.00	190,555,000	1947	1.00
29,130,000	1936 S	2.00	99,000,000	1947 S	1.00
40,620,000	1936 D	1.75	194,750,000	1947 D	.50
309,179,320	1937	1.75	317,570,000	1948	.75
34,500,000	1937 S	2.00	81,735,000	1948 S	1.25
50,430,000	1937 D	2.00	172,637,500	1948 D	.60
156,696,734	1938	1.85	217,490,000	1949	1.15
15,180,000	1938 S	4.00	64,290,000	1949 S	2.75
20,010,000	1938 D	3.00	154,370,500	1949 D	.85
316,479,520	1939	1.25	272,686,386	1950	.75
52,070,000	1939 S	1.75	118,505,000	1950 S	1.15
15,160,000	1939 D	6.00	334,950,000	1950 D	.50
586,825,872	1940	1.00	294,633,500	1951	2.00
112,940,000	1940 S	.90	100,890,000	1951 S	1.50
81,390,000	1940 D	1.00	625,355,000	1951 D	.50
887,039,100	1941	.75	186,856,980	1952	.85
92,360,000	1941 S	4.00	137,800,004	1952 S	1.25
128,700,000	1941 D	3.00	746,130,000	1952 D	.50
657,828,600	1942	.50	256,883,800	1953	.50
85,590,000	1942 S	5.00	181,835,000	1953 S	.75
206,698,000	1942 D	.70	700,515,000	1953 D	.40
684,628,670	1943 zinc-steel	1.00	96,190,000	1954 S	.50
191,550,000	1943 S zinc-steel	2.00	251,552,500	1954 D	.35
217,660,000	1943 D zinc-steel	1.00	330,958,200	1955	.30
1,435,400,000	1944 copper	.75	44,610,000	1955 S	.60
71,873,350	1954	1.00	563,257,500	1955 D	.25
282,760,000	1944 S copper	.65	420,926,081	1956	.25
430,587,000	1944 D copper	.60	1,098,201,100	1956 D	.25
1,040,515,000	1945 copper	.40	282,540,000	1957	.25

LINCOLN HEAD CENTS (continued)

1955 Double die
VF 350.00 Unc 1500.00

QUANTITY	YEAR	MS-65
1,051,342,000	1957 D	.25
252,595,000	1958	.25
800,953,300	1958 D	.20
619,715,000	1959	.20
1,279,760,000	1959 D	.20
586,405,000	1960 Small date	6.50
	1960 Large date	.20
1,580,884,000	1960 D Small date	.50
	1960 D Large date	.20
756,373,244	1961	.20
1,753,266,700	1961 D	.20
609,263,019	1962	.20
1,793,148,400	1962 D	.20
757,185,645	1963	.20
1,774,020,400	1963 D	.20
2,648,575,000	1964	.15
3,799,071,500	1964 D	.15
1,494,884,900	1965	.15
2,185,886,200	1966	.15
3,048,667,100	1967	.15
1,707,880,970	1968	.15
2,886,269,600	1968 D	.15
258,270,001	1968 S	.15
1,136,910,000	1969	.15
4,002,832,200	1969 D	.15
544,375,000	1969 S	.15
1,898,315,000	1970	.15
2,891,438,900	1970 D	.15
693,192,814	1970 S	.15
1,919,490,000	1971	.15
2,911,045,600	1971 D	.15
528,354,192	1971 S	.10
	1972 Double strike	275.00
2,933,255,000	1972	.15
2,665,071,400	1972 D	.15
380,200,104	1972 S	.15
3,728,245,000	1973	.15
3,549,576,588	1973 D	.15
319,937,634	1973 S	.15
4,232,140,523	1974	.15
4,235,098,000	1974 D	.15
412,039,228	1974 S	.15
5,451,476,142	1975	
4,505,275,300	1975 D	.10
2,845,450	1975 S (proof only)	
4,674,292,426	1976	.10
4,221,592,455	1976 D	.10

QUANTITY	YEAR	UNC.
4,149,730	1975 S (proof only)	
4,469,930,000	1977	.10
4,194,062,300	1977 D	.10
3,251,152	1977 S (proof only)	
5,558,605,000	1978	.10
4,280,233,400	1978 D	.10
3,127,781	1978 S (proof only)	
6,018,515,000	1979	.10
4,139,357,254	1979 D	.10
3,677,175	1979 S (proof only)	
7,414,705,000	1980	.10
5,140,098,660	1980 D	.10
3,554,806	1980 S (proof only)	
7,491,750,000	1981	.10
5,373,235,677	1981 D	.10
4,063,083	1981 S (proof only)	
10,712,525,000	1982 Large Date	.10
	1982 Small Date	.15
6,012,979,368	1982 D	.10
3,857,479	1982 S (proof only)	
7,752,355,000	1983 Double Die	
	Reverse	200.00
	1983	.10
6,467,198,428	1983 D	.10
3,228,648	1983 S (proof only)	
8,151,079,000	1984	.10
5,569,238,906	1984 D	.10
3,065,110	1984 S (proof only)	
5,648,489,887	1985	.10
5,287,399,926	1985 D	.10
3,362,662	1985 S (proof only)	
4,491,395,493	1986	.10
4,442,866,698	1986 D	.10
3,010,497	1986 S (proof only)	
4,682,246,693	1987	.10
4,879,389,514	1987 D	.10
3,792,233	1987 S (proof only)	
6,092,810,000	1988	.10
5,253,740,443	1988 D	.10
3,262,948	1988 S (proof only)	
7,261,535,000	1989	.10
5,345,467,111	1989 D	.10
3,215,728	1989 S (proof only)	
6,851,765,000	1990	.10
4,922,894,533	1990 D	.10
3,299,559	1990 S (proof only)	
5,165,940,000	1991	.10
4,158,442,076	1991 D	.10
2,867,787	1991 S (proof only)	
4,648,905,000	1992	.10
4,448,673,300	1992 D	.10
4,176,560	1992 S (proof only)	.10
5,684,705,000	1993	.10
6,426,650,571	1993 D	.10
3,394,792	1993 S (proof only)	
6,500,850,000	1994	.10
7,131,765,000	1994 D	.10
3,269,923	1994 S (proof only)	.10
6,411,440,000	1995	.10
7,128,560,000	1995 D	.10
	1995 S (proof only)	
	1996	.10
	1996 D	.10
	1996 S (proof only)	
	1997	.10
	1997 D	.10
	1997 S (proof only)	

Two Cent Pieces

TWO CENTS—BRONZE

QUANTITY	YEAR	GOOD TO VERY GOOD	VERY FINE	EXT. FINE	FINE	UNC.	PROOF -63
19,847,500	1864 small motto	$55.00	$85.00	$110.00	$200.00	$550.00	
	1864 large motto	6.00	8.00	12.50	30.00	225.00	1000.00
13,640,000	1865	6.00	8.00	12.50	30.00	225.00	900.00
3,177,000	1866	6.00	8.00	12.50	30.00	235.00	900.00
2,938,750	1867	6.00	8.00	12.50	30.00	235.00	900.00
2,803,750	1868	6.00	8.00	12.50	30.00	235.00	900.00
1,546,500	1869	6.00	8.00	12.50	30.00	235.00	900.00
861,250	1870	7.50	15.00	25.00	50.00	300.00	900.00
721,250	1871	8.50	17.50	27.50	60.00	350.00	900.00
65,000	1872	65.00	160.00	165.00	225.00	850.00	1400.00
?	1873 only proofs were struck						2500.00

Three Cent Pieces

THREE CENTS—SILVER

1851–1853   1854–1873

The "O" mint mark is to the right of the "III" on the reverse.

QUANTITY	YEAR	GOOD TO VERY GOOD	VERY FINE	EXT. FINE	FINE	UNC.	PROOF -63
5,447,400	1851	$9.00	$13.00	$25.00	$45.00	$275.00	
720,000	1851 O	12.50	25.00	50.00	75.00	425.00	
18,663,500	1852	9.00	13.00	25.00	45.00	275.00	
11,400,000	1853	9.00	13.00	25.00	45.00	275.00	
671,000	1854	13.00	20.00	30.00	70.00	450.00	
139,000	1855	17.50	27.50	50.00	125.00	550.00	3250.00
1,458,000	1856	13.00	20.00	30.00	60.00	450.00	2500.00
1,042,000	1857	11.00	16.00	30.00	65.00	450.00	2500.00
1,604,000	1858	11.00	16.00	30.00	65.00	500.00	2500.00
365,000	1859	12.50	16.00	25.00	55.00	275.00	800.00
287,000	1860	12.50	16.00	25.00	55.00	275.00	800.00
498,000	1861	12.50	16.00	25.00	55.00	275.00	800.00
363,550	1862	12.50	16.00	25.00	55.00	275.00	900.00
21,460	1863	(all remaining years struck as proofs only)					950.00
470	1864						950.00
8,500	1865						950.00

The 1851 silver 3 cents in proof sold for $61,600 at the May 1996 Eliasberg sale.

QUANTITY	YEAR	GOOD TO VERY GOOD	VERY FINE	EXT. FINE	FINE	UNC.	PROOF -63
22,725	1866						900.00
4,625	1867						900.00
4,100	1868						900.00
5,100	1869						900.00
4,000	1870						900.00
4,260	1871						900.00
1,950	1872						900.00
600	1873						1250.00

THREE CENTS—NICKEL

QUANTITY	YEAR	GOOD TO VERY GOOD	VERY FINE	EXT. FINE	FINE	UNC.	PROOF -63
11,382,000	1865	$5.50	$7.00	$9.00	$15.00	$135.00	$1200.00
4,801,000	1866	5.50	7.00	9.00	15.00	135.00	500.00
3,915,000	1867	5.50	7.00	9.00	15.00	150.00	400.00
3,252,000	1868	5.50	7.00	9.00	15.00	150.00	400.00
1,604,000	1869	5.50	8.00	11.00	15.00	150.00	400.00
1,335,000	1870	5.50	8.50	10.00	16.00	150.00	400.00
604,000	1871	6.00	9.00	11.00	17.50	175.00	400.00
862,000	1872	6.00	9.00	11.00	17.50	175.00	400.00
1,173,000	1873	6.00	9.00	11.00	17.50	150.00	400.00
790,000	1874	6.00	9.00	11.00	25.00	175.00	400.00
228,000	1875	7.50	12.50	17.50	25.00	200.00	400.00
162,000	1876	8.00	12.00	17.50		225.00	400.00
?	1877 only proofs were struck						1750.00
2,350	1878 only proofs were struck						900.00
41,200	1879	35.00	40.00	50.00	60.00	275.00	400.00
24,955	1880	40.00	45.00	70.00	80.00	275.00	400.00
1,080,575	1881	6.00	8.00	10.00	15.00	135.00	400.00
25,300	1882	37.50	50.00	60.00	70.00	275.00	400.00
10,609	1883	75.00	100.00	125.00	150.00	300.00	400.00
5,642	1884	100.00	150.00	175.00	200.00	400.00	700.00
4,790	1885	175.00	225.00	250.00	300.00	425.00	800.00
4,290	1886 only proofs were struck						800.00
7,961	1887	150.00	175.00	200.00	225.00	300.00	800.00
	1887 over 86—only proofs were struck						625.00
41,083	1888	35.00	37.50	45.00	50.00	250.00	425.00
21,561	1889	40.00	50.00	55.00	70.00	300.00	425.00

These now obsolete denominations were each introduced to fill a specific need. The two cent piece was an attempt to cope with the desperate shortage of small coins that occurred near the close of the Civil War. The theory was that a coin press could produce just as many two cent pieces as one cent pieces in a given time, but the face value of the coins going into circulation would be double. Once the deficiency was made up, the larger coins proved to be awkward. The silver three cent piece came into being along with the 3¢ letter rate with the thought that it would be convenient for buying stamps. The nickel three cent piece which came later was intended to redeem the three cent paper notes issued during the Civil War. Neither of the three cent coins was really practical and after the first few years they were struck in small quantities only until they were finally discontinued.

Nickel Five Cents

Though nickel was suggested for American coins as early as 1837, the first five-cent nickels were not issued until 1866.

NICKEL FIVE CENTS—SHIELD TYPE

1866–1867   **1867–1883**

QUANTITY	YEAR	GOOD TO VERY GOOD	FINE	VERY FINE	EXT. FINE	UNC.	PROOF -63
14,742,500	1866	$11.00	$18.50	$32.50	$85.00	$415.00	$2500.00
30,909,500	1867						
	with rays	13.50	25.00	35.00	90.00	425.00	8000.00
	1867 without rays	8.00	12.50	17.50	35.00	150.00	425.00
28,817,000	1868	8.00	12.50	17.50	35.00	150.00	550.00
16,395,000	1869	8.00	12.50	17.50	35.00	150.00	550.00
4,806,000	1870	10.00	14.00	20.00	37.50	175.00	550.00
561,000	1871	35.00	45.00	55.00	85.00	250.00	725.00
6,036,000	1872	9.00	15.00	17.50	30.00	150.00	550.00
4,550,000	1873	9.50	12.50	20.00	35.00	150.00	550.00
3,538,000	1874	11.00	17.50	18.00	40.00	150.00	550.00
2,097,000	1875	12.50	22.50	27.50	50.00	200.00	550.00
2,530,000	1876	12.00	20.00	25.00	40.00	150.00	550.00
?500	1877 only proofs were struck						1750.00
2,350	1878 only proofs were struck						1000.00
29,100	1879	85.00	100.00	135.00	175.00	450.00	750.00
19,955	1880	100.00	135.00	150.00	200.00	500.00	800.00
72,375	1881	85.00	125.00	140.00	200.00	425.00	750.00
11,476,600	1882	9.00	12.50	20.00	30.00	175.00	425.00
1,456,919	1883	10.00	12.50	20.00	30.00	175.00	425.00

LIBERTY HEAD NICKELS

1883   **1883–1912**

The variety without "CENTS" was issued first, but unscrupulous people goldplated them and passed them off as $5 gold pieces. To remedy the situation, the word "CENTS" was added to the later issues and continued to appear on subsequent dates.

LIBERTY HEAD NICKELS (continued)

QUANTITY	YEAR	GOOD	VERY GOOD	FINE	VERY FINE	EXT. FINE	UNC.	PROOF -63
5,479,519	1883 without "Cents"	$2.25	$3.25	$3.50	$6.00	$9.00	$45.00	$350.00
16,032,983	1883 with "Cents"	6.50	8.50	17.50	25.00	37.50	125.00	300.00
11,273,942	1884	7.00	9.00	18.50	27.50	45.00	150.00	250.00
1,476,490	1885	125.00	200.00	225.00	300.00	400.00	800.00	1100.00
3,330,290	1886	35.00	50.00	75.00	100.00	200.00	400.00	650.00
15,263,652	1887	3.50	5.00	12.50	20.00	40.00	125.00	300.00
10,720,483	1888	6.50	10.00	17.50	22.50	37.50	125.00	300.00
15,881,361	1889	3.50	5.00	12.50	20.00	35.00	110.00	300.00
16,259,272	1890	4.50	6.00	15.00	22.50	37.50	110.00	300.00
16,834,350	1891	3.50	5.00	12.50	20.00	35.00	110.00	300.00
11,699,642	1892	3.50	5.00	12.50	20.00	35.00	110.00	300.00
13,370,195	1893	3.50	5.00	12.50	20.00	35.00	125.00	300.00
5,413,132	1894	7.00	9.00	18.50	27.50	45.00	125.00	300.00
9,979,884	1895	2.50	5.00	12.50	17.50	30.00	125.00	300.00
8,842,920	1896	3.00	6.00	15.00	20.00	25.00	125.00	325.00
20,428,735	1897	1.00	2.00	4.00	7.00	22.50	110.00	300.00
12,532,087	1898	1.00	2.00	4.00	7.00	22.50	110.00	300.00
26,029,031	1899	.75	1.75	4.00	6.50	22.50	110.00	300.00
27,255,995	1900	.75	1.00	3.00	6.00	20.00	100.00	300.00
26,480,213	1901	.75	1.00	3.00	6.00	20.00	100.00	300.00
31,480,579	1902	.75	1.00	3.00	6.00	20.00	100.00	300.00
28,006,725	1903	.75	1.00	3.00	6.00	20.00	100.00	300.00
21,404,984	1904	.75	1.00	3.00	6.00	20.00	100.00	300.00
29,827,276	1905	.75	1.00	3.00	6.00	20.00	100.00	300.00
38,613,725	1906	.75	1.00	3.00	6.00	20.00	100.00	300.00
39,214,800	1907	.75	1.00	3.00	6.00	20.00	100.00	300.00
22,686,177	1908	.75	1.00	3.00	6.00	20.00	100.00	300.00
11,590,526	1909	.75	1.00	3.00	6.00	20.00	100.00	300.00
30,169,353	1910	.75	1.00	3.00	6.00	20.00	100.00	300.00
39,559,372	1911	.75	1.00	3.00	6.00	20.00	100.00	300.00
26,236,714	1912	.75	1.00	3.00	6.00	20.00	100.00	300.00
8,474,000	*1912 D	2.50	3.50	12.50	15.00	50.00	200.00	
238,000	*1912 S	50.00	55.00	100.00	150.00	250.00	650.00	
5 Known	1913 (an outstanding rarity) Sold for $1,485,000 at the May 1996 Eliasberg sale, the record at auction for any U.S. coin.							

*Mint mark to left of "CENTS" on reverse.

The mint marks are under "Five cents" on the reverse.

1913   1913–1938

BUFFALO NICKELS

QUANTITY	YEAR	GOOD	VERY GOOD	FINE	VERY FINE	EXT. FINE	UNC.
30,993,520	1913 Type 1 —buffalo on mound	$3.00	$3.25	$5.00	$7.00	$12.00	$50.00
2,105,000	1913 S Type 1	7.00	10.00	12.00	20.00	25.00	100.00
5,337,000	1913 D Type 1	4.50	6.00	10.00	12.00	17.50	85.00
29,858,700	1913 Type 2 buffalo on line	2.50	3.50	4.00	5.00	10.00	50.00
1,209,000	1913 S Type 2	50.00	55.00	70.00	90.00	120.00	300.00

BUFFALO NICKELS (continued)

QUANTITY	YEAR	GOOD	VERY GOOD	FINE	VERY FINE	EXT. FINE	UNC.
4,156,000	1913 D						
	Type 2	32.50	37.50	50.00	65.00	75.00	200.00
20,665,738	1914	3.00	4.50	5.50	7.50	12.50	50.00
3,470,000	1914 S	4.50	6.00	8.50	14.00	28.00	100.00
3,912,000	1914 D	20.00	28.00	37.50	50.00	80.00	250.00
20,987,270	1915	1.65	2.50	3.75	5.25	12.00	50.00
1,505,000	1915 S	8.50	12.50	22.50	55.00	75.00	250.00
7,569,500	1915 D	6.00	7.50	15.00	28.00	45.00	120.00
63,498,066	1916	.75	1.00	1.75	3.00	6.50	35.00
11,860,000	1916 S	3.25	4.25	7.00	17.50	37.50	120.00
13,333,000	1916 D	4.25	5.50	9.00	15.00	38.50	115.00
51,424,029	1917	.85	1.00	1.75	3.50	12.00	42.50
4,193,000	1917 S	3.50	6.00	10.00	32.50	57.50	225.00
9,910,800	1917 D	4.00	6.00	11.00	34.00	57.50	215.00
32,086,314	1918	.65	1.25	2.35	5.50	16.00	80.00
4,882,000	1918 S	3.00	6.00	11.00	32.50	65.00	225.00
8,362,000	1918 D	4.00	6.50	12.00	35.00	75.00	285.00
	1918 D over 7	275.00	350.00	650.00	1000.00	2400.00	20,000.00
60,868,000	1919	.60	.80	1.50	3.15	8.00	37.50
7,521,000	1919 S	2.50	5.00	10.00	35.00	75.00	275.00
8,006,000	1919 D	3.50	6.50	16.00	45.00	85.00	330.00
63,093,000	1920	.55	.75	1.25	3.00	7.50	42.50
9,689,000	1920 S	1.75	3.00	16.00	27.50	70.00	200.00
9,418,000	1920 D	3.00	5.00	10.00	47.50	75.00	300.00
10,663,000	1921	.90	1.20	3.25	6.25	16.50	80.00
1,557,000	1921 S	12.00	16.50	35.00	100.00	165.00	650.00
35,715,000	1923	.45	.65	1.15	3.00	8.00	40.00
6,142,000	1923 S	1.65	2.50	6.00	22.50	47.50	175.00
21,620,000	1924	.45	.65	1.25	4.00	9.00	55.00
1,437,000	1924 S	4.50	6.50	15.00	120.00	225.00	800.00
5,258,000	1924 D	2.25	3.25	8.00	45.00	70.00	250.00
35,565,100	1925	.45	.70	1.25	3.00	6.50	40.00
6,256,000	1925 S	2.25	4.00	6.00	20.00	50.00	225.00
4,450,000	1925 D	3.50	5.25	12.00	40.00	67.50	275.00
44,693,000	1926	.45	.55	1.00	1.50	5.00	30.00
970,000	1926 S	6.00	8.00	15.00	60.00	300.00	850.00
5,638,000	1926 D	2.00	3.75	9.00	40.00	85.00	175.00
37,981,000	1927	.45	.55	1.00	1.50	5.00	30.00
3,430,000	1927 S	1.10	1.50	4.00	12.50	50.00	175.00
5,730,000	1927 D	1.00	1.50	2.75	12.00	32.50	90.00
23,411,000	1928	.50	.55	1.00	2.25	5.00	30.00
6,936,000	1928 S	.75	1.00	2.00	3.00	12.00	67.50
6,436,000	1928 D	.65	.75	1.50	5.00	12.00	45.00
36,446,000	1929	.40	.55	.90	1.65	3.65	27.50
7,754,000	1929 S	.50	.60	1.00	1.65	7.50	35.00
8,370,000	1929 D	.55	1.00	1.50	3.75	10.00	55.00
22,849,000	1930	.40	.50	1.00	1.65	4.00	30.00
5,435,000	1930 S	.65	.85	1.65	2.00	6.50	55.00
1,200,000	1931 S	3.75	4.50	5.50	7.00	14.00	75.00
20,213,000	1934	.30	.40	.65	1.50	3.75	27.50
7,480,003	1934 D	.50	.60	1.00	2.50	6.50	45.00
58,264,000	1935	.30	.40	.50	.65	1.50	19.00
10,300,000	1935 S	.35	.40	.50	1.25	3.40	25.00
12,092,000	1935 D	.40	.45	.65	2.00	5.00	40.00
119,001,420	1936				1.00	1.75	18.50
14,930,000	1936 S				1.00	2.35	22.00
24,418,000	1936 D				.75	2.25	22.00
79,485,769	1937				.75	1.50	17.50
5,635,000	1937 S				.75	1.75	17.50
17,826,000	1937 D				.75	2.00	17.50
	1937 D three-legged buffalo				200.00	300.00	1250.00
7,020,000	1938 D				1.25	1.75	17.50

JEFFERSON NICKELS

QUANTITY	YEAR	EXT. FINE	UNC.
19,515,365	1938	$.75	$1.75
4,105,000	1938 S	3.50	7.75
5,376,000	1938 D	2.25	6.00
120,627,535	1939	.35	1.35
6,630,000	1939 S	2.50	17.50
3,514,000	1939 D	8.00	35.00
176,499,158	1940	.35	1.00
39,690,000	1940 S	.65	2.00
43,540,000	1940 D	.50	1.75
203,283,720	1941	.40	1.00
43,445,000	1941 S	.50	2.50
53,432,000	1941 D	.50	2.50
49,818,600	1942	.50	2.00
13,938,000	1942 D	2.50	17.50

Wartime Silver Content

QUANTITY	YEAR	EXT. FINE	UNC.
57,900,600	1942 P	4.00	15.00
32,900,000	1942 S	2.50	10.00
271,165,000	1943 P	1.50	4.00
104,060,000	1943 S	1.50	5.00
15,294,000	1943 D	2.50	5.00
119,150,000	1944 P	1.75	4.00
21,640,000	1944 S	2.00	7.50
32,309,000	1944 D	2.00	6.00
119,408,100	1945 P	1.75	4.00
58,939,000	1945 S	1.50	4.00
37,158,000	1945 D	1.50	4.00

The mint marks are to the right of the building or above it on the reverse until 1968, then on the obverse near the date.

Prewar Nickel Content

QUANTITY	YEAR	MS-65
161,116,000	1946	1.00
13,560,000	1946 S	1.75
45,292,200	1946 D	1.00
95,000,000	1947	.75
24,720,000	1947 S	1.50
37,822,000	1947 D	1.25
89,348,000	1948	1.00
11,300,000	1948 S	1.65
44,734,000	1948 D	1.50
60,652,000	1949	1.00
9,716,000	1949 S	3.00
35,238,000	1949 D	1.75
9,847,386	1950	3.00
2,630,030	1950 D	14.00
26,689,500	1951	1.50
7,776,000	1951 S	4.00
20,460,000	1951 D	2.25
64,069,980	1952	.85
20,572,000	1952 S	1.25
30,638,000	1952 D	2.50
46,772,800	1953	.50
19,210,900	1953 S	1.00
59,878,600	1953 D	.85
47,917,350	1954	.35
29,384,000	1954 S	.35
117,183,060	1954 D	.30
8,266,200	1955	1.75
74,464,100	1955 D	.35
35,397,081	1956	.30
67,222,040	1956 D	.30
38,408,000	1957	.30
136,828,900	1957 D	.30
17,088,000	1958	.60
168,249,120	1958 D	.30
27,248,000	1959	.40

QUANTITY	YEAR	MS-65
160,738,240	1959 D	.25
55,416,000	1960	.20
192,582,180	1960 D	.20
76,668,244	1961	.20
229,372,760	1961 D	.20
100,602,019	1962	.20
280,195,720	1962 D	.20
178,851,645	1963	.20
276,829,460	1963 D	.20
1,024,672,000	1964	.20
1,787,297,160	1964 D	.20
133,771,380	1965	.20
153,946,700	1966	.20
107,325,800	1967	.20
91,227,880	1968 D	.20
100,396,001	1968 S	.20
202,807,500	1969 D	.20
120,164,000	1969 S	.20
515,485,380	1970 D	.15
241,464,814	1970 S	.15
106,884,000	1971	.15
316,144,800	1971 D	.15
3,224,138	1971 S (proof only)	
202,036,000	1972	.15
351,694,600	1972 D	.15
3,267,667	1972 S (proof only)	
384,396,000	1973	.15
261,405,400	1973 D	.15
2,769,624	1973 S (proof only)	
601,752,000	1974	.15
277,373,000	1974 D	.15
2,617,350	1974 S (proof only)	
181,772,000	1975	.15
401,875,300	1975 D	.15
	1975 S (proof only)	
367,124,000	1976	.15

JEFFERSON NICKELS (continued)

QUANTITY	YEAR	MS-65	QUANTITY	YEAR	MS-65
563,964,147	1976 D	.15	771,360,000	1988	.15
	1976 S (proof only)		663,771,652	1988 D	.15
585,376,000	1977	.15	3,262,948	1988 S (proof only)	
297,313,422	1977 D	.15	898,812,000	1989	.15
	1977 S (proof only)		570,842,474	1989 D	.15
391,308,000	1978	.15	3,215,728	1989 S (proof only)	
313,092,780	1978 D	.15	661,636,000	1990	.15
3,127,781	1978 S (proof only)		663,938,503	1990 D	.15
463,188,000	1979	.15	3,299,559	1990 S (proof only)	
325,867,672	1979 D	.15	614,104,000	1991	.15
3,677,175	1979 S (proof only)		436,496,678	1991 D	.15
593,004,000	1980	.15	2,867,787	1991 S (proof only)	
502,323,448	1980 D	.15	399,552,000	1992	.15
3,554,806	1980 S (proof only)		450,565,113	1992 D	.15
657,504,000	1981	.15	4,176,560	1992 S (proof only)	
364,801,843	1981 D	.15	412,076,000	1993	.15
4,063,083	1981 S (proof only)		406,084,135	1993 D	.15
292,355,000	1982	.15	3,394,792	1993 S (proof only)	
373,726,544	1982 D	.15	722,160,000	1994	.15
3,857,479	1982 S (proof only)		715,726,110	1994 D	.15
561,615,000	1983	.15		1994 S (proof only)	
536,726,276	1983 D	.15	3,269,923	1995	.15
3,228,648	1983 S (proof only)		744,156,000	1995 D	.15
746,769,000	1984	.15	888,112,000	1995 S (proof only)	
517,675,146	1984 D	.15		1996	.15
3,065,110	1984 S (proof only)			1996 D	.15
647,114,962	1985	.15		1996 (proof only)	
459,747,446	1985 D	.15		1997	.15
3,362,662	1985 S (proof only)			1997 D	.15
536,883,493	1986	.15		1997 (proof only)	
61,819,144	1986 D	.15			
3,010,497	1986 S (proof only)				
371,499,481	1987	.15			
410,590,604	1987 D	.15			
3,792,233	1987 S (proof only)				

Note: 25,000 "Matte Finish" 1997 Jefferson nickels were struck for the U.S. Botanic Garden issue of that year.

Half Dimes

Flowing Hair
1794–1795

Draped Bust
1796–1797   **1800–1805**

HALF DIMES—FLOWING HAIR TYPE

QUANTITY	YEAR	ABOUT GOOD TO GOOD	VERY GOOD	FINE	VERY FINE
86,416	1794	$325.00	$700.00	$1300.00	$2250.00
	1795	300.00	600.00	1100.00	1600.00

HALF DIMES—DRAPED BUST TYPE

QUANTITY	YEAR	ABOUT GOOD TO GOOD	VERY GOOD	FINE	VERY FINE
10,230	1796	$400.00	$850.00	$1300.00	$2000.00
	1796 over 5	450.00	1000.00	1400.00	2250.00
44,527	1797 13 stars	350.00	800.00	1200.00	1500.00
	1797 15 stars	325.00	750.00	1100.00	1400.00
	1797 16 stars	325.00	750.00	1100.00	1400.00
24,000	1800	225.00	500.00	750.00	1100.00

QUANTITY	YEAR	ABOUT GOOD TO GOOD	VERY GOOD	FINE	VERY FINE
	1800 LIBERTY	225.00	500.00	750.00	1100.00
33,910	1801	225.00	500.00	750.00	1100.00
13,010	1802 extremely rare	2250.00	5000.00	15,000.00	25,000.00
37,850	1803	225.00	500.00	750.00	1000.00
15,600	1805	250.00	650.00	950.00	1650.00

HALF DIMES—CAPPED BUST TYPE

QUANTITY	YEAR	GOOD TO VERY GOOD	FINE	VERY FINE	EXT. FINE	UNC.
1,230,000	1829	$20.00	$27.50	$40.00	$85.00	$500.00
1,240,000	1830	20.00	27.50	40.00	80.00	450.00
1,242,700	1831	20.00	27.50	40.00	80.00	450.00
965,000	1832	20.00	27.50	40.00	80.00	450.00
1,370,000	1833	20.00	27.50	40.00	80.00	450.00
1,480,000	1834	20.00	27.50	40.00	80.00	450.00
2,760,000	1835	20.00	27.50	40.00	80.00	450.00
1,900,000	1836	20.00	27.50	40.00	80.00	450.00
2,276,000	1837 large 5c	20.00	27.50	40.00	80.00	450.00
	1837 small 5c	27.50	60.00	85.00	200.00	1750.00

1837–1838   1838–1859

The mint marks are under the wreath, or within it, on the reverse.

HALF DIMES—LIBERTY SEATED TYPE
Without stars

2,255,000	1837	$45.00	$75.00	$100.00	$225.00	$850.00
?	1838 O	55.00	120.00	250.00	650.00	3000.00

With stars, no drapery from elbow

2,255,000	1838	8.00	12.00	25.00	55.00	450.00
1,069,150	1839	8.00	12.00	25.00	55.00	450.00
1,096,550	1839 O	9.00	15.00	30.00	65.00	500.00
1,344,085	**1840	8.00	12.00	25.00	55.00	450.00
935,000	**1840 O	10.00	20.00	40.00	85.00	550.00

With drapery from elbow

	1840	12.50	17.50	40.00	100.00	700.00
	1840 O	20.00	35.00	60.00	125.00	850.00
1,150,000	1841	7.50	12.00	20.00	50.00	375.00
815,000	1841 O	10.00	17.50	35.00	70.00	550.00
815,000	1842	8.00	12.00	22.00	50.00	340.00
350,000	1842 O	12.00	25.00	75.00	150.00	750.00
1,165,000	1843	8.00	12.00	25.00	50.00	340.00
430,000	1844	8.00	15.00	25.00	50.00	375.00
220,000	1844 O	30.00	75.00	225.00	500.00	1000.00
1,564,000	1845	8.00	12.00	25.00	45.00	340.00

**Includes 1840 half dimes with drapery from elbow

HALF DIMES—LIBERTY SEATED TYPE (continued)

QUANTITY	YEAR	GOOD TO VERY GOOD	FINE	VERY FINE	EXT. FINE	UNC.
27,000	1846	85.00	250.00	400.00	800.00	1750.00
1,274,000	1847	8.00	12.00	25.00	45.00	340.00
668,000	1848	8.00	12.00	25.00	45.00	340.00
600,000	1848 O	12.00	25.00	55.00	90.00	575.00
1,309,000	1849	8.00	12.00	25.00	45.00	340.00
	1849 over 48	10.00	15.00	35.00	65.00	450.00
140,000	1849 O	35.00	67.50	150.00	365.00	1200.00
955,000	1850	8.00	12.00	25.00	50.00	300.00
690,000	1850 O	10.00	20.00	55.00	100.00	700.00
781,000	1851	8.00	12.00	25.00	50.00	375.00
860,000	1851 O	10.00	20.00	50.00	75.00	675.00
1,000,500	1852	8.00	12.00	25.00	50.00	375.00
260,000	1852 O	15.00	40.00	75.00	200.00	1250.00
13,345,020	1853 no arrows	17.50	45.00	80.00	150.00	650.00
	1853 arrows	8.00	12.00	20.00	50.00	300.00
2,360,000	1853 O no arrows	100.00	175.00	300.00	600.00	2500.00
	1853 O arrows	8.00	10.00	25.00	50.00	475.00
5,740,000	1854 arrows	8.00	10.00	25.00	50.00	300.00
1,560,000	1854 O arrows	8.00	12.00	30.00	60.00	500.00
1,750,000	1855 arrows	8.00	10.00	25.00	40.00	475.00
600,000	1855 O arrows	10.00	20.00	50.00	90.00	650.00
4,880,000	1856	7.00	10.00	20.00	40.00	300.00
1,100,000	1856 O	7.00	10.00	20.00	45.00	500.00
1,380,000	1857 O	7.00	10.00	20.00	50.00	500.00
3,500,000	1858	7.00	10.00	20.00	40.00	275.00
1,660,000	1858 O	7.00	10.00	20.00	45.00	400.00
340,000	1859	10.00	17.50	35.00	65.00	350.00
560,000	1859 O	7.00	12.50	27.50	65.00	415.00

1860–1873

QUANTITY	YEAR	GOOD TO VERY GOOD	FINE	VERY FINE	EXT. FINE	UNC.
799,000	1860 no stars	7.50	11.00	15.00	35.00	300.00
1,060,000	1860 O	7.50	12.50	20.00	50.00	350.00
3,281,000	1861	7.50	11.00	15.00	35.00	315.00
1,492,550	1862	7.50	11.00	15.00	35.00	315.00
18,460	1863	37.50	75.00	135.00	200.00	700.00
100,000	1863 S	20.00	30.00	50.00	115.00	675.00
48,470	1864	200.00	300.00	350.00	500.00	1500.00
90,000	1864 S	25.00	65.00	85.00	165.00	825.00
13,500	1865	75.00	125.00	215.00	315.00	1000.00
120,000	1865 S	15.00	25.00	50.00	100.00	700.00
10,725	1866	55.00	125.00	200.00	325.00	800.00
120,000	1866 S	15.00	30.00	50.00	115.00	700.00
8,625	1867	80.00	150.00	275.00	350.00	1000.00
120,000	1867 S	14.00	32.50	55.00	140.00	625.00
85,900	1868	15.00	35.00	60.00	150.00	650.00
280,000	1868 S	8.00	15.00	25.00	50.00	450.00
208,600	1869	8.00	15.00	22.50	45.00	400.00
230,000	1869 S	8.00	12.00	20.00	45.00	400.00
536,600	1870	6.50	10.00	15.00	35.00	340.00
1,488,860	1871	6.50	10.00	15.00	30.00	300.00
161,000	1871 S	17.50	30.00	65.00	110.00	450.00
2,947,950	1872	6.50	9.00	15.00	30.00	275.00
837,000	1872 S in wreath	6.50	9.00	15.00	32.50	285.00
	1872 S below wreath	6.50	9.00	15.00	32.50	285.00
712,600	1873	6.50	9.00	15.00	32.50	285.00
324,000	1873 S	6.50	9.00	15.00	32.50	285.00

Dimes

DIMES—DRAPED BUST TYPE

1795–1797   **1798–1807**

QUANTITY	YEAR	ABOUT GOOD TO GOOD	VERY GOOD	FINE	VERY FINE
22,135	1796	$550.00	$1250.00	$1850.00	$2750.00
25,261	1797 13 stars	425.00	1100.00	1350.00	2150.00
	1797 16 stars	450.00	1150.00	1400.00	2350.00
27,550	1798 over 97	225.00	475.00	900.00	1275.00
	1798	225.00	475.00	900.00	1275.00
21,760	1800	200.00	450.00	850.00	1000.00
34,640	1801	225.00	500.00	1000.00	1250.00
10,975	1802	235.00	550.00	1000.00	1350.00
33,040	1803	225.00	500.00	900.00	1200.00
8,265	1804	325.00	550.00	1500.00	3250.00
120,780	1805	175.00	425.00	800.00	1000.00
165,000	1807	175.00	425.00	800.00	1000.00

DIMES—CAPPED BUST TYPE

QUANTITY	YEAR	ABOUT GOOD TO GOOD	VERY GOOD	FINE	VERY FINE	UNC.
44,710	1809	$50.00	$125.00	$225.00	$425.00	$3800.00
65,180	1811 over 09	35.00	75.00	100.00	215.00	3350.00
421,500	1814	25.00	40.00	55.00	100.00	2500.00
942,587	1820	22.50	32.50	50.00	80.00	1800.00
1,186,512	1821	22.50	30.00	45.00	75.00	1750.00
100,000	1822	100.00	150.00	300.00	500.00	6500.00
440,000	1823 over 22	25.00	35.00	50.00	80.00	2250.00
?	1824 over 22	22.50	40.00	65.00	100.00	2250.00
510,000	1825	25.00	32.50	50.00	80.00	1400.00
1,215,000	1827	15.00	32.50	45.00	75.00	1400.00
125,000	1828 large date	30.00	50.00	75.00	125.00	1750.00
	1828 small date	25.00	35.00	55.00	80.00	1750.00
	1829 large 10c	22.50	40.00	60.00	140.00	1100.00
	1829 medium 10c	17.50	35.00	45.00	125.00	1050.00
	1829 small 10c	17.50	35.00	45.00	125.00	1050.00
510,000	1830	17.50	35.00	50.00	125.00	850.00
771,350	1831	17.50	35.00	45.00	125.00	800.00
522,500	1832	17.50	35.00	45.00	125.00	800.00
485,000	1833	17.50	35.00	45.00	125.00	800.00
635,000	1834	17.50	35.00	45.00	125.00	800.00
1,410,000	1835	17.50	35.00	45.00	125.00	800.00
1,190,000	1836	17.50	35.00	45.00	125.00	800.00
1,042,000	* 1837	17.50	35.00	45.00	125.00	800.00

*Includes Liberty Seated dimes of 1837

DIMES—LIBERTY SEATED TYPE

1837–1838   **1838–1860**

The mint marks are under the wreath or within it, on the reverse.

QUANTITY	YEAR	GOOD TO VERY GOOD	FINE	VERY FINE	EXT. FINE	UNC.
			Without stars			
	1837	$42.50	$80.00	$135.00	$300.00	$1100.00
402,434	1838 O	50.00	120.00	200.00	350.00	2250.00
		With stars, no drapery from elbow				
1,992,500	1838	17.50	32.50	50.00	125.00	1000.00
1,053,115	1839	7.50	15.00	25.00	60.00	425.00
1,243,272	1839 O	8.00	20.00	35.00	55.00	500.00
1,358,580	** 1840	7.50	14.00	25.00	55.00	425.00
1,175,000	1840 O	8.50	20.00	35.00	65.00	850.00
	1841 very rare					
		With drapery from elbow				
	1840	17.50	35.00	55.00	120.00	800.00
1,622,500	1841	6.00	10.00	25.00	50.00	350.00
2,007,500	1841 O	7.50	15.00	25.00	50.00	500.00
1,887,500	1842	6.00	10.00	20.00	45.00	450.00
2,020,000	1842 O	10.00	20.00	30.00	80.00	550.00
1,370,000	1843	6.00	10.00	20.00	45.00	450.00
150,000	1843 O	40.00	110.00	350.00	600.00	2000.00
72,500	1844	40.00	80.00	160.00	375.00	1750.00
1,755,000	1845	6.00	10.00	20.00	35.00	400.00
230,000	‡‡ 1845 O	37.50	100.00	160.00	500.00	2000.00
31,300	1846	65.00	120.00	200.00	425.00	850.00
245,000	1847	12.50	20.00	45.00	90.00	1000.00
451,500	1848	9.00	17.50	35.00	75.00	500.00
839,000	1849	6.00	12.00	25.00	75.00	600.00
300,000	1849 O	15.00	30.00	65.00	200.00	2000.00
1,931,500	1850	6.00	12.00	25.00	45.00	400.00
510,000	1850 O	15.00	30.00	55.00	125.00	1200.00
1,026,500	1851	6.00	12.00	25.00	50.00	425.00
400,000	1851 O	12.50	20.00	45.00	150.00	1250.00
1,535,500	1852	6.00	12.00	20.00	45.00	450.00
430,000	1852 O	15.00	30.00	50.00	200.00	1500.00
12,173,010	‡‡ 1853	30.00	55.00	85.00	175.00	1000.00
		With arrows at date				
	1853	5.50	12.00	25.00	50.00	400.00
1,100,000	1853 O	8.00	15.00	35.00	80.00	800.00
4,470,000	1854	6.00	12.00	22.50	45.00	475.00
1,770,000	1854 O	6.50	17.50	27.50	50.00	500.00
2,075,000	1855	6.00	12.00	22.50	45.00	475.00
		Without arrows at date				
5,780,000	1856	5.50	12.00	20.00	35.00	400.00
1,180,000	1856 O	5.50	12.00	20.00	35.00	550.00
70,000	1856 S	40.00	80.00	125.00	500.00	2500.00
5,580,000	1857	5.50	12.00	20.00	25.00	350.00
1,540,000	1857 O	5.50	12.50	25.00	40.00	475.00
1,540,000	1858	5.50	12.00	20.00	35.00	350.00
290,000	1858 O	10.00	25.00	40.00	75.00	700.00
60,000	1858 S	45.00	85.00	150.00	400.00	1250.00
430,000	1859	5.50	12.00	20.00	35.00	425.00

**Includes 1840 dimes with drapery from elbow
‡‡ A "Superb" 1845-O dime sold for $90,200 at the May 1996 Eliasberg sale.
†† Includes 1853 dimes with arrows at date

1860–1891

QUANTITY	YEAR	GOOD TO VERY GOOD	FINE	VERY FINE	EXT. FINE	UNC.
480,000	1859 O	5.50	12.50	25.00	45.00	450.00
140,000	1860 S	17.50	45.00	125.00	225.00	1000.00
607,000	1860	$5.50	$12.00	$15.00	$27.50	$275.00
40,000	1860 O rare	450.00	750.00	1000.00	2500.00	11,000.00
1,924,000	1861	5.50	12.00	15.00	27.50	275.00
172,500	1861 S	16.00	35.00	70.00	150.00	1000.00
847,550	1862	5.50	12.00	15.00	27.50	265.00
180,750	1862 S	15.00	37.50	65.00	135.00	1000.00
14,460	1863	50.00	100.00	175.00	300.00	1000.00
157,500	1863 S	20.00	40.00	75.00	165.00	1000.00
11,470	1864	55.00	115.00	150.00	275.00	1000.00
230,000	1864 S	55.00	30.00	55.00	140.00	1050.00
10,500	1865	15.00	125.00	225.00	325.00	1100.00
175,000	1865 S	15.00	32.50	65.00	175.00	1000.00
8,725	1866	90.00	225.00	300.00	500.00	1300.00
135,000	1866 S	15.00	35.00	60.00	150.00	1100.00
6,625	1867	175.00	300.00	500.00	625.00	1500.00
140,000	1867 S	15.00	35.00	55.00	140.00	1100.00
466,250	1868	5.50	12.50	25.00	55.00	500.00
260,000	1868 S	12.00	25.00	45.00	75.00	425.00
256,600	1869	5.50	12.00	17.50	40.00	450.00
450,000	1869 S	12.00	25.00	35.00	100.00	425.00
471,500	1870	5.50	12.00	15.00	35.00	400.00
50,000	1870 S	70.00	125.00	200.00	350.00	2750.00
753,610	1871	5.50	12.00	15.00	35.00	300.00
320,000	1871 S	12.50	30.00	60.00	125.00	1000.00
20,100	1871 CC rare	275.00	750.00	1000.00	2000.00	6500.00
2,396,450	1872	5.50	12.00	15.00	35.00	275.00
190,000	1872 S	12.50	30.00	60.00	125.00	800.00
24,000	1872 CC	150.00	450.00	675.00	1200.00	3500.00
3,947,100	1873 no arrows	5.50	12.00	15.00	40.00	300.00
	1873 arrows	12.50	30.00	45.00	100.00	750.00
455,000	1873 S arrows	20.00	45.00	65.00	110.00	750.00
31,191	1873 CC arrows	425.00	800.00	1000.00	1750.00	22,500.00
***	1873 CC no arrows					(unique)
2,940,700	1874 arrows	15.00	135.00	50.00	100.00	750.00
240,000	1874 S arrows	22.50	50.00	80.00	140.00	850.00
10,817	1874 CC arrows (very rare)	325.00	1250.00	2000.00	4250.00	22,500.00

Without arrows at date

QUANTITY	YEAR	GOOD TO VERY GOOD	FINE	VERY FINE	EXT. FINE	UNC.
10,350,700	1875	5.50	12.00	15.00	30.00	235.00
9,070,000	1875 S in wreath	5.50	12.00	15.00	30.00	235.00
	1875 S below wreath	5.50	12.00	15.00	30.00	235.00
4,645,000	1875 CC in wreath	5.50	12.00	15.00	30.00	275.00
	1875 CC below wreath	5.50	12.50	17.50	35.00	300.00
11,461,150	1876	5.50	9.00	12.50	30.00	225.00
10,420,000	1876 S	5.50	9.00	12.50	30.00	225.00
8,270,000	1876 CC	5.50	9.00	12.50	30.00	250.00
7,310,510	1877	5.50	9.00	12.50	30.00	225.00
2,340,000	1877 S	5.50	9.00	12.50	30.00	225.00

*** The 1873–CC no arrows dime realized $550,00 at the May 1996 Eliasberg sale.

DIMES—LIBERTY SEATED TYPE (continued)

QUANTITY	YEAR	GOOD TO VERY GOOD	VERY FINE	EXT. FINE	FINE	UNC.
7,700,000	1877 CC	5.50	10.00	15.00	35.00	325.00
1,678,800	1878	5.50	10.00	12.50	32.50	250.00
200,000	1878 CC	22.50	50.00	85.00	150.00	675.00
15,100	1879	65.00	100.00	200.00	300.00	725.00
37,355	1880	45.00	85.00	175.00	200.00	550.00
24,975	1881	50.00	90.00	185.00	225.00	575.00
3,911,100	1882	5.50	9.00	12.50	30.00	250.00
7,675,712	1883	5.50	9.00	12.50	30.00	250.00
3,366,380	1884	5.50	9.00	12.50	30.00	250.00
564,969	1884 S	11.00	22.50	40.00	75.00	400.00
2,533,427	1885	5.50	9.00	12.50	30.00	235.00
43,690	1885 S	200.00	300.00	400.00	625.00	3750.00
6,377,570	1886	5.50	9.00	12.50	30.00	225.00
206,524	1886 S	11.00	27.50	50.00	80.00	500.00
11,283,939	1887	5.50	9.00	12.50	30.00	225.00
4,454,450	1887 S	5.50	9.00	12.50	30.00	235.00
5,496,487	1888	5.50	9.00	12.50	30.00	225.00
1,720,000	1888 S	5.50	9.00	15.00	35.00	235.00
7,380,711	1889	5.50	9.00	12.50	30.00	225.00
972,678	1889 S	11.00	25.00	60.00	90.00	400.00
9,911,541	1890	5.50	9.00	12.50	30.00	225.00
1,423,076	1890 S	5.50	9.00	15.00	32.50	275.00
15,310,600	1891	5.50	9.00	12.50	30.00	225.00
4,540,000	1891 O	5.50	9.00	15.00	35.00	275.00
3,196,116	1891 S	5.50	9.00	12.50	30.00	275.00

DIMES—LIBERTY HEAD TYPE

The mint marks are under the wreath on the reverse.

QUANTITY	YEAR	GOOD	VERY GOOD	FINE	VERY FINE	EXT. FINE	UNC.	PROOF
12,121,245	1892	$2.00	$3.75	$5.75	$10.00	$25.00	$150.00	$750.00
3,841,700	1892 O	4.50	8.00	10.00	17.50	30.00	200.00	
990,710	1892 S	25.00	35.00	45.00	60.00	90.00	325.00	
3,340,792	1893	4.00	6.00	9.00	15.00	25.00	200.00	825.00
1,760,000	1893 O	12.00	17.50	25.00	35.00	50.00	275.00	
2,491,401	1893 S	5.50	7.00	13.50	20.00	35.00	275.00	
1,330,972	1894	7.00	10.00	15.00	25.00	35.00	225.00	825.00
720,000	1894 O	30.00	42.50	70.00	100.00	200.00	1000.00	
24	*1894 S ext. rare						100,000.00*	
690,880	1895	35.00	50.00	80.00	100.00	150.00	450.00	825.00
440,000	1895 O	100.00	125.00	200.00	300.00	375.00	1750.00	
1,120,000	1895 S	13.50	20.00	27.50	40.00	65.00	350.00	
2,000,762	1896	5.50	8.00	12.50	20.00	32.50	215.00	650.00
610,000	1896 O	40.00	50.00	70.00	90.00	150.00	500.00	
575,056	1896 S	32.50	45.00	65.00	100.00	200.00	725.00	
10,869,264	1897	1.50	2.25	5.50	8.00	20.00	175.00	625.00
666,000	1897 O	32.50	40.00	60.00	80.00	175.00	625.00	
1,342,844	1897 S	7.50	13.50	22.50	37.50	60.00	275.00	
16,320,735	1898	1.50	2.00	4.25	7.50	17.50	175.00	625.00
2,130,000	1898 O	4.00	6.25	12.50	27.50	55.00	250.00	
1,702,507	1898 S	4.00	6.25	12.50	25.00	50.00	225.00	
19,580,846	1899	1.35	1.75	4.25	10.00	20.00	165.00	625.00
2,650,000	1899 O	3.75	7.00	15.00	25.00	50.00	250.00	
1,867,493	1899 S	4.00	6.50	12.50	20.00	40.00	250.00	

* An 1894 S sold for $451,000 at the May 1996 Eliasberg sale.

QUANTITY	YEAR	GOOD	GOOD	VERY FINE	FINE	VERY FINE	UNC.	EXT. PROOF
17,600,912	1900	1.25	2.00	5.00	7.00	17.50	125.00	625.00
2,010,000	1900 O	5.00	8.00	15.00	25.00	55.00	250.00	
5,168,270	1900 S	2.00	3.25	6.00	10.00	22.50	150.00	
18,860,478	1901	1.25	1.50	3.50	7.00	15.00	150.00	625.00
5,620,000	1901 O	1.85	3.25	7.00	15.00	40.00	375.00	
593,022	1901 S	30.00	55.00	85.00	125.00	190.00	750.00	
21,380,777	1902	1.25	2.00	4.25	10.00	20.00	175.00	625.00
4,500,000	1902 O	1.75	3.25	7.00	15.00	30.00	235.00	
2,070,000	1902 S	3.50	7.00	12.50	25.00	50.00	275.00	
19,500,755	1903	1.50	1.75	5.00	10.00	20.00	175.00	625.00
8,180,000	1903 O	1.75	2.75	6.50	12.50	27.50	225.00	
613,300	1903 S	25.00	35.00	55.00	70.00	135.00	575.00	
14,601,027	1904	1.35	1.75	5.25	10.00	25.00	175.00	625.00
800,000	1904 S	17.50	27.50	40.00	55.00	90.00	575.00	
14,552,350	1905	1.25	1.50	5.00	10.00	17.50	175.00	625.00
3,400,000	1905 O	1.75	3.75	10.00	15.00	35.00	225.00	
6,855,199	1905 S	1.50	2.50	5.50	12.00	25.00	225.00	
19,958,406	1906	1.25	1.50	3.00	8.00	17.50	175.00	625.00
4,060,000	1906 D	1.50	2.50	7.00	12.50	25.00	185.00	
2,610,000	1906 O	2.65	5.50	12.50	22.50	32.50	175.00	
3,136,640	1906 S	2.00	3.75	7.50	12.50	30.00	175.00	
22,220,575	1907	1.25	1.75	3.00	9.00	20.00	175.00	625.00
4,080,000	1907 D	1.50	3.50	7.00	12.50	30.00	175.00	
5,058,000	1907 O	1.50	2.75	6.50	12.00	27.50	185.00	
3,178,470	1907 S	1.50	2.75	7.00	12.50	27.50	185.00	
10,600,545	1908	1.25	1.50	3.75	10.00	25.00	175.00	625.00
7,490,000	1908 D	1.25	1.75	3.50	9.00	22.50	175.00	
1,789,000	1908 O	3.50	6.50	12.50	20.00	35.00	200.00	
3,220,000	1908 S	1.50	2.75	7.00	12.00	25.00	180.00	625.00
10,240,650	1909	1.25	1.75	3.50	10.00	22.50	175.00	
954,000	1909 D	3.75	6.50	14.00	27.50	50.00	225.00	
2,287,000	1909 O	2.75	3.75	9.00	17.50	32.50	235.00	
1,000,000	1909 S	4.25	7.75	17.50	35.00	55.00	235.00	625.00
11,520,551	1910	1.35	1.65	3.00	9.00	22.50	175.00	
3,490,000	1910 D	1.65	2.50	5.00	11.00	27.50	200.00	
1,240,000	1910 S	2.50	4.25	7.75	17.50	32.50	225.00	625.00
18,870,543	1911	1.25	1.75	3.00	7.50	22.50	175.00	
11,209,000	1911 D	1.25	1.40	3.00	7.50	22.50	175.00	
3,520,000	1911 S	1.50	2.25	3.75	11.00	27.50	185.00	625.00
19,350,700	1912	1.25	1.75	2.75	7.50	27.50	175.00	
11,760,000	1912 D	1.35	1.75	2.75	7.50	27.50	175.00	
3,420,000	1912 S	1.75	2.35	4.25	7.75	25.00	185.00	625.00
19,760,622	1913	1.25	1.65	2.75	6.75	22.50	175.00	
510,000	1913 S	7.50	13.00	27.50	45.00	90.00	300.00	700.00
17,360,655	1914	1.25	1.75	2.75	7.50	22.50	175.00	
11,908,000	1914 D	1.25	1.75	2.75	7.50	22.50	175.00	
2,100,000	1914 S	1.75	2.75	7.00	11.00	27.50	185.00	700.00
5,620,450	1915	1.25	1.75	3.75	10.00	22.50	175.00	
960,000	1915 S	2.50	3.25	10.00	16.50	32.50	190.00	
18,490,000	1916	1.25	1.75	3.25	9.00	22.50	175.00	
5,820,000	1916 S	1.25	1.75	3.25	9.00	22.50	175.00	

*A Proof specimen fetched $275,000.00 at a 1/16/90 auction.

DIMES—MERCURY HEAD TYPE

The mint marks are to the left of the fasces on the reverse.

DIMES—MERCURY HEAD TYPE (continued)

QUANTITY	YEAR	GOOD	VERY GOOD	FINE	VERY FINE	EXT. FINE	UNC.
22,180,080	1916	$1.00	$2.50	$3.50	$5.50	$7.50	$35.00
264,0000	1916 D	275.00	350.00	800.00	1250.00	2000.00	3750.00
10,450,000	1916 S	2.75	3.75	5.50	7.00	13.50	37.50
55,230,000	1917	1.20	1.35	1.75	2.50	6.25	30.00
9,402,000	1917 D	2.15	4.50	7.75	12.00	30.00	125.00
27,330,000	1917 S	1.25	1.65	2.00	3.50	7.25	65.00
26,680,000	1918	1.10	1.35	3.75	7.50	20.00	70.00
22,674,800	1918 D	1.25	1.50	4.25	8.00	16.50	100.00
19,300,000	1918 S	1.10	1.35	2.35	7.00	16.50	80.00
35,740,000	1919	1.00	1.25	2.00	3.25	7.50	45.00
9,939,000	1919 D	1.75	3.00	8.00	15.00	32.50	125.00
8,850,000	1919 S	1.75	3.25	8.00	15.00	32.50	135.00
59,030,000	1920	1.00	1.50	1.50	1.75	4.00	30.00
19,171,000	1920 D	1.10	1.65	2.15	4.75	11.00	80.00
13,820,000	1920 S	1.10	1.25	2.00	4.50	12.00	80.00
1,230,000	1921	16.50	25.00	50.00	90.00	350.00	900.00
1,080,000	1921 D	27.50	40.00	75.00	150.00	400.00	850.00
50,130,000	1923	1.00	1.10	1.20	1.50	3.50	25.00
6,440,000	1923 S	1.10	1.50	3.75	6.50	25.00	100.00
24,010,000	1924	1.00	1.10	1.25	2.00	5.00	50.00
6,810,000	1924 D	1.10	1.65	3.75	5.50	18.00	110.00
7,120,000	1924 S	1.00	1.35	2.50	5.50	18.00	100.00
25,610,000	1925	1.00	1.15	1.35	2.00	5.00	50.00
5,117,000	1925 D	2.25	4.25	9.00	22.50	70.00	250.00
5,850,000	1925 S	1.10	1.35	2.00	6.25	22.50	125.00
32,160,000	1926	1.00	1.15	1.30	1.50	4.00	25.00
6,828,000	1926 D	1.10	1.50	2.50	5.00	15.00	80.00
1,520,000	1926 S	6.50	8.50	16.50	22.50	125.00	625.00
28,080,000	1927	1.00	1.15	1.25	1.50	3.50	25.00
4,812,000	1927 D	1.15	2.75	5.50	20.00	35.00	200.00
4,770,000	1927 S	1.10	1.35	2.00	5.50	17.50	150.00
19,480,000	1928	1.00	1.15	1.25	1.50	3.50	35.00
4,161,000	1928 D	1.25	2.50	4.00	15.00	35.00	125.00
7,400,000	1928 S	1.10	1.25	1.50	3.75	11.00	75.00
25,970,000	1929	1.00	1.10	1.20	1.40	3.00	25.00
5,034,000	1929 D	1.10	1.25	2.40	3.25	6.50	30.00
4,730,000	1929 S	1.00	1.15	1.65	2.75	4.25	50.00
6,770,000	1930	1.00	1.15	1.50	1.75	4.50	40.00
1,843,000	1930 S	2.25	3.00	4.00	5.00	15.00	150.00
3,150,000	1931	1.20	1.30	1.75	3.25	7.25	60.00
1,260,000	1931 D	7.00	8.00	9.00	14.00	22.50	125.00
1,800,000	1931 S	2.25	3.50	4.00	4.75	12.50	85.00
24,080,000	1934	1.00	1.15	1.35	1.40	4.00	32.50
6,772,000	1934 D	1.00	1.30	1.50	2.00	6.00	75.00
58,830,000	1935	1.00	1.10	1.20	1.30	1.75	20.00
10,477,000	1935 D	1.00	1.15	1.30	2.00	7.00	40.00
15,840,000	1935 S	1.00	1.10	1.20	1.30	2.25	25.00
87,504,130	1936				1.25	1.50	12.50
16,132,000	1936 D				1.35	5.00	30.00
9,210,000	1936 S				1.25	2.75	20.00
56,865,756	1937				1.00	1.50	12.00
14,146,000	1937 D				1.10	1.50	40.00
9,740,000	1937 S				1.10	1.50	25.00
22,198,728	1938				1.00	1.40	12.50
5,537,000	1938 D				1.25	2.25	22.50
8,090,000	1938 S				1.25	2.25	20.00
67,749,321	1939				1.10	1.65	10.00
24,394,000	1939 D				1.10	1.65	12.50
10,540,000	1939 S				1.35	3.00	25.00
65,361,827	1940				1.10	1.50	8.00
21,198,000	1940 D				1.10	1.50	15.00
21,560,000	1940 S				1.10	1.50	12.50
175,106,557	1941				1.10	1.50	8.00
45,634,000	1941 D				1.10	1.50	15.00
43,090,000	1941 S				1.10	1.50	12.50

1942

The 1942/41 dime very clearly shows the numeral "1" at the front edge of the "2" in the date. The second "1" is close to the "4" as on the regular 1941 dimes.

QUANTITY	YEAR	VERY FINE	EXT. FINE	UNC.
205,432,329	1942 over 1	275.00	350.00	1250.00
	1942			7.50
60,740,000	1942 D	1.10	1.50	12.50
49,300,000	1942 S	1.10	1.50	17.50
191,710,000	1943	1.10	1.50	6.00
71,949,000	1943 D	1.10	1.50	6.00
60,400,000	1943 S	1.10	1.50	10.00
231,410,000	1944	1.10	1.50	6.00
62,224,000	1944 D	1.10	1.50	6.00
49,490,000	1944 S	1.10	1.50	6.00
159,130,000	1945	1.10	1.50	6.00
40,245,000	1945 D	1.10	1.50	11.00
41,920,000	1945 S	1.10	1.50	15.00

DIMES—ROOSEVELT TYPE

QUANTITY	YEAR	EXT. FINE	MS-63
255,250,000	1946	$1.15	$2.00
61,043,500	1946 D	1.15	2.50
27,900,000	1946 S	1.15	3.50
121,520,000	1947	1.15	2.50
46,835,000	1947 D	1.15	5.00
38,840,000	1947 S	1.15	4.00

The mint marks are at the left bottom of the torch on the reverse.

QUANTITY	YEAR	MS-65	QUANTITY	YEAR	MS-65
74,950,000	1948	3.50	85,780,000	1959	1.25
52,841,000	1948 D	3.50	164,919,790	1959 D	1.25
35,520,000	1948 S	5.00	70,390,000	1960	1.25
30,940,000	194	17.50	200,160,400	1960 D	1.25
26,034,000	1949 D	8.00	96,758,244	1961	1.25
13,510,000	1949 S	25.00	209,146,550	1961 D	1.25
50,181,500	1950	3.50	75,668,019	1962	1.25
46,803,000	1950 D	3.00	334,948,380	1962 D	1.25
20,440,000	1950 S	15.00	126,725,645	1963	1.25
103,937,602	1951	2.50	421,476,530	1963 D	1.25
52,191,800	1951 D	2.00	929,360,000	1964	1.25
31,630,000	1951 S	10.00	1,357,517,180	1964 D	1.25
99,122,073	1952	2.50	1,649,780,570	1965	.25
122,100,000	1952 D	2.50	1,380,474,957	1966	.25
44,419,500	1952 S	5.00	2,244,007,320	1967	.25
53,618,920	1953	2.00	424,470,400	1968	.25
136,400,000	1953 D	1.75	480,748,280	1968 D	.25
39,180,000	1953 S	2.75	3,041,509	1968 S (proof only)	
114,243,503	1954	2.00	145,790,000	1969	.25
106,397,000	1954 D	2.00	563,323,870	1969 D	.25
22,860,000	1954 S	2.00	2,934,631	1969 S (proof only)	
12,828,381	1955	2.50	345,570,000	1970	.25
13,959,000	1955 D	1.75	754,942,100	1970 D	.25
18,510,000	1955 S	1.75	2,632,810	1970 S (proof only)	
108,821,081	1956	1.50	162,690,000	1971	.25
108,015,100	1956 D	1.50	377,914,240	1971 D	.25
160,160,000	1957	1.50	3,244,138	1971 S (proof only)	
113,354,330	1957 D	1.50	431,540,000	1972	.25
31,910,000	1958	1.75	330,290,000	1972 D	.25
136,564,600	1958 D	1.25	3,267,667	1972 S (proof only)	

DIMES—ROOSEVELT TYPE (continued)

QUANTITY	YEAR	MS-65	QUANTITY	YEAR	MS-65
315,670,000	1973	.25	473,326,974	1986 D	.20
455,032,426	1973 D	.25	3,010,497	1986 S (proof only)	
2,769,624	1973 S (proof only)		762,709,481	1987	.20
470,248,000	1974	.25	653,203,402	1987 D	.20
571,083,000	1974 D	.25	3,792,233	1987 S (proof only)	
2,617,350	1974 S (proof only)		1,030,550,000	1988	.20
585,673,900	1975	.25	962,385,489	1988 D	.20
313,705,300	1975 D	.25	3,262,938	1988 S (proof only)	
2,845,450	1975 S (proof only)		1,298,400,000	1989	.20
568,760,000	1976	.25	896,535,597	1989 D	.20
695,222,774	1976 D	.25	3,215,728	1989 S (proof only)	
4,149,730	1976 (proof only)		1,034,340,000	1990	.20
796,930,000	1977	.25	839,995,824	1990 D	.20
376,607,228	1977 D	.25	3,299,559	1990 S (proof only)	
3,251,152	1977 S (proof only)		927,220,000	1991	.20
663,980,000	1978	.20	601,241,114	1991 D	.20
282,847,540	1978 D	.20	2,867,787	1991 S (proof only)	
3,127,781	1978 S (proof only)		593,500,000	1992	.20
315,440,000	1979	.20	616,273,932	1992 D	.20
390,921,184	1979 D	.20	2,858,981	1992 S (proof only)	
3,677,175	1979 S (proof only)		766,180,000	1993	.20
735,170,000	1980	.20	750,110,166	1993D	.20
719,354,321	1980 D	.20	2,633,439	1993S (proof only)	
3,554,806	1980 S (proof only)		1,189,000,000	1994	.20
676,650,000	1981	.20	1,303,268,110	1994 D	.20
712,284,143	1981 D	.20	2,484,594	1994 S (proof only)	
4,063,083	1981 S (proof only)		1,125,500,000	1995	.20
519,475,000	1982	.20	1,274,890,000	1995 D	.20
542,713,584	1982 D	.20		1995 S (proof only)	
3,857,479	1982 S (proof only)			1996	.20
647,025,000	1983	.20		1996 D	.20
730,129,224	1983 D	.20		1996 S (proof only)	
3,228,648	1983 S (proof only)			1997	.20
856,669,000	1984	.20		1997 D	.20
704,803,976	1984 D	.20		1997 S (proof only)	
3,065,110	1984 S (proof only)				
705,200,962	1985	.20			
587,979,970	1985 D	.20			
3,362,662	1985 S (proof only)				
682,649,693	1986	.20			

Twenty Cents

These silver coins were issued for a very short time, from 1875 to 1878. The difference between this coin and the popular quarter was too slight to make the twenty-cent piece useful. A peculiarity of this coin is that it had a smooth edge instead of the usual corrugated edge.

TWENTY CENT PIECES

The mint marks are under the eagle on the reverse.

QUANTITY	YEAR	GOOD TO VERY GOOD	FINE	VERY FINE	EXT. FINE	UNC.	PROOF
39,700	1875	$60.00	$80.00	$130.00	$215.00	$1000.00	$2500.00
1,155,000	1875 S	55.00	70.00	125.00	185.00	1000.00	
133,290	1875 CC	65.00	70.00	130.00	215.00	1100.00	
15,900	1876	80.00	115.00	165.00	250.00	1250.00	
10,000	1876 CC (extremely rare)						2500.00
510	1877 only proofs were struck						4000.00
600	1878 only proofs were struck						3750.00

Quarters

QUARTERS—DRAPED BUST TYPE

1796

1804–1807

QUANTITY	YEAR	ABOUT GOOD TO GOOD	VERY GOOD	FINE	VERY FINE
5,894	1796 rare	$1300.00	$2750.00	$5000.00	$10,500.00
6,738	1804	320.00	800.00	1800.00	4000.00
121,394	1805	135.00	200.00	300.00	900.00
206,124	1806 over 5	125.00	165.00	300.00	900.00
	1806	100.00	165.00	275.00	800.00
220,643	1807	100.00	165.00	275.00	800.00

QUARTERS—CAPPED BUST TYPE

QUANTITY	YEAR	ABOUT GOOD TO GOOD	VERY GOOD	FINE	VERY FINE	UNC.
69,232	1815	$40.00	$55.00	$85.00	$265.00	$3250.00
361,174	1818 over 15	45.00	55.00	85.00	275.00	2750.00
	1818	40.00	55.00	85.00	265.00	2250.00
144,000	1819	40.00	55.00	80.00	235.00	2000.00
127,444	1820	40.00	55.00	80.00	235.00	2000.00
216,851	1821	40.00	55.00	80.00	235.00	1800.00
64,080	1822	40.00	65.00	90.00	275.00	2500.00
	1822 25 over 50c (rare)	300.00	425.00	700.00	1250.00	8500.00

QUANTITY	YEAR	ABOUT GOOD TO GOOD	VERY GOOD	FINE	VERY FINE	UNC.
17,000	1823 over 22 (extremely rare)	2000.00	5000.00	10,000.00	17,500.00	
?	1824	45.00	55.00	85.00	250.00	3200.00
168,000	1825 over 22	40.00	50.00	75.00	175.00	2600.00
	1825 over 23	40.00	50.00	75.00	175.00	2400.00
	1825 over 24	40.00	50.00	75.00	175.00	2700.00
4,000	1827 extremely rare, Superior August 1990 Sale, Proof					42,000.00
102,000	1828	40.00	50.00	65.00	200.00	2500.00
?	1828 25 over 50c	70.00	120.00	200.00	315.00	3200.00

QUANTITY	YEAR	GOOD TO VERY GOOD	FINE	VERY FINE	EXT. FINE	UNC.
398,000	1831	40.00	50.00	85.00	200.00	1100.00
320,000	1832	40.00	50.00	85.00	200.00	1100.00
156,000	1833	40.00	55.00	110.00	300.00	1200.00
286,000	1834	40.00	50.00	90.00	200.00	1100.00
1,952,000	1835	40.00	50.00	85.00	200.00	1100.00
472,000	1836	40.00	50.00	85.00	200.00	1100.00
252,400	1837	40.00	50.00	85.00	200.00	1200.00
832,000*	1838	40.00	50.00	85.00	200.00	1100.00

QUARTERS—LIBERTY SEATED TYPE

1838–1865   **1866–1891**

Without drapery from elbow
The mint marks are under the eagle on the reverse.

QUANTITY	YEAR					
	*1838	$13.50	$25.00	$50.00	$165.00	$1700.00
491,146	1839	13.50	22.50	45.00	160.00	1600.00
425,200	**1840 O	13.50	22.50	45.00	150.00	1300.00

With drapery from elbow

QUANTITY	YEAR					
188,127	1840	13.50	27.50	50.00	150.00	1200.00
	**1840 O	12.50	25.00	45.00	160.00	1250.00
120,000	1841	25.00	45.00	70.00	175.00	900.00
452,000	1841 O	15.00	30.00	60.00	150.00	900.00
88,000	1842	37.50	85.00	130.00	250.00	1500.00
769,000	1842 O large date	15.00	25.00	50.00	80.00	1100.00
	1842 O small date	50.00	200.00	400.00	800.00	3000.00

*Includes 1838 Liberty Seated quarters.
**Includes 1840 O quarters with drapery from elbow.

QUANTITY	YEAR	GOOD TO VERY GOOD	FINE	VERY FINE	EXT. FINE	UNC.
645,600	1843	15.00	25.00	35.00	75.00	700.00
968,000	1843 O	15.00	25.00	50.00	125.00	800.00
421,400	1844	15.00	25.00	35.00	75.00	700.00
740,000	1844 O	15.00	25.00	35.00	90.00	950.00
922,000	1845	15.00	25.00	35.00	75.00	700.00
510,000	1846	15.00	25.00	35.00	75.00	675.00
734,000	1847	15.00	25.00	35.00	75.00	675.00
368,000	1847 O	20.00	40.00	50.00	150.00	850.00
146,000	1848	20.00	40.00	70.00	200.00	1000.00
340,000	1849	20.00	40.00	50.00	125.00	900.00
?	1849 O	225.00	550.00	850.00	1500.00	4500.00
190,800	1850	15.00	35.00	70.00	120.00	900.00
412,000	1850 O	15.00	37.50	80.00	135.00	1000.00
160,000	1851	15.00	35.00	75.00	125.00	800.00
88,000	1851 O	125.00	350.00	550.00	1200.00	2750.00
177,060	1852	15.00	40.00	80.00	150.00	750.00
			Without drapery from elbow			
96,000	1852 O	200.00	350.00	550.00	1100.00	3250.00
?	1853 over 52 Rare					
		With arrows at date. Rays over eagle.				
15,254,220	1853	15.00	22.50	45.00	100.00	1100.00
1,332,000	1853 O	15.00	32.50	50.00	120.00	1300.00
		With arrows at date. Without rays.				
12,380,000	1854	12.00	17.50	35.00	75.00	800.00
1,484,000	1854 O	12.00	17.50	35.00	100.00	900.00
2,857,000	1855	12.00	17.50	35.00	75.00	850.00
176,000	1855 O	60.00	110.00	180.00	350.00	1600.00
396,400	1855 S	55.00	100.00	170.00	300.00	1500.00
		Without arrows at date				
7,264,000	1856	12.00	17.50	35.00	60.00	550.00
968,000	1856 O	12.00	17.50	35.00	75.00	850.00
286,000	1856 S	27.50	55.00	120.00	235.00	1200.00
9,644,000	1857	12.00	17.50	35.00	55.00	450.00
1,180,000	1857 O	12.00	17.50	35.00	60.00	800.00
82,000	1857 S	40.00	70.00	150.00	250.00	1600.00
7,368,000	1858	12.00	17.50	35.00	55.00	450.00
520,000	1858 O	12.00	17.50	35.00	55.00	850.00
121,000	1858 S	35.00	65.00	140.00	325.00	1500.00
1,344,000	1859	12.00	17.50	30.00	60.00	750.00
260,000	1859 O	12.00	17.50	40.00	85.00	1050.00
80,000	1859 S	60.00	150.00	275.00	475.00	2500.00
805,400	1860	12.00	17.50	30.00	50.00	500.00
388,000	1860 O	12.00	17.50	40.00	80.00	1000.00
56,000	1860 S	80.00	235.00	400.00	650.00	2500.00
4,854,600	1861	12.00	17.50	35.00	55.00	475.00
96,000	1861 S	40.00	75.00	150.00	250.00	2500.00
932,550	1862	12.00	17.50	30.00	55.00	500.00
67,000	1862 S	40.00	80.00	140.00	300.00	1900.00
192,060	1863	20.00	32.50	50.00	120.00	775.00
94,070	1864	35.00	60.00	150.00	200.00	1000.00
20,000	1864 S	130.00	300.00	450.00	900.00	3000.00
59,300	1865	45.00	80.00	115.00	225.00	900.00
41,000	1865 S	55.00	85.00	200.00	400.00	2500.00
		With motto over eagle				
17,525	1866	125.00	250.00	400.00	550.00	1300.00
28,005	1866 S	80.00	200.00	350.00	500.00	2000.00
20,620	1867	100.00	175.00	300.00	425.00	1200.00
48,000	1867 S	50.00	150.00	250.00	300.00	2000.00
30,000	1868	80.00	140.00	275.00	350.00	900.00
96,000	1868 S	65.00	110.00	180.00	240.00	1500.00
16,600	1869	150.00	340.00	400.00	550.00	1250.00
76,000	1869 S	65.00	150.00	250.00	300.00	1400.00
87,400	1870	40.00	80.00	140.00	225.00	850.00
8,340	1870 CC	725.00	2000.00	2750.00	5000.00	8000.00
171,232	1871	17.50	45.00	75.00	120.00	700.00
30,900	1871 S	125.00	325.00	550.00	825.00	2750.00
10,890	1871 CC	525.00	1000.00	2000.00	2750.00	8000.00

CATALOG OF UNITED STATES COINS **51**

QUARTERS—LIBERTY SEATED TYPE (continued)

QUANTITY	YEAR	GOOD TO VERY GOOD	FINE	VERY FINE	EXT. FINE	UNC.
182,950	1872	15.00	45.00	70.00	125.00	550.00
83,000	1872 S	200.00	425.00	750.00	1100.00	4250.00
9,100	1872 CC	325.00	625.00	850.00	2500.00	6500.00
1,484,300*	1873 no arrows	15.00	30.00	75.00	150.00	800.00
16,462**	1873 CC no arrows	800.00	1000.00	2000.00	4250.00	
	With arrows at date					
*	1873	27.50	50.00	90.00	235.00	1000.00
156,000	1873 S	35.00	75.00	120.00	275.00	1250.00
**	1873 CC	725.00	1000.00	2250.00	4500.00	10,000.00
471,900	1874	22.50	40.00	75.00	185.00	1000.00
392,000	1874 S	30.00	50.00	90.00	215.00	1000.00
	Without arrows at date					
4,293,500	1875	10.00	15.00	25.00	50.00	375.00
680,000	1875 S	12.50	25.00	45.00	85.00	500.00
140,000	1875 CC	37.50	85.00	150.00	400.00	1500.00
17,817,150	1876	10.00	12.00	20.00	50.00	375.00
8,596,000	1876 S	9.00	12.00	20.00	50.00	400.00
4,944,000	1876 CC	10.00	20.00	35.00	75.00	450.00
10,911,710	1877	9.00	12.50	20.00	50.00	350.00
8,996,000	1877 S	9.00	12.50	20.00	50.00	375.00
4,192,000	1877 CC	10.00	15.00	25.00	80.00	500.00
2,260,800	1878	9.00	12.50	22.50	55.00	400.00
140,000	1878 S	60.00	70.00	125.00	225.00	1600.00
996,000	1878 CC	17.50	30.00	45.00	85.00	575.00
14,700	1879	70.00	150.00	175.00	225.00	650.00
14,955	1880	70.00	150.00	175.00	225.00	650.00
12,975	1881	75.00	160.00	185.00	265.00	700.00
16,300	1882	70.00	150.00	175.00	225.00	650.00
15,439	1883	70.00	150.00	175.00	225.00	650.00
8,875	1884	100.00	185.00	250.00	325.00	850.00
14,530	1885	70.00	150.00	175.00	225.00	750.00
5,886	1886	150.00	225.00	300.00	450.00	850.00
10,710	1887	125.00	175.00	225.00	350.00	700.00
10,833	1888	125.00	175.00	225.00	350.00	700.00
1,216,000	1888 S	10.00	12.50	22.50	50.00	400.00
12,711	1889	80.00	150.00	200.00	265.00	700.00
80,590	1890	45.00	70.00	90.00	150.00	600.00
3,920,600	1891	10.00	12.50	22.50	50.00	365.00
68,000	1891 O	125.00	220.00	375.00	500.00	2500.00
2,216,000	1891 S	10.00	16.00	27.50	55.00	375.00

*includes 1873 quarters with arrows.
**includes 1873 CC quarters with arrows.

QUARTERS—LIBERTY HEAD (BARBER) TYPE

The mint marks are under the eagle on the reverse.

QUANTITY	YEAR	GOOD	VERY GOOD	FINE	VERY FINE	EXT. FINE	UNC.	PROOF
8,237,245	1892	$3.00	$7.00	$10.00	$25.00	$55.00	$250.00	$850.00
2,640,000	1892 O	6.00	10.00	12.00	30.00	60.00	325.00	

QUANTITY	YEAR	GOOD	VERY GOOD	FINE	VERY FINE	EXT. FINE	UNC.	PROOF
964,079	1892 S	12.50	20.00	35.00	50.00	85.00	400.00	
5,444,815	1893	2.50	5.25	10.00	25.00	55.00	300.00	850.00
3,396,000	1893 O	3.00	7.50	12.50	30.00	65.00	320.00	
1,454,535	1893 S	7.00	11.00	16.00	37.50	70.00	350.00	
3,432,972	1894	2.50	5.50	10.00	25.00	55.00	300.00	850.00
2,852,000	1894 O	3.25	7.50	14.00	27.50	65.00	320.00	
2,648,821	1894 S	2.50	7.50	14.00	27.50	65.00	340.00	
4,440,880	1895	2.50	5.00	10.00	25.00	55.00	300.00	850.00
2,816,000	1895 O	3.00	7.150	14.00	27.50	65.00	400.00	
1,764,681	1895 S	6.00	10.00	16.00	32.50	65.00	340.00	
3,874,762	1896	2.50	5.00	10.00	25.00	55.00	300.00	850.00
1,484,000	1896 O	5.00	10.00	25.00	40.00	85.00	700.00	
188,039	1896 S	125.00	200.00	350.00	460.00	750.00	3000.00	
8,140,731	1897	2.50	4.00	10.00	22.50	55.00	300.00	850.00
1,414,800	1897 O	7.00	11.00	20.00	40.00	80.00	700.00	
542,229	1897 S	12.50	20.00	30.00	50.00	90.00	550.00	
11,100,735	1898	2.50	4.00	10.00	20.00	50.00	300.00	850.00
1,868,000	1898 O	3.50	7.00	15.00	30.00	60.00	425.00	
1,020,592	1898 S	6.00	10.00	16.00	30.00	55.00	475.00	
12,624,846	1899	2.50	4.00	10.00	22.50	50.00	300.00	850.00
2,644,000	1899 O	3.00	5.00	12.00	27.50	55.00	375.00	
708,000	1899 S	7.00	15.00	25.00	37.50	70.00	400.00	
10,016,912	1900	2.50	4.00	10.00	22.50	55.00	300.00	850.00
3,416,000	1900 O	5.00	11.00	15.00	25.00	60.00	350.00	
1,858,585	1900 S	2.50	5.00	12.50	22.50	50.00	350.00	
8,892,813	1901	2.50	4.00	10.00	22.50	45.00	300.00	850.00
1,612,000	1901 O	10.00	17.50	40.00	70.00	135.00	550.00	
72,664	1901 S	450.00	800.00	1000.00	1500.00	3500.00	10,000.00	
12,197,744	1902	2.50	4.00	9.00	22.50	55.00	300.00	850.00
4,748,000	1902 O	2.75	4.50	14.00	25.00	60.00	325.00	
1,524,612	1902 S	7.00	12.00	17.50	35.00	65.00	375.00	
9,670,064	1903	2.75	4.50	10.00	22.50	55.00	300.00	850.00
3,500,000	1903 O	2.75	5.00	12.50	35.00	70.00	375.00	
1,036,000	1903 S	7.00	12.00	25.00	55.00	70.00	425.00	
9,588,813	1904	2.75	4.50	10.00	22.50	55.00	300.00	850.00
2,456,000	1904 O	5.00	9.00	16.50	30.00	75.00	500.00	
4,968,250	1905	2.75	4.50	10.00	22.50	55.00	300.00	850.00
1,230,000	1905 O	5.50	12.00	20.00	40.00	65.00	375.00	
1,884,000	1905 S	4.00	6.50	12.50	27.50	60.00	325.00	
3,656,435	1906	2.75	5.00	10.00	22.50	60.00	300.00	850.00
3,280,000	1906 D	3.00	5.50	12.50	27.50	60.00	325.00	
2,056,000	1906 O	5.00	9.00	14.00	32.50	65.00	325.00	
7,192,575	1907	2.50	4.00	9.00	22.50	60.00	300.00	850.00
2,484,000	1907 D	3.50	6.50	12.50	27.50	60.00	325.00	
4,560,000	1907 O	2.75	6.50	12.00	25.00	55.00	325.00	
1,360,000	1907 S	3.50	6.50	12.50	27.50	65.00	325.00	
4,232,545	1908	2.50	4.50	10.00	22.50	55.00	300.00	850.00
5,788,000	1908 D	2.50	4.50	10.00	22.50	55.00	325.00	
6,244,000	1908 O	2.50	4.50	10.00	22.50	55.00	325.00	
784,000	1908 S	7.00	14.00	17.50	35.00	80.00	475.00	
9,268,650	1909	2.50	3.50	7.50	25.00	55.00	300.00	850.00
5,114,000	1909 D	2.50	3.50	7.50	25.00	55.00	325.00	
712,000	1909 O	10.00	17.50	35.00	70.00	125.00	600.00	
1,348,000	1909 S	2.75	4.25	9.00	24.00	55.00	350.00	
2,244,551	1910	2.50	3.50	9.00	24.00	55.00	300.00	850.00
1,500,000	1910 D	2.75	4.25	10.00	25.00	60.00	325.00	
3,720,543	1911	2.50	3.50	9.00	24.00	55.00	300.00	850.00
933,600	1911 D	3.50	5.50	17.50	35.00	70.00	325.00	
988,000	1911 S	3.50	4.25	12.50	25.00	65.00	340.00	
4,400,700	1912	2.50	3.50	9.00	24.00	55.00	300.00	850.00
708,000	1912 S	3.50	6.00	14.00	30.00	70.00	400.00	
484,613	1913	10.00	15.00	40.00	100.00	300.00	1200.00	900.00
1,450,800	1913 D	3.50	4.25	12.50	32.50	65.00	300.00	
40,000	1913 S	200.00	350.00	550.00	800.00	1500.00	3750.00	
6,244,610	1914	2.50	3.50	9.00	24.00	55.00	300.00	850.00
3,046,000	1914 D	2.50	3.50	9.00	24.00	55.00	300.00	
264,000	1914 S	12.50	15.00	30.00	60.00	200.00	625.00	

CATALOG OF UNITED STATES COINS **53**

QUARTERS—LIBERTY HEAD (BARBER) TYPE (continued)

QUANTITY	YEAR	GOOD	VERY GOOD	FINE	VERY FINE	EXT. FINE	UNC.	PROOF
3,480,450	1915	2.50	3.50	9.00	24.00	55.00	300.00	1050.00
3,694,000	1915 D	2.50	3.50	9.00	24.00	55.00	325.00	
704,000	1915 S	3.00	5.00	12.50	27.50	60.00	375.00	
1,788,000	1916	2.50	3.50	9.00	24.00	55.00	300.00	
6,540,800	1916 D	2.50	3.50	9.00	24.00	55.00	325.00	

QUARTERS—STANDING LIBERTY TYPE

1916–1917   1917–1930

The mint marks are above and to the left of the date on the obverse.

QUANTITY	YEAR	GOOD	VERY GOOD	FINE	VERY FINE	EXT. FINE	UNC.
52,000	1916	$750.00	$1100.00	$1400.00	$1750.00	$2250.00	$5000.00
8,792,000	1917 type I*	7.50	10.00	15.00	25.00	55.00	225.00
1,509,200	1917 D type I*	7.50	11.00	17.50	27.50	60.00	250.00
1,952,000	1917 S type I*	7.50	11.00	17.50	27.50	60.00	250.00
13,880,000	1917 type II**	7.50	11.00	15.00	24.00	50.00	175.00
6,224,400	1719 D type II**	12.50	16.00	25.00	30.00	55.00	200.00
5,552,000	1917 S type II**	12.00	17.50	27.50	30.00	60.00	220.00
14,240,000	1819	7.00	10.00	14.00	20.00	40.00	165.00
7,380,000	1918 D	10.00	16.00	20.00	30.00	45.00	175.00
11,072,000	1819 S	7.00	10.00	15.00	22.50	40.00	140.00
?	1918 S (over 17)	500.00	625.00	1250.00	2000.00	3250.00	12,500.00
11,324,000	1919	10.00	15.00	20.00	30.00	40.00	150.00
1,944,000	1919 D	30.00	45.00	55.00	85.00	125.00	425.00
1,836,000	1919 S	30.00	50.00	55.00	80.00	150.00	400.00
27,860,000	1920	5.50	8.00	10.00	15.00	27.50	125.00
3,586,400	1920 D	12.50	20.00	30.00	42.00	70.00	200.00
6,380,000	1920 S	8.00	11.00	15.00	25.00	40.00	150.00
1,916,000	1921	40.00	65.00	115.00	140.00	200.00	400.00
9,716,000	1923	8.00	12.50	15.00	20.00	40.00	140.00
1,360,000	1923 S	60.00	90.00	125.00	200.00	300.00	500.00
10,920,000	1924	5.00	7.00	10.00	12.50	25.00	120.00
3,112,000	1924 D	16.00	24.00	30.00	40.00	50.00	130.00
2,860,000	1924 S	11.00	14.00	20.00	30.00	50.00	150.00
12,280,000	1925	3.00	4.00	4.50	9.00	25.00	100.00
11,316,000	1926	3.00	4.00	4.50	9.00	25.00	100.00
1,716,000	1926 D	3.25	4.00	7.00	14.00	35.00	115.00
2,700,000	1926 S	3.25	4.00	7.50	16.00	40.00	215.00
11,912,000	1927	3.00	4.00	4.50	9.00	25.00	100.00
976,400	1927 D	5.00	7.00	15.00	30.00	55.00	165.00
396,000	1927 S	10.00	15.00	50.00	150.00	625.00	4250.00
6,336,000	1928	3.00	4.00	4.50	9.00	22.50	100.00
1,627,600	1928 D	3.25	5.00	5.00	9.00	22.50	125.00
2,644,000	1928 S	3.00	4.00	4.75	9.00	22.50	120.00
11,140,000	1929	3.00	4.00	4.50	9.00	25.00	100.00
1,358,000	1929 D	3.25	4.50	6.00	9.00	25.00	120.00
1,764,000	1929 S	3.00	4.00	5.00	9.00	22.50	110.00
5,632,000	1930	3.00	4.00	5.00	9.00	22.50	100.00
1,556,000	1930 S	3.25	4.50	5.00	9.00	22.50	125.00

*stars at sides of eagle **3 stars below eagle

QUARTERS—WASHINGTON TYPE

The mint marks are under the eagle
on the reverse.

QUANTITY	YEAR	VERY GOOD	FINE	VERY FINE	EXT. FINE	UNC.
5,404,000	1932	$3.25	$3.75	$4.00	$5.00	$35.00
436,800	1932 D	45.00	55.00	65.00	125.00	500.00
408,000	1932 S	45.00	50.00	55.00	70.00	275.00
31,912,052	1934	2.75	3.25	3.50	5.00	30.00
3,527,200	1934 D	2.50	5.50	8.00	20.00	125.00
32,484,000	1935	2.50	3.25	3.50	4.00	18.00
5,780,000	1935 D	2.75	3.75	8.00	15.00	125.00
5,660,000	1935 S	2.75	3.75	7.00	11.00	70.00
41,303,837	1936	2.50	3.00	3.25	3.75	20.00
5,374,000	1936 D	2.75	6.50	15.00	40.00	250.00
3,828,000	1936 S	2.50	3.00	3.75	10.00	80.00
19,701,542	1937	2.50	3.00	3.25	4.00	30.00
7,189,600	1937 D	2.50	3.00	3.50	5.00	45.00
1,652,000	1937 S	6.50	8.50	11.00	22.50	110.00
9,480,045	1938	2.50	3.00	6.50	14.00	55.00
2,832,000	1938 S	2.75	5.00	6.50	11.00	65.00
33,548,795	1939	2.50	3.25	3.50	4.50	15.00
7,092,000	1939 D	2.75	3.50	3.75	4.75	32.50
2,628,000	1939 S	3.00	3.50	4.50	11.00	55.00
35,715,246	1940	2.50	3.00	3.25	4.50	16.00
2,797,600	1940 D	2.75	3.75	6.50	14.00	80.00
8,244,000	1940 S	2.75	3.25	4.00	4.50	20.00
79,047,287	1941	2.50	3.00	3.75	4.00	7.50
16,714,800	1941 D	2.50	3.00	3.75	4.50	25.00
16,080,000	1941 S	2.50	3.00	3.75	4.50	20.00

QUANTITY	YEAR	VERY FINE	EXT. FINE	MS-63
102,117,123	1942	2.50	4.00	10.00
17,487,200	1942 D	2.75	5.00	24.00
19,384,000	1942 S	3.75	7.00	65.00
99,700,000	1943	2.50	4.00	8.50
16,095,600	1943 D	3.00	5.00	40.00
21,700,000	1943 S	3.00	5.00	45.00
104,956,000	1944	2.50	3.75	6.00
14,600,000	1944 D	2.50	3.75	12.00
12,560,000	1944 S	3.00	4.00	13.50
74,372,000	1945	2.50	3.75	8.00
12,341,600	1945 D	2.50	3.75	11.00
17,004,001	1945 S	2.50	3.75	10.00
53,436,000	1946	2.50	3.75	6.00
9,072,800	1946 D	2.50	3.75	12.50
4,204,000	1946 S	3.00	4.25	10.00
22,556,000	1947	2.50	3.75	7.00
15,338,400	1947 D	2.50	3.75	7.00
5,532,000	1947 S	2.75	4.25	9.00
35,196,000	1948	2.50	3.75	7.00
16,766,800	1948 D	2.50	3.75	7.50
15,960,000	1948 S	2.50	3.75	7.00
9,312,000	1949	5.00	5.00	25.00
10,068,400	1949 D	3.00	4.50	12.50
24,971,512	1950	2.50	3.75	5.50
21,075,600	1950 D	2.50	3.75	6.00
10,284,600	1950 S	2.50	3.75	10.00
43,505,602	1951	2.50	3.75	5.50
35,354,800	1951 D	2.50	3.75	7.00
8,948,000	1951 S	3.00	3.00	12.50

QUARTERS—WASHINGTON TYPE (continued)

QUANTITY	YEAR	VERY GOOD	FINE	VERY FINE	EXT. FINE	UNC.
38,862,073	1952			2.50	4.25	5.50
49,795,200	1952 D			2.50	3.75	5.00
13,707,800	1952 S			2.50	3.75	9.00
18,664,920	1953			2.50	3.75	5.50
56,112,400	1953 D			2.50	3.75	5.00
14,016,000	1953 S			2.50	2.50	7.00
54,645,503	1954			2.50	2.50	5.00
46,305,000	1954 D			2.50	2.50	5.00
11,834,722	1954 S			2.50	2.50	5.00
18,558,381	1955			2.50	3.00	5.50
3,182,400	1955 D			3.00	2.50	7.00
44,325,081	1956				2.50	3.50
32,334,500	1956 D				2.50	3.50
46,720,000	1957				2.50	3.50
77,924,160	1957 D				2.50	3.50
6,360,000	1958				2.50	5.00
78,124,900	1958 D				2.50	3.50
24,374,000	1959				2.50	3.50
62,054,232	1959 D				2.50	3.50
29,164,000	1960				2.50	3.50
63,000,324	1960 D				2.50	3.50
40,064,244	1961				2.50	3.50
83,656,928	1961 D				2.50	3.50
39,374,019	1962				50	3.50
127,554,756	1962 D				.50	3.50
77,391,645	1963				.50	3.50
135,288,184	1963 D				.50	3.50
570,390,585	1964				.50	3.50
704,135,528	1964 D				.50	3.50

QUANTITY	YEAR	UNC.	QUANTITY	YEAR	UNC.
1,817,357,540	1965	.75	215,048,000	1972	.60
818,836,911	1966	.75	311,067,732	1972 D	
1,524,031,848	1967	.75	3,267,667	1972 S (proof only)	.60
220,731,500	1968	.75	346,924,000	1973	.60
101,534,500	1968 D	.90	232,977,400	1973 D	
3,041,509	1968 S (proof only)		2,796,624	1973 S (proof only)	
176,212,000	1969	.60	*	1974	.60
114,372,000	1969 D	.75	*	1974 D	.60
2,934,631	1969 S (proof only)		2,617,350	1974 S (proof only)	
136,420,000	1970	.60	809,784,016	1976 Copper-nickel clad	1.00
417,341,364	1970 D	.60	860,118,839	1976 D Copper-nickel clad	1.00
2,632,810	1970 S (proof only)		7,059,099	1976 S Copper-nickel clad (proof)	
109,284,000	1971	.60			
258,634,428	1971 D	.60	**11,000,000	1976 S Silver clad	5.00
3,224,138	1971 S (proof only)	.60	**4,000,000	1976 S Silver Clad (proof)	

*Mintage continued into 1975—struck simultaneously with Bicentennial coins dated 1776–1976.
**Approximate mintage. Not all released.

Bicentennial coins dated 1776–1976.

QUANTITY	YEAR	MS-63
468,556,000	1977	.50
256,524,978	1977 D	.50
3,251,152	1977 S (proof only)	
521,452,000	1978	.50
287,373,152	1978 D	.50
3,127,781	1978 S (proof only)	
515,708,000	1979	.50
489,789,780	1979 D	.50
3,677,175	1979 S (proof only)	
635,832,000	1980	.50
518,327,427	1980 D	.50
3,554,806	1980 S (proof only)	
601,716,000	1981	.50
575,722,833	1981 D	.50
4,063,083	1981 S (proof only)	
500,931,000	1982	.50
480,042,788	1982 D	.50
3,857,479	1982 S (proof only)	
673,535,000	1983	.50
617,806,446	1983 D	.50
3,228,648	1983 S (proof only)	
676,545,000	1984	.50
546,483,064	1984 D	.50
3,065,110	1984 S (proof only)	
775,818,962	1985	.50
519,962,888	1985 D	.50
3,362,662	1985 S (proof only)	
551,199,333	1986	.50
504,298,660	1986 D	.50
3,010,497	1986 S (proof only)	
582,499,481	1987	.50
655,594,696	1987 D	.50
3,792,233	1987 S (proof only)	
562,052,000	1988	.50

QUANTITY	YEAR	MS-63
	1988 S (proof only)	
596,810,688	1988 D	.50
512,868,000	1989	.50
896,535,597	1989 D	.50
3,220,194	1989 S (proof only)	
613,792,000	1990	.50
927,638,181	1990 D	.50
3,299,559	1990 S (proof only)	
570,968,000	1991	.50
630,966,693	1991 D	.50
2,867,787	1991 S (proof only)	
384,764,000	1992	.50
389,777,107	1992 D	.50
2,858,981	1992 S (proof only)	
639,276,000	1993	.50
645,476,128	1993 D	.50
2,633,439	1993 S (proof only)	
825,600,000	1994	.50
800,034,110	1994 D	.50
2,484,594	1994 S (proof only)	
1,004,336,000	1995	150
1,103,216,000	1995 D	.50
	1995 S (proof only)	
	1996	.50
	1996 D	.50
	1996 S (proof only)	
	1997	.50
	1997 D	.50
	1997 S (proof only)	

Half Dollars

HALF DOLLARS—FLOWING HAIR TYPE

QUANTITY	YEAR	GOOD TO VERY GOOD	FINE	VERY FINE
23,464	1794	$1000.00	$2500.00	$3750.00
299,680	1795	550.00	750.00	1500.00

HALF DOLLARS—DRAPED BUST TYPE

1796–1797   **1801–1807**

QUANTITY	YEAR	GOOD TO VERY GOOD	FINE	VERY FINE
?	1796 15 stars, rare	$8500.00	$15,000.00	$25,000.00
?	1796 16 stars, rare	8500.00	15,000.00	25,000.00
3,918	1797 rare	8000.00	12,500.00	22,500.00
30,289	1801	200.00	500.00	850.00
29,890	1802	165.00	400.00	650.00
31,715	1803	125.00	250.00	550.00
156,519	1805 over 4	150.00	375.00	575.00
211,722	1805	80.00	200.00	400.00
839,576	1806 over 5	85.00	175.00	400.00
	1806 over 9 (inverted 6)	135.00	285.00	500.00
	1806	75.00	185.00	450.00
301,076	1807 bust right	75.00	150.00	400.00

HALF DOLLARS—CAPPED BUST TYPE

QUANTITY	YEAR	FINE	VERY FINE	EXT. FINE	UNC
750,500	1807 bust left	$125.00	$275.00	$500.00	$2250.0
	1807 50 over 20	75.00	175.00	325.00	1750.0
1,368,600	1808 over 7	60.00	100.00	250.00	1100.0
	1808	37.50	70.00	175.00	1000.0
1,405,810	1809	35.00	65.00	175.00	900.0
1,276,276	1810	35.00	65.00	150.00	850.0
1,203,644	1811	35.00	65.00	160.00	900.0
	1811 as 18.11	65.00	135.00	160.00	1100.0
1,628,059	1812 over 11	60.00	100.00	175.00	1100.
	1812	40.00	65.00	160.00	1000.0
1,241,903	1813	40.00	65.00	150.00	950.0

QUANTITY	YEAR	FINE	VERY FINE	EXT. FINE	UNC.
1,039,075	1814 over 13	50.00	80.00	200.00	1000.00
	1814	40.00	65.00	175.00	850.00
47,015	1815 over 12	650.00	1100.00	1650.00	6500.00
1,215,567	1817 over 13	65.00	175.00	500.00	1500.00
	1817	40.00	70.00	150.00	850.00
	1817 as 181.7	50.00	85.00	200.00	950.00
1,960,322	1818	40.00	75.00	125.00	800.00
	1818 over 17	40.00	75.00	125.00	900.00
2,208,000	1819 over 18	40.00	80.00	100.00	900.00
	1819	35.00	75.00	85.00	850.00
751,122	1820 over 19	50.00	90.00	175.00	900.00
	1820	50.00	100.00	185.00	1000.00
1,305,797	1821	40.00	70.00	120.00	800.00
1,559,573	1822	40.00	70.00	120.00	800.00
	1822 over 21	100.00	175.00	300.00	1250.00
1,694,200	1823 over 22	100.00	150.00	150.00	1000.00
	1823	35.00	70.00	†20.00	800.00
3,504,954	1824 over other dates	35.00	70.00	100.00	850.00
	1824 over 21	35.00	65.00	100.00	800.00
	1824	35.00	65.00	90.00	700.00
2,934,166	1825	35.00	65.00	90.00	700.00
4,004,180	1826	35.00	65.00	90.00	700.00
5,493,400	1827 over 26	32.50	50.00	80.00	700.00
	1827	32.50	50.00	75.00	700.00
3,075,200	1828	32.50	45.00	70.00	650.00
3,712,156	1829 over 27	32.50	55.00	75.00	700.00
	1829	30.00	45.00	70.00	650.00
4,764,800	1830	27.50	45.00	70.00	650.00
5,873,660	1831	27.50	45.00	70.00	650.00
4,797,000	1832	27.50	45.00	70.00	650.00
5,206,000	1833	27.50	45.00	70.00	650.00
6,412,004	1834	27.50	45.00	70.00	650.00
5,352,006	1835	27.50	45.00	70.00	650.00
6,546,200	1836 lettered edge	27.50	45.00	70.00	650.00
	1836 milled edge	500.00	1100.00	2000.00	6500.00
3,629,820	1837	55.00	100.00	200.00	1000.00
3,546,000	1838	55.00	100.00	200.00	1000.00
20	1838 O (extremely rare)				50,000.00
3,334,560	*1839	55.00	100.00	200.00	1000.00
162,976	1839 O mint mark on obv.	200.00	325.00	500.00	3750.00

*includes 1839 Liberty Seated half dollars

HALF DOLLARS—LIBERTY SEATED TYPE

1839–1865   1866–1891

The mint marks are under the eagle on the reverse.

HALF DOLLARS—LIBERTY SEATED TYPE (continued)

QUANTITY (see above)	YEAR	GOOD TO VERY GOOD	FINE	VERY FINE	EXT. FINE	UNC.
	1839 no drapery	$45.00	$80.00	$150.00	$350.00	$5000.00
	1839 with drapery	20.00	30.00	50.00	80.00	500.00
1,435,008	1840 small letters	15.00	25.00	40.00	75.00	500.00
	1840 large letters	40.00	70.00	120.00	200.00	550.00
855,100	1840 O	20.00	25.00	50.00	85.00	600.00
310,000	1841	20.00	40.00	65.00	125.00	650.00
401,000	1841 O	20.00	40.00	50.00	85.00	650.00
2,012,764	1842	20.00	35.00	45.00	80.00	600.00
?	1842 O small date (rare)	200.00	500.00	1000.00	3500.00	Rare
957,000	1842 O large date	20.00	35.00	50.00	85.00	600.00
3,844,000	1843	20.00	35.00	45.00	80.00	575.00
2,268,000	1843 O	20.00	35.00	45.00	80.00	550.00
1,766,000	1844	20.00	35.00	45.00	80.00	550.00
2,005,000	1844 O	17.50	30.00	40.00	80.00	550.00
589,000	1845	20.00	35.00	45.00	90.00	600.00
2,094,000	1845 O	17.50	30.00	45.00	85.00	550.00
2,210,000	1846 horizontal 6 error	65.00	120.00	165.00	300.00	1000.00
	1846	17.50	30.00	45.00	85.00	550.00
2,304,000	1846 O small date	17.50	30.00	45.00	85.00	550.00
	1846 O large date	45.00	125.00	300.00	425.00	1300.00
1,156,000	1847 over 46	500.00	1000.00	1750.00	5000.00	Rare
	1847	17.50	30.00	45.00	85.00	575.00
2,584,000	1847 O	17.50	30.00	45.00	85.00	575.00
580,000	1848	17.50	30.00	45.00	85.00	575.00
3,180,000	1848 O	17.50	30.00	45.00	85.00	575.00
1,252,000	1849	17.50	30.00	45.00	85.00	575.00
2,310,000	1849 O	17.50	30.00	45.00	85.00	575.00
227,000	1850	45.00	85.00	135.00	250.00	850.00
2,456,000	1850 O	17.50	30.00	45.00	90.00	600.00
200,750	1851	35.00	85.00	125.00	250.00	850.00
402,000	1851 O	25.00	50.00	75.00	125.00	600.00
77,130	1852	75.00	225.00	400.00	625.00	1350.00
144,000	1852 O	40.00	75.00	125.00	250.00	1100.00
?	1853 no arrows (extremely rare)					
3,532,708	1853 arrows	20.00	45.00	90.00	250.00	2250.00
1,328,000	1853 O arrows	20.00	45.00	90.00	250.00	2250.00
2,982,000	1854	15.00	30.00	50.00	80.00	750.00
5,240,000	1854 O	15.00	25.00	40.00	75.00	750.00
759,500	1855	15.00	30.00	50.00	100.00	750.00
3,688,000	1855 O	15.00	25.00	40.00	90.00	750.00
129,950	1855 S rare	175.00	350.00	625.00	1250.00	6250.00
938,000	1856	16.00	30.00	50.00	75.00	550.00
2,658,000	1856 O	15.00	30.00	50.00	75.00	550.00
211,000	1856 S	25.00	40.00	100.00	200.00	1000.00
1,988,000	1857	15.00	30.00	50.00	85.00	550.00
818,000	1857 O	16.00	35.00	50.00	85.00	550.00
158,000	1857 S	30.00	50.00	100.00	200.00	1250.00
4,226,000	1858	15.00	25.00	40.00	70.00	500.00
7,294,000	1858 O	15.00	25.00	40.00	70.00	500.00
476,000	1858 S	20.00	35.00	50.00	100.00	750.00
748,000	1859	15.00	25.00	40.00	70.00	500.00
2,834,000	1859 O	14.00	25.00	40.00	70.00	500.00
566,000	1859 S	17.50	35.00	55.00	120.00	800.00
303,700	1860	15.00	25.00	40.00	85.00	750.00
1,290,000	1860 O	15.00	25.00	40.00	75.00	625.00
472,000	1860 S	17.50	30.00	50.00	85.00	650.00
2,888,400	1861	15.00	25.00	40.00	75.00	500.00
2,532,633	*1861 O	15.00	25.00	40.00	75.00	500.00
939,500	1861 S	15.00	25.00	40.00	75.00	550.00
252,350	1862	20.00	35.00	80.00	175.00	825.00
1,352,000	1862 S	17.50	30.00	45.00	90.00	750.00
503,660	1863	17.50	30.00	45.00	90.00	750.00

QUANTITY	YEAR	GOOD TO VERY GOOD	FINE	VERY FINE	EXT. FINE	UNC.
916,000	1863 S	17.50	30.00	45.00	90.00	750.00
379,570	1864	17.50	30.00	45.00	90.00	750.00
658,000	1864 S	17.50	30.00	45.00	90.00	750.00
511,900	1865	17.50	30.00	45.00	90.00	800.00
675,000	1865 S	17.50	30.00	45.00	100.00	875.00
745,625	1866 motto	15.00	25.00	35.00	90.00	800.00
1,054,000	1866 S no motto	65.00	135.00	275.00	70.00	800.00
	1866 S motto	15.00	25.00	37.50	450.00	4250.00
424,325	1867	15.00	25.00	37.50	75.00	525.00
1,196,000	1867 S	15.00	25.00	37.50	75.00	525.00
378,200	1868	15.00	25.00	37.50	75.00	525.00
1,160,000	1868 S	15.00	25.00	37.50	75.00	525.00
795,900	1869	15.00	25.00	37.50	75.00	525.00
656,000	1869 S	15.00	25.00	37.50	75.00	525.00
600,900	1870	15.00	25.00	37.50	75.00	525.00
1,004,000	1870 S	15.00	25.00	37.50	75.00	525.00
54,617	1870 CC	325.00	1100.00	1500.00	3750.00	7500.00
1,165,350	1871	15.00	25.00	37.50	50.00	525.00
2,178,000	1871 S	15.00	25.00	37.50	65.00	575.00
139,950	1871 CC	100.00	200.00	400.00	750.00	4750.00
881,550	1872	15.00	25.00	40.00	75.00	525.00
580,000	1872 S	15.00	25.00	40.00	75.00	550.00
272,000	1872 CC	65.00	125.00	250.00	425.00	2250.00
2,617,500	1873 no arrows	15.00	25.00	40.00	75.00	525.00
	1873 arrows	30.00	65.00	125.00	200.00	875.00
337,060	1873 CC no arrows	75.00	150.00	250.00	500.00	2500.00
	1873 CC arrows	70.00	125.00	225.00	350.00	2250.00
233,000	1873 S	35.00	65.00	125.00	250.00	1100.00
2,360,300	1874	27.50	55.00	115.00	225.00	1100.00
394,000	1874 S	40.00	85.00	135.00	275.00	1500.00
59,000	1874 CC	125.00	275.00	525.00	1000.00	4750.00
6,027,500	1875	15.00	25.00	37.50	75.00	475.00
3,200,000	1875 S	15.00	25.00	37.50	75.00	500.00
1,008,000	1875 CC	17.50	30.00	50.00	85.00	575.00
8,419,150	1876	15.00	25.00	37.50	70.00	500.00
4,528,000	1876 S	15.00	25.00	37.50	70.00	475.00
1,956,000	1876 CC	17.50	35.00	50.00	110.00	650.00
8,304,510	1877	15.00	25.00	37.50	70.00	550.00
5,356,000	1877 S	15.00	25.00	37.50	70.00	575.00
1,420,000	1877 CC	17.50	35.00	55.00	100.00	600.00
1,378,400	1878	15.00	25.00	40.00	70.00	500.00
12,000	1878 S	2000.00	3500.00	5000.00	10,000.00	27,500.00
62,000	1878 CC	175.00	300.00	650.00	1250.00	3750.00
5,900	1879	125.00	175.00	275.00	350.00	1000.00
9,755	1880	100.00	150.00	200.00	275.00	825.00
10,975	1881	100.00	150.00	200.00	275.00	825.00
5,500	1882	125.00	200.00	250.00	375.00	900.00
9,039	1883	100.00	150.00	200.00	275.00	825.00
5,275	1884	125.00	200.00	275.00	350.00	900.00
6,130	1885	125.00	200.00	275.00	350.00	900.00
5,886	1886	135.00	175.00	275.00	400.00	900.00
5,710	1887	125.00	200.00	275.00	400.00	900.00
12,833	1888	100.00	150.00	200.00	275.00	850.00
12,711	1889	100.00	150.00	200.00	275.00	850.00
12,590	1890	100.00	150.00	200.00	275.00	850.00
200,600	1891	20.00	35.00	75.00	85.00	600.00

*All but 300,000 of these coins were struck after the Confederate forces seized the New Orleans Mint.

HALF DOLLARS—LIBERTY HEAD (BARBER) TYPE

The mint marks are to the left of "half dollar" on the reverse.

QUANTITY	YEAR	GOOD	VERY GOOD	FINE	VERY FINE	EXT. FINE	UNC.	PROOF
935,245	1892	$8.00	$12.50	$30.00	$50.00	$130.00	$500.00	$1100.00
390,000	1892 O	80.00	90.00	130.00	230.00	325.00	850.00	
1,029,028	1892 S	60.00	85.00	125.00	200.00	300.00	900.00	
1,826,792	1893	8.00	12.50	30.00	50.00	130.00	580.00	1000.00
1,389,000	1893 O	17.50	25.00	40.00	75.00	130.00	700.00	
740,000	1893 S	45.00	65.00	90.00	135.00	200.00	825.00	
1,148,972	1894	8.00	15.00	27.50	45.00	130.00	625.00	1000.00
2,138,000	1894 O	8.00	15.00	30.00	50.00	140.00	700.00	
4,048,690	1894 S	6.00	9.00	25.00	42.50	125.00	650.00	
1,835,218	1895	6.00	9.00	27.50	42.50	125.00	600.00	1000.00
1,766,000	1895 O	9.00	12.50	35.00	45.00	135.00	650.00	
1,108,086	1895 S	15.00	25.00	27.50	60.00	135.00	650.00	
950,762	1896	7.00	12.00	35.00	45.00	135.00	650.00	1000.00
924,000	1896 O	15.00	20.00	35.00	65.00	175.00	800.00	
1,140,948	1896 S	37.50	50.00	75.00	120.00	225.00	850.00	
2,480,731	1897	6.50	9.00	17.50	40.00	160.00	700.00	1000.00
632,000	1897 O	40.00	55.00	75.00	125.00	225.00	900.00	
933,900	1897 S	40.00	60.00	80.00	135.00	250.00	900.00	
2,956,735	1898	6.50	9.00	15.00	40.00	125.00	600.00	1000.00
874,000	1898 O	12.00	17.50	35.00	50.00	160.00	700.00	
2,358,550	1898 S	7.50	11.00	20.00	50.00	130.00	650.00	
5,538,846	1899	5.50	7.50	15.00	37.50	120.00	550.00	1000.00
1,724,000	1899 O	6.00	8.50	20.00	50.00	120.00	575.00	
1,686,411	1899 S	9.00	12.50	25.00	50.00	120.00	600.00	
4,762,912	1900	6.25	7.00	12.00	37.50	120.00	550.00	1000.00
2,744,000	1900 O	6.25	7.50	12.50	40.00	130.00	600.00	
2,560,322	1900 S	7.00	10.00	12.50	40.00	125.00	600.00	
4,268,813	1901	6.25	7.50	12.00	37.50	115.00	500.00	1000.00
1,124,000	1901 O	6.00	10.00	20.00	55.00	200.00	900.00	
847,044	1901 S	11.00	20.00	50.00	125.00	250.00	1200.00	
4,922,777	1902	6.25	7.50	12.50	37.50	115.00	525.00	1000.00
2,526,000	1902 O	6.25	7.50	12.50	37.50	115.00	650.00	
1,460,670	1902 S	6.25	8.00	15.00	40.00	115.00	600.00	
2,278,755	1903	6.25	7.50	25.00	37.50	115.00	550.00	1000.00
2,100,000	1903 O	6.25	7.50	17.50	37.50	115.00	650.00	
1,920,772	1903 S	5.00	8.00	20.00	40.00	115.00	650.00	
2,992,670	1904	5.50	7.00	12.50	37.50	115.00	500.00	1000.00
1,117,600	1904 O	6.25	9.00	15.00	40.00	140.00	850.00	
553,038	1904 S	11.00	20.00	37.50	80.00	200.00	900.00	
662,727	1905	6.25	11.00	25.00	55.00	150.00	650.00	1000.00
505,000	1905 O	10.00	17.50	35.00	70.00	175.00	650.00	
2,494,000	1905 S	5.50	6.50	12.50	37.50	125.00	600.00	
2,638,675	1906	6.25	7.00	12.50	37.50	125.00	550.00	1000.00
4,028,000	1906 D	6.25	7.00	12.50	37.50	115.00	525.00	
2,446,000	1906 O	6.25	7.00	12.50	37.50	115.00	550.00	
1,740,154	1906 S	6.50	7.50	13.50	40.00	120.00	600.00	
2,598,575	1907	6.25	7.00	12.50	37.50	115.00	575.00	1000.00
3,856,000	1907 D	6.25	7.00	12.50	37.50	115.00	575.00	
3,946,600	1907 O	6.25	7.00	12.50	37.50	115.00	600.00	
1,250,000	1907 S	6.25	7.00	13.50	37.50	115.00	600.00	

QUANTITY	YEAR	GOOD	VERY GOOD	FINE	VERY FINE	EXT. FINE	UNC.	PROOF
1,354,545	1908	6.25	7.00	13.50	37.50	115.00	575.00	1000.00
3,280,000	1908 D	6.25	7.00	12.50	37.50	115.00	575.00	
5,360,000	1908 O	6.25	7.00	12.50	37.50	115.00	600.00	
1,644,828	1908 S	6.25	7.00	13.50	37.50	115.00	625.00	
2,368,650	1909	6.25	7.00	12.50	37.50	115.00	550.00	1000.00
925,400	1909 O	6.25	7.00	13.50	37.50	115.00	750.00	
1,764,000	1909 S	6.25	7.00	12.50	37.50	115.00	600.00	
418,551	1910	7.00	12.50	22.50	50.00	135.00	700.00	1100.00
1,948,000	1910 S	6.25	7.00	12.50	37.50	115.00	575.00	
1,406,543	1911	6.25	7.00	12.50	37.50	115.00	575.00	1000.00
695,080	1911 D	6.25	7.00	14.00	40.00	115.00	575.00	
1,272,000	1911 S	6.25	7.00	12.50	37.50	115.00	550.00	
1,550,700	1912	6.25	7.00	12.50	37.50	115.00	550.00	1000.00
2,300,800	1912 D	6.25	7.00	12.50	37.50	115.00	550.00	
1,370,000	1912 S	6.25	7.00	12.50	37.50	115.00	600.00	
188,627	1913	15.00	20.00	37.50	70.00	150.00	750.00	1200.00
534,000	1913 D	6.25	8.00	12.50	45.00	115.00	575.00	
604,000	1913 S	6.25	7.50	14.00	40.00	125.00	625.00	
124,610	1914	25.00	30.00	50.00	90.00	190.00	800.00	1400.00
992,000	1914 S	6.25	7.00	12.50	40.00	115.00	600.00	
138,450	1915	18.00	25.00	45.00	80.00	150.00	875.00	1200.00
1,170,400	1915 D	6.25	7.00	12.50	37.50	115.00	550.00	
1,604,000	1915 S	6.25	7.00	12.50	37.50	115.00	550.00	

HALF DOLLARS—WALKING LIBERTY TYPE

The mint marks are to the left of "half dollar" on the reverse.

QUANTITY	YEAR	GOOD	VERY GOOD	FINE	VERY FINE	EXT. FINE	UNC.
608,000	1916	$15.00	$24.00	$40.00	$75.00	$150.00	$325.00
1,014,400	1916 D on obv	10.00	15.00	27.50	55.00	120.00	300.00
508,000	1916 S on obv	35.00	40.00	90.00	200.00	300.00	725.00
12,992,000	1917	6.50	7.50	9.00	12.50	30.00	150.00
765,400	1917 D on obv	7.00	12.00	35.00	60.00	120.00	450.00
1,940,000	1917 D on rev	6.50	8.50	20.00	40.00	100.00	525.00
952,000	1917 S on obv	8.00	15.00	40.00	100.00	225.00	1000.00
5,554,000	1917 S on rev	6.50	8.00	10.00	20.00	40.00	300.00
6,634,000	1918	6.50	7.50	7.50	20.00	100.00	325.00
3,853,040	1918 D	6.50	8.00	8.50	35.00	100.00	650.00
10,282,000	1918 S	6.50	7.50	7.50	17.50	70.00	325.00
962,000	1919	7.00	9.00	20.00	85.00	200.00	1000.00
1,165,000	1919 D	7.00	9.00	20.00	100.00	275.00	1650.00
1,552,000	1919 S	6.50	7.50	18.00	75.00	240.00	1800.00
6,372,000	1920	6.50	7.00	10.00	17.50	45.00	250.00
1,551,000	1920 D	6.50	7.50	12.50	70.00	150.00	1000.00
4,624,000	1920 S	6.50	7.50	12.00	35.00	90.00	900.00
246,000	1921	40.00	55.00	90.00	220.00	650.00	1900.00
208,000	1921 D	65.00	80.00	125.00	225.00	750.00	2100.00
548,000	1921 S	12.00	17.50	37.50	200.00	650.00	6500.00
2,178,000	1923 S	6.50	7.00	9.00	40.00	110.00	900.00
2,392,000	1927 S	6.50	7.00	9.00	25.00	65.00	650.00
1,940,000	1928 S		6.50	7.00	25.00	90.00	750.00

CATALOG OF UNITED STATES COINS   **63**

HALF DOLLARS—WALKING LIBERTY TYPE (continued)

QUANTITY	YEAR	GOOD	VERY GOOD	FINE	VERY FINE	EXT. FINE	UNC.
1,001,200	1929 D		7.00	8.00	20.00	45.00	350.00
1,902,000	1929 S		6.50	7.00	12.50	40.00	350.00
1,786,000	1933 S		6.50	7.00	17.50	50.00	400.00
6,964,000	1934		6.50	7.00	9.00	11.00	65.00
2,361,400	1934 D		6.50	7.50	10.00	30.00	225.00
3,652,000	1934 S		6.50	7.00	8.00	25.00	300.00
9,162,000	1935		6.50	7.00	8.00	10.00	60.00
3,003,800	1935 D		6.50	7.00	7.50	25.00	210.00
3,854,000	1935 S		6.50	7.00	7.50	30.00	250.00
12,617,901	1936		6.50	7.00	7.50	10.00	55.00
4,252,400	1936 D		6.50	7.00	8.00	15.00	120.00
3,884,000	1936 S		6.50	7.00	8.00	20.00	175.00
9,527,728	1937		6.50	7.00	7.50	9.00	55.00
1,760,001	1937 D		6.50	7.00	8.00	27.50	225.00
2,090,000	1937 S		6.50	7.00	7.50	20.00	175.00
4,118,152	1938		6.50	7.50	8.00	12.50	90.00
491,600	1938 D		27.50	30.00	37.50	75.00	450.00
6,820,808	1939		6.50	7.00	7.50	9.00	65.00
4,267,800	1939 D		6.50	7.00	7.50	10.00	65.00
2,552,000	1939 S		6.50	7.00	7.50	15.00	100.00
9,167,279	1940				6.50	9.00	55.00
4,550,000	1940 S				6.50	12.00	85.00
24,207,412	1941				6.50	8.00	50.00
11,248,400	1941 D				6.50	8.50	60.00
8,098,000	1941 S				8.00	15.00	175.00
47,839,120	1942				6.50	8.00	50.00
10,973,800	1942 D				7.50	10.00	65.00
12,708,000	1942 S				7.50	12.50	110.00
53,190,000	1943				6.50	8.00	55.00
11,346,000	1943 D				6.50	9.00	60.00
13,450,000	1943 S				6.50	8.50	55.00
28,206,000	1944				6.50	7.50	45.00
9,769,000	1944 D				6.50	9.00	65.00
8,904,000	1944 S				6.50	9.00	70.00
31,502,000	1945				6.50	8.00	50.00
9,966,800	1945 D				6.50	9.00	65.00
10,156,000	1945 S				6.50	9.00	70.00
12,118,000	1946				6.50	9.00	55.00
2,151,100	1946 D				6.50	9.00	65.00
3,724,000	1946 S				6.50	9.00	75.00
4,094,000	1947				6.50	10.00	70.00
3,900,000	1947 D				6.50	10.00	70.00

HALF DOLLARS—FRANKLIN TYPE

The mint marks are above the Liberty Bell on the reverse.

QUANTITY	YEAR	VERY FINE	EXT. FINE	UNC.
3,006,814	1948	$6.50	$7.50	$20.00
4,028,600	1948 D	6.50	7.50	17.50
5,714,000	1949	6.50	8.00	45.00
4,120,600	1949 D	6.50	8.00	40.00
3,744,000	1949 S	7.00	11.00	70.00
7,793,509	1950	6.50	7.50	40.00
8,031,600	1950 D	6.50	7.50	30.00
16,859,602	1951	6.50	7.50	17.50
9,475,200	1951 D	6.50	7.50	30.00
13,696,000	1951 S	6.50	7.50	22.00
21,274,073	1952	6.50	7.50	15.00
25,395,600	1952 D	6.50	7.50	11.00
5,526,000	1952 S	6.50	7.50	30.00
2,796,920	1953	6.50	8.00	22.50
20,900,400	1953 D	6.50	7.50	14.00
4,148,000	1953 S	6.50	7.50	25.00
13,421,503	1954	6.50	7.50	12.50
25,445,580	1954 D	6.50	7.50	12.00
4,993,400	1954 S	6.50	7.50	15.00
2,876,381	1955	6.50	9.00	18.50

QUANTITY	YEAR	EXT. FINE	UNC.	QUANTITY	YEAR	EXT. FINE	UNC.
4,213,081	1956	$6.50	$12.50	18,215,812	1960 D	$6.50	$8.50
5,150,000	1957	6.50	12.50	11,318,244	1961	6.50	8.50
19,966,850	1957 D	6.50	10.00	20,276,442	1961 D	6.50	7.50
4,042,000	1958	6.50	12.00	12,932,019	1962	6.50	7.50
23,962,412	1958 D	6.50	10.00	70,473,281	1962 D	6.50	7.50
6,200,000	1959	6.50	10.00	77,391,645	1963	6.50	7.50
13,053,750	1959 D	6.50	10.00	135,288,184	1963 D	6.50	7.50
6,024,000	1960	6.50	10.00				

HALF DOLLARS—KENNEDY TYPE

The mint marks are near the claw holding the laurel wreath on the reverse.

QUANTITY	YEAR	MS-65	QUANTITY	YEAR	MS-65
273,304,004	1964	$7.50	302,097,424	1971 D	2.00
156,205,446	1964 D	7.50	3,267,667	1971 S (proof only)	
63,519,366	1965	4.00	153,180,000	1972	2.00
106,723,349	1966	3.75	141,890,000	1972 D	2.00
295,046,978	1967	3.75	3,267,667	1972 S (proof only)	
246,951,930	1968 D	3.75	64,964,000	1973	2.00
3,041,509	1968 S (proof only)		83,171,400	1973 D	2.00
129,881,800	1969 D	3.75	2,769,624	1973 S (proof only)	
2,934,631	1969 S (proof only)		*	1974	2.00
2,150,000	1970 D	30.00	*	1974 D	2.00
2,632,810	1970 S (proof only)		2,617,350	1974 S (proof only)	
155,164,000	1971	2.00			

*Mintage continued into 1975—struck simultaneously with Bicentennial coins dated 1776–1976.

Mintage of Bicentennial coins dated 1776–1976 began in March 1975.

QUANTITY	YEAR	MS-65
234,308,000	1976 Copper-nickel clad	1.50
287,565,248	1976 D Copper-nickel clad	1.50
	1976 S Copper-nickel clad (proof)	
*4,239,722	1976 S Silver clad	10.00
	1976 S Silver clad (proof)	

*Approximate mintage. Not all released.

QUANTITY	YEAR	MS-65
43,598,000	1977	1.00
31,449,106	1977 D	1.00
3,251,152	1977 S (proof only)	
14,350,000	1978	1.00
13,765,799	1978 D	1.00
3,127,781	1978 S (proof only)	
68,312,000	1979	1.00
15,815,422	1979 D	1.00
3,677,175	1979 S (proof only)	
44,134,000	1980	1.00
33,456,449	1980 D	1.00
3,554,806	1980 S (proof only)	
29,544,000	1981	1.00
27,839,533	1981 D	1.00
4,063,083	1981 S (proof only)	
10,819,000	1982	1.00
13,140,102	1982 D	1.00
3,857,479	1982 S (proof only)	
34,139,000	1983	1.00
32,472,244	1983 D	1.00
3,228,648	1983 S (proof only)	
26,029,000	1984	1.00
26,262,158	1984 D	1.00
3,065,110	1984 S (proof only)	
18,706,962	1985	1.00
19,814,034	1985 D	1.00
3,362,662	1985 S (proof only)	
13,107,633	1986	1.00
15,366,145	1986 D	1.00
3,010,497	1986 S (proof only)	
	1987	1.00
	1987 D	1.00
3,792,233	1987 S (proof only)	

QUANTITY	YEAR	MS-65
13,626,000	1988	1.00
12,000,096	1988 D	1.00
3,262,948	1988 S (proof only)	
24,542,000	1989	1.00
23,000,216	1989 D	1.00
3,215,728	1989 S (proof only)	
22,278,000	1990	1.00
20,096,242	1990 D	1.00
3,299,559	1990 S (proof only)	
14,874,000	1991	1.00
15,054,678	1991 D	1.00
2,867,787	1991 S (proof only)	
17,628,000	1992	1.00
17,000,106	1992 D	1.00
2,858,981	1992 S (proof only)	
15,510,000	1993	1.00
15,000,006	1993 D	1.00
2,633,439	1993 S (proof only)	
23,718,000	1994	1.00
23,828,110	1994 D	1.00
2,484,594	1994 S (proof only)	
26,496,000	1995	1.00
26,288,000	1995 D	1.00
	1995 S (proof only)	
	1996	1.00
	1996 D	1.00
	1996 S (proof only)	
	1997	1.00
	1997 D	1.00
	1997 S (proof only)	

While the Kennedy half dollars are struck ostensibly for circulation, most are held as souvenirs.

Silver Dollars

DOLLARS—FLOWING HAIR TYPE

QUANTITY	YEAR	GOOD TO VERY GOOD	FINE	VERY FINE
1,758	1794 very rare	$6500.00	$15,000.00	$26,500.00
160,295	*1795	700.00	1100.00	2100.00

*This coin is included in quantity for 1795 draped bust type.

Silver Dollar—Flowing Hair Type

1795–1798

1798–1804

DOLLARS—DRAPED BUST TYPE

QUANTITY	YEAR	GOOD TO VERY GOOD	FINE	VERY FINE
184,013	1795	$600.00	$1200.00	$2000.00
72,920	1796	375.00	800.00	1300.00
7,776	1797 stars 10 and 6	500.00	1000.00	1400.00
	1797 stars 9 and 7	500.00	1000.00	1500.00
327,536	1798 small eagle, 15 stars	450.00	850.00	1250.00
	1798 small eagle, 13 stars	450.00	850.00	1250.00
327,536	1798 large eagle	400.00	750.00	1100.00
423,515	1799 over 98, 15 stars	400.00	750.00	1100.00
	1799 over 98, 13 stars	400.00	750.00	1000.00
	1799 stars 7 and 6	400.00	750.00	1000.00
	1799 stars 8 and 5	400.00	750.00	1000.00
220,920	1800	400.00	750.00	1000.00
54,454	1801	400.00	750.00	1000.00
41,650	1802 over 1	400.00	750.00	1000.00
	1802	400.00	700.00	950.00
66,064	1803	350.00	700.00	900.00
	1804 outstanding rarity			375,000.00

*A very rare 1804 Proof sold for $990,000.00 at a 7/7/89 auction

DOLLARS—LIBERTY SEATED TYPE

1840–1865   1866–1873

The mint marks are under the eagle on the reverse.

QUANTITY	YEAR	GOOD TO VERY GOOD	FINE	VERY FINE	EXT. FINE	UNC.
61,005	1840	$125.00	$175.00	$250.00	$375.00	$1400.00
173,000	1841	100.00	125.00	185.00	250.00	1000.00
184,618	1842	100.00	125.00	185.00	250.00	1000.00
165,100	1843	100.00	125.00	185.00	250.00	1000.00
20,000	1844	125.00	150.00	225.00	375.00	1750.00
24,500	1845	125.00	150.00	225.00	375.00	1750.00
110,600	1846	100.00	125.00	185.00	250.00	1000.00
59,000	1846 O	110.00	150.00	275.00	500.00	2500.00
140,750	1847	100.00	125.00	185.00	250.00	1000.00
15,000	1848	175.00	250.00	300.00	550.00	2250.00
62,600	1849	110.00	165.00	225.00	365.00	1500.00
7,500	1850	225.00	300.00	500.00	900.00	3750.00
40,000	1850 O	175.00	250.00	375.00	750.00	3500.00
1,300	1851	1300.00	2000.00	3250.00	6250.00	14,000.00
1,100	1852					12,500.00
46,110	1853	150.00	200.00	250.00	425.00	1500.00
33,140	1854	165.00	300.00	500.00	800.00	2750.00
26,000	1855	150.00	400.00	600.00	850.00	3000.00
63,500	1856	125.00	265.00	350.00	500.00	2250.00
94,000	1857	150.00	225.00	325.00	425.00	1800.00
80	1858	Struck in proof only, 7500.00				
256,500	1859	125.00	250.00	300.00	350.00	2000.00
360,000	1859 O	100.00	125.00	165.00	250.00	950.00
20,000	1859 S	175.00	300.00	425.00	750.00	3500.00
218,930	1860	100.00	125.00	200.00	325.00	1200.00
515,000	1860 O	90.00	115.00	150.00	250.00	900.00
78,500	1861	125.00	200.00	300.00	425.00	2000.00
12,090	1862	200.00	375.00	625.00	725.00	2000.00
27,660	1863	150.00	250.00	400.00	500.00	1750.00
31,170	1864	150.00	250.00	400.00	500.00	1750.00
47,000	1865	140.00	225.00	350.00	475.00	1700.00
49,625	1866 motto	140.00	225.00	350.00	475.00	1650.00
60,325	1867	140.00	225.00	350.00	475.00	1650.00
182,700	1868	125.00	200.00	275.00	375.00	1600.00
424,300	1869	120.00	175.00	225.00	300.00	1500.00
433,000	1870	120.00	175.00	225.00	300.00	1400.00
?	1870 S	Extremely rare	Stacks's Nov. 1989 Sale, VF, $77,000			
12,462	1870 CC	300.00	375.00	500.00	800.00	3000.00
1,115,760	1871	90.00	125.00	150.00	225.00	1100.00
1,376	1871 CC	700.00	1100.00	2000.00	3500.00	17,500.00
1,106,450	1872	100.00	125.00	175.00	300.00	1100.00
9,000	1872 S	200.00	350.00	500.00	850.00	3750.00
3,150	1872 CC	425.00	800.00	1500.00	1800.00	8500.00
293,600	1873	100.00	125.00	150.00	225.00	1250.00
2,300	1873 CC	1000.00	1750.00	2250.00	8500.00	22,500.00
700	1873 S	Extremely rare	Unknown in any collection			

DOLLARS—LIBERTY HEAD (MORGAN) TYPE

The mint mark is on the reverse under the eagle.

QUANTITY	YEAR	FINE	VERY FINE	EXT. FINE	UNC.	PROOF
10,509,550	1878 8 feathers	$14.00	$17.50	$22.50	$65.00	$1750.00
	1878 7 feathers		13.50	15.00	40.00	4500.00
	1878 7 over 8 feathers	20.00	25.00	28.00	65.00	
9,774,000	1878 S		16.50	18.50	50.00	
2,212,000	1878 CC	17.50	30.00	37.50	125.00	
14,807,100	1879		15.00	16.50	45.00	1750.00
2,887,000	1879 O	14.00	15.00	16.50	70.00	
9,110,000	1879 S		13.50	15.00	50.00	
756,000	1879 CC	35.00	75.00	225.00	1100.00	
12,601,355	1880		13.50	14.00	45.00	1750.00
5,305,000	1880 O	13.50	14.00	16.00	75.00	
8,900,000	1880 S		13.50	15.00	40.00	
591,000	1880 CC	50.00	65.00	85.00	150.00	
9,163,975	1881		13.50	15.00	40.00	1750.00
5,708,000	1881 O	13.50	15.00	16.00	40.00	
12,760,000	1881 S	13.50	15.00	16.00	40.00	
296,000	1881 CC	70.00	80.00	100.00	200.00	
11,101,100	1882		13.50	15.00	40.00	1750.00
6,090,000	1882 O	13.50	15.00	16.00	40.00	
9,250,000	1882 S		13.50	15.00	40.00	
1,133,000	1882 CC	25.00	35.00	40.00	100.00	
12,291,039	1883		13.50	15.00	40.00	1500.00
8,725,000	1883 O		13.50	14.00	30.00	
6,250,000	1883 S	15.00	17.50	27.50	400.00	
1,204,000	1883 CC	25.00	30.00	40.00	100.00	
14,070,875	1884		14.00	15.00	55.00	1500.00
9,730,000	1884 O		13.50	14.00	35.00	
3,200,000	1884 S	16.50	20.00	35.00	2000.00	
1,136,000	1884 CC	30.00	40.00	55.00	90.00	
17,787,767	1885		13.50	15.00	35.00	1500.00
9,185,000	1885 O		13.50	15.00	35.00	
1,497,000	1885 S	15.00	17.50	30.00	125.00	
228,000	1885 CC	125.00	150.00	175.00	265.00	
19,963,886	1886		13.50	15.00	37.50	1500.00
10,710,000	1886 O	14.00	15.00	20.00	350.00	
750,000	1886 S	20.00	24.00	28.00	200.00	
20,290,710	1887		13.50	14.00	30.00	1500.00
11,550,000	1887 O	14.00	15.00	16.00	55.00	
1,771,000	1887 S	15.00	17.50	25.00	90.00	
19,183,833	1888		13.50	15.00	35.00	1500.00
12,150,000	1888 O	14.00	15.00	17.50	35.00	
657,000	1888 S	25.00	27.50	35.00	175.00	
21,726,811	1889		14.00	17.50	35.00	1500.00
11,875,000	1889 O	$13.50	15.00	20.00	100.00	

DOLLARS—LIBERTY HEAD (MORGAN) TYPE (continued)

QUANTITY	YEAR	FINE	VERY FINE	EXT. FINE	UNC.	PROOF
700,000	1889 S	22.50	27.50	35.00	180.00	
350,000	1889 CC	150.00	250.00	550.00	7000.00	
16,802,590	1890		17.50	22.50	50.00	1650.00
10,701,000	1890 O	13.50	15.00	17.50	85.00	
8,230,373	1890 S	13.50	15.00	18.50	100.00	
2,309,041	1890 CC	25.00	35.00	50.00	250.00	
8,694,206	1891	14.00	16.00	17.50	100.00	1500.00
7,954,529	1891 O	14.00	16.00	25.00	150.00	
5,296,000	1891 S	14.00	16.50	17.50	100.00	
1,618,000	1891 CC	25.00	30.00	45.00	200.00	
1,037,245	1892	15.00	17.50	25.00	135.00	1500.00
2,744,000	1892 O	15.00	17.50	25.00	150.00	
1,200,000	1892 S	18.00	40.00	150.00	6250.00	
1,352,000	1892 CC	30.00	50.00	110.00	415.00	
378,792	1893	45.00	55.00	75.00	300.00	1750.00
300,000	1893 O	50.00	90.00	175.00	1000.00	
100,000	1893 S	650.00	1100.00	3500.00	26,500.00	
677,000	1893 CC	50.00	95.00	280.00	1100.00	
110,972	1894	225.00	350.00	475.00	1200.00	3250.00
1,723,000	1894 O	15.00	17.50	35.00	650.00	
1,260,000	1894 S	17.50	22.50	75.00	400.00	
12,880	1895 rare			8500.00	12,500.00	
450,000	1895 O	60.00	100.00	250.00	4500.00	
400,000	1895 S	80.00	150.00	375.00	1500.00	
9,976,762	1896	13.50	15.00	17.50	40.00	1500.00
4,900,000	1896 O	14.00	16.00	30.00	475.00	
5,000,000	1896 S	15.00	25.00	80.00	500.00	
2,822,731	1897	14.00	15.00	17.50	50.00	1500.00
4,004,000	1897 O	14.00	15.00	18.00	475.00	
5,825,000	1897 S	14.00	16.00	18.00	90.00	
5,884,735	1898	14.00	15.00	17.50	40.00	1500.00
4,440,000	1898 O	14.00	15.00	17.50	32.50	
4,102,000	1898 S	15.00	17.50	20.00	250.00	
330,846	1899	30.00	35.00	45.00	125.00	1500.00
12,290,000	1899 O		14.00	16.00	40.00	
2,562,000	1899 S	14.00	16.50	30.00	250.00	
8,830,912	1900		14.00	16.00	35.00	1250.00
12,590,000	1900 O		14.00	16.00	50.00	
3,540,000	1900 S	15.00	18.00	25.00	140.00	
6,962,813	1901	17.50	25.00	80.00	1000.00	2800.00
13,320,000	1901 O		14.00	16.00	35.00	
2,284,000	1901 S	15.00	18.00	25.00	320.00	
7,994,777	1902	14.00	16.00	17.50	70.00	1500.00
8,636,000	1902 O		14.00	16.00	30.00	
1,530,000	1902 S	32.50	50.00	75.00	250.00	
4,652,755	1903	15.00	17.50	22.50	70.00	1500.00
4,450,000	1903 O	90.00	125.00	140.00	300.00	
1,241,000	1903 S	18.00	25.00	200.00	1750.00	
2,788,650	1904	15.00	17.50	20.00	200.00	1500.00
3,720,000	1904 O	14.00	16.00	18.00	35.00	
2,304,000	1904 S	16.00	22.50	75.00	850.00	
44,690,000	1921			14.00	20.00	
21,695,000	1921 S			14.00	40.00	
20,345,000	1921 D			14.00	45.00	

DOLLARS—PEACE TYPE

QUANTITY	YEAR	VERY FINE	EXT. FINE	UNC.
1,006,473	1921	$30.00	$40.00	$200.00
51,737,000	1922	14.00	15.00	25.00
15,063,000	1922 D	14.00	15.00	30.00
17,475,000	1922 S	14.00	15.00	30.00
30,800,000	1923	14.00	15.00	17.50
6,811,000	1923 D	14.00	15.00	45.00
19,020,000	1923 S	14.00	15.00	50.00
11,811,000	1924	14.00	15.00	25.00

The mint marks are at the bottom to the left of the eagle's wing on the reverse.

QUANTITY	YEAR	VERY FINE	EXT. FINE	UNC.
1,728,000	1924 S	15.00	25.00	125.00
10,198,000	1925	14.00	15.00	25.00
1,610,000	1925 S	15.00	20.00	125.00
1,939,000	1926	14.00	16.50	30.00
2,348,700	1926 D	14.00	16.00	65.00
6,980,000	1926 S	14.00	16.00	40.00
848,000	1927	20.00	30.00	75.00
1,268,900	1927 D	15.00	25.00	200.00
866,000	1927 S	17.50	25.00	225.00
360,649	1928	125.00	150.00	250.00
1,632,000	1928 S	14.00	15.00	150.00
954,057	1934	17.50	25.00	75.00
1,569,000	1934 D	15.00	20.00	100.00
1,011,000	1934 S	40.00	150.00	1200.00
1,576,000	1935	15.00	20.00	55.00
1,964,000	1935 S	16.00	30.00	150.00

DOLLARS—EISENHOWER TYPE

QUANTITY	YEAR	MS-65	QUANTITY	YEAR	MS-65
47,799,000	1971	$2.75	2,000,056	1973	$12.50
68,587,424	1971 D	2.50	2,000,000	1973 D	12.50
6,668,526	1971 S	9.00	1,883,140	1973 S	10.00
75,890,000	1972	2.50	27,366,000	1974	2.35
95,548,511	1972 D	2.35	35,466,000	1974 D	2.35
2,193,056	1972 S	12.50	1,900,000	1974 S	12.50

DOLLARS—EISENHOWER TYPE (continued)

QUANTITY	YEAR	MS-65
4,019,000	1976 Copper-nickel clad, Variety I	$8.00
113,318,000	1976 Copper-nickel clad, Variety II	5.00
21,048,710	1976 D Copper-nickel clad, Variety I	6.00
82,179,564	1976 D Copper-nickel clad, Variety II	5.00
2,845,450	1976 S Copper-nickel clad, Variety I (proof)	
4,149,730	1976 S Copper-nickel clad, Variety II (proof)	
4,000,000	1976 S Silver clad, Variety I (proof)	
*4,149,730	1976 S Silver clad, Variety I	12.50
12,596,000	1977	2.35
32,983,006	1977 D	2.35
3,251,152	1977 S (proof only)	
25,702,000	1978	2.35
33,012,890	1978 D	2.35
3,127,781	1978 S (proof only)	

DOLLARS—SUSAN B. ANTHONY TYPE

QUANTITY	YEAR	MS-65
360,222,000	1979	1.75
288,015,744	1979 D	1.75
109,576,000	1979 S	1.75
3,677,175	1979 S (proof)	
27,610,000	1980	2.00
41,628,708	1980 D	2.00
20,422,000	1980 S	2.50
3,554,806	1980 S (proof)	
3,000,000	1981	5.00
3,250,000	1981 D	5.00
3,492,000	1981 S	5.00
4,063,083	1981 S (proof)	

Trade Dollars

These silver coins were issued from 1873 to 1885 for use in the Orient. From 1879 to 1885 Trade Dollars were issued only as proofs, apparently for collectors. It is said that Trade Dollars are still circulating in the Orient—some of them mutilated by "chopmarks" made to check their content.

TRADE DOLLARS

1873 —1885

The mint marks are under the eagle on the reverse.

QUANTITY	YEAR	GOOD TO VERY GOOD	FINE	VERY FINE	EXT. FINE	UNC.	PROOF
397,500	1873	$55.00	$70.00	$85.00	$125.00	$700.00	$2750.00
703,000	1873 S	55.00	70.00	100.00	150.00	750.00	
124,500	1873 CC	60.00	80.00	120.00	350.00	1250.00	
987,800	1874	55.00	70.00	80.00	130.00	700.00	2750.00
2,549,000	1874 S	55.00	60.00	70.00	100.00	550.00	
1,373,200	1874 CC	60.00	70.00	80.00	120.00	800.00	
218,900	1875	75.00	100.00	200.00	300.00	1200.00	2750.00
4,487,000	1875 S	55.00	60.00	70.00	120.00	600.00	
1,573,700	1875 CC	60.00	70.00	85.00	130.00	700.00	
456,150	1876	55.00	70.00	80.00	120.00	650.00	2750.00
5,227,000	1876 S	55.00	60.00	70.00	100.00	550.00	
509,000	1876 CC	60.00	70.00	100.00	200.00	1000.00	
3,039,710	1877	55.00	60.00	70.00	100.00	600.00	2750.00
9,519,000	1877 S	55.00	60.00	70.00	100.00	575.00	
534,000	1877 CC	65.00	100.00	130.00	250.00	1100.00	
900	1878 Proofs only						3000.00
4,162,000	1878 S	55.00	60.00	75.00	100.00	550.00	
97,000	1878 CC	200.00	325.00	500.00	850.00	5500.00	
1,541	1879 Proofs only						3000.00
1,987	1880 Proofs only						3000.00
960	1881 Proofs only						3000.00
1,097	1882 Proofs only						3000.00
979	1883 Proofs only						3000.00
10	1884 Proofs only						75,000.00
5	1885 Proofs only						165,000.00

GOLD COINS

There are a number of reasons why gold coins are scarce and have substantial values. Gold is intrinsically much more valuable than silver, and there have been times when it was desirable to melt down gold coins for what the metal would bring.

Remember, also, that up to the time gold was discovered in California in 1848, the metal was scarce in the United States. Consequently the early issues of gold coins were small and the coins correspondingly scarce. Then, too, gold coins never circulated to more than a very limited extent; collectors did not come across these coins in ordinary usage.

Still another reason for the present-day scarcity of gold coins is the Presidential Order of 1933 which removed gold coins from circulation. (The order, by the way, made a careful distinction in favor of coin collectors by allowing them to continue acquiring gold coins as part of their hobby.)

Gold coins were struck in the following denominations:

Gold Dollars	1849–1889
Quarter Eagles ($2.50)	1796–1929
Three-Dollar Gold Pieces	1854–1889
Half Eagles ($5)	1795–1929
Eagles ($10)	1795–1933
Double Eagles ($20)	1849–1933

New interpretations and amendments concerning the 1933 order were issued beginning in 1954 until finally all restrictions on ownership of gold were removed as of January 1975. U.S. citizens may now buy, sell, or hold gold in any form.

After a lapse of more than 50 years, the United States resumed gold coinage in 1984 with a $10 denomination commemorating the 1984 Los Angeles Summer Olympics. A $5 gold coin was released in 1986 to commemorate the centennial of the Statue of Liberty. Additional $5 cold coin commemoratives were issued to mark the 1987 Constitutional Bicentennial, the 1988 Seoul Olympics, the 1989 Congress Bicentennial, the 1991 Mount Rushmore Golden Anniversary, the 1992 Barcelona Summer Olympics, the 1992 Columbus 500th Anniversary, the 1993 Bill of Rights Bicentennial, the 1994 World Cup Soccer Tournament, the 1996 Atlanta Summer Olympics, and the 1997 Jackie Robinson, among others.

Gold Dollars

These coins were first issued when gold became plentiful after the California Gold Rush. They are very small, weighing only 25.8 grains. (A silver dollar weighs over 400 grains.) Due to the highly unpredictable and volatile nature of the current precious metals markets, prices for gold and silver coins may fluctuate significantly.

LIBERTY HEAD TYPE

QUANTITY	YEAR	FINE	VERY FINE	UNC.
658,567	1849 open wreath—small head and stars	$125.00	$200.00	$600.00
	1849 open wreath—large head and stars	125.00	200.00	600.00
	1849 closed wreath	200.00	300.00	650.00
?	1849 C open wreath (extremely rare)		100,000.00	
11,634	1849 C closed wreath	275.00	550.00	3750.00
21,588	1849 D open wreath	285.00	575.00	4250.00
215,000	1849 O open wreath	225.00	350.00	900.00
481,953	1850	150.00	225.00	600.00
6,966	1850 C	375.00	675.00	5500.00
8,382	1850 D	365.00	650.00	5000.00
14,000	1850 O	250.00	325.00	2250.00
3,317,671	1851	150.00	200.00	600.00
41,267	1851 C	275.00	450.00	2250.00
9,882	1851 D	300.00	475.00	3500.00
290,000	1851 O	175.00	225.00	725.00
2,045,351	1852	125.00	200.00	550.00
9,434	1852 C	285.00	475.00	3250.00
6,360	1852 D	325.00	625.00	5000.00
140,000	1852 O	150.00	250.00	850.00
4,076,051	1853	150.00	250.00	550.00
11,515	1853 C	265.00	500.00	5250.00
6,583	1853 D	350.00	625.00	6500.00
290,000	1853 O	150.00	275.00	750.00
1,639,445*	1854	140.00	225.00	500.00
2,935	1854 D	550.00	825.00	12,500.00
14,632	1854 S	300.00	425.00	2100.00

*includes Indian-Headdress Dollars of 1854

INDIAN-HEADDRESS TYPE

QUANTITY	YEAR	FINE	VERY FINE	UNC.
783,943	1854	200.00	375.00	3250.00
758,269	1855	200.00	350.00	3250.00
9,803	1855 C	650.00	1100.00	12,000.00
1,811	1855 D	1900.00	3250.00	22,500.00
55,000	1855 O	400.00	600.00	6000.00
24,600	1856 S	450.00	700.00	7250.00

LARGER INDIAN-HEADDRESS TYPE

1,762,936	1856	150.00	225.00	600.00
1,460	1856 D	2500.00	4000.00	22,500.00

LARGER INDIAN-HEADDRESS TYPE (continued)

QUANTITY	YEAR	FINE	VERY FINE	UNC.
774,789	1857	$150.00	$200.00	$425.00
13,280	1857 C	300.00	525.00	5500.00
3,533	1857 D	500.00	850.00	8500.00
10,000	1857 S	350.00	550.00	6250.00
117,995	1858	175.00	225.00	625.00
3,477	1858 D	600.00	875.00	7250.00
10,000	1858 S	325.00	450.00	3750.00
168,244	1859	175.00	200.00	500.00
5,235	1859 C	375.00	600.00	7500.00
4,952	1859 D	500.00	800.00	7500.00
15,000	1859 S	300.00	425.00	5500.00
36,668	1860	175.00	250.00	550.00
1,556	1860 D	2300.00	2750.00	25,000.00
13,000	1860 S	300.00	375.00	3250.00
527,499	1861	150.00	225.00	600.00
?	1861 D	5000.00	7250.00	32,500.00
1,326,865	1862	185.00	200.00	500.00
6,250	1863	325.00	475.00	3750.00
5,950	1864	325.00	425.00	1750.00
3,725	1865	325.00	425.00	2000.00
7,180	1866	300.00	425.00	1300.00
5,250	1867	300.00	450.00	1500.00
10,525	1868	250.00	325.00	1200.00
5,925	1869	285.00	425.00	1300.00
6,335	1870	275.00	350.00	1200.00
3,000	1870 S	300.00	600.00	3250.00
3,930	1871	285.00	425.00	1100.00
3,530	1872	285.00	425.00	1100.00
125,125	1873	225.00	350.00	750.00
198,820	1874	150.00	225.00	450.00
420	1875	2000.00	3000.00	8500.00
3,425	1876	200.00	325.00	1100.00
3,920	1877	250.00	400.00	1000.00
3,020	1878	225.00	350.00	1100.00
3,030	1879	225.00	350.00	1000.00
1,636	1880	200.00	300.00	1000.00
7,660	1881	200.00	300.00	800.00
5,040	1882	200.00	300.00	800.00
10,840	1883	150.00	250.00	625.00
6,206	1884	175.00	275.00	650.00
12,205	1885	150.00	250.00	650.00
6,016	1886	175.00	275.00	650.00
8,543	1887	175.00	275.00	650.00
16,080	1888	175.00	275.00	650.00
30,729	1889	175.00	275.00	650.00

Quarter Eagles ($2.50)

The handsome Indian Head Type in the quarter eagle and half eagle series is unique in United States coinage in that the design and legends are incused. This means they are sunk below the surface of the coin instead of being in relief (raised above the surface of the coin).

LIBERTY CAP TYPE

LIBERTY CAP TYPE

QUANTITY	YEAR	FINE	VERY FINE	UNC.
963	1796 no stars	$9000.00	$15,000.00	$85,000.00
432	1796 with stars	7500.00	13,500.00	60,000.00
1,756	1797	5000.00	9000.00	37,500.00
614	1798	3500.00	5000.00	20,000.00
2,612	1802 over 1	2500.00	3750.00	16,500.00
3,327	1804	2750.00	4000.00	18,500.00
1,781	1805	2500.00	3500.00	16,000.00
1,616	1806 over 4	2500.00	3250.00	17,000.00
	1806 over 5	4000.00	7500.00	25,000.00
6,812	1807	2500.00	3250.00	16,000.00

LIBERTY HEAD WITH MOTTO OVER EAGLE

2,710	1808	6500.00	13,000.00	40,000.00
6,448	1821 reduced size	2000.00	3500.00	14,000.00
2,600	1824 over 21	2000.00	3750.00	15,000.00
4,434	1825	2000.00	3750.00	14,000.00
760	1826 over 25	3000.00	5500.00	22,500.00
2,800	1827	2000.00	3000.00	15,500.00
3,403	1829	2000.00	3000.00	12,000.00
4,540	1830	2000.00	3000.00	12,000.00
4,520	1831	2000.00	3000.00	12,000.00
4,400	1832	2000.00	3000.00	12,000.00
4,160	1833	2000.00	3000.00	12,000.00
4,000	1834	3750.00	5500.00	28,500.00

RIBBON TYPE WITHOUT MOTTO

The mint mark—only on 1838 and 1839—is above the date on the obverse.

112,324	1834	200.00	285.00	2400.00
131,402	1835	200.00	285.00	2250.00
547,986	1836	200.00	285.00	2250.00
45,080	1837	225.00	300.00	2300.00
47,030	1838	225.00	300.00	2300.00
7,908	1838 C	550.00	850.00	15,000.00
27,021	1839	225.00	300.00	3750.00
18,173	1839 C	500.00	750.00	10,000.00
13,674	1839 D	500.00	800.00	10,500.00
17,781	1839 O	400.00	600.00	5750.00

QUARTER EAGLES–CORONET TYPE WITHOUT MOTTO

The mint mark is below the eagle on the reverse.

QUANTITY	YEAR	FINE	VERY FINE	UNC.
18,859	1840	$175.00	$250.00	$2750.00
12,838	1840 C	285.00	525.00	8500.00
3,532	1840 D	400.00	800.00	12,500.00
26,200	1840 O	250.00	500.00	4500.00
?	1841	(an outstanding rarity; Proof $100,000.00)		
10,297	1841 C	325.00	525.00	7500.00
4,164	1841 D	400.00	1000.00	12,000.00
2,823	1842	375.00	875.00	12,500.00
6,737	1842 C	375.00	800.00	10,000.00
4,643	1842 D	375.00	1000.00	12,500.00
19,800	1842 O	300.00	525.00	7500.00
100,546	1843	200.00	375.00	1400.00
26,096	1843 C	375.00	625.00	6500.00
36,209	1843 D	325.00	600.00	5000.00
368,002	1843 O	175.00	275.00	1250.00
6,784	1844	275.00	500.00	5250.00
11,622	1844 C	275.00	575.00	7500.00
17,732	1844 D	275.00	500.00	6250.00
91,051	1845	200.00	285.00	1000.00
19,460	1845 D	350.00	600.00	7500.00
4,000	1845 O	625.00	1100.00	13,500.00
21,598	1846	200.00	400.00	2750.00
4,808	1846 C	550.00	850.00	10,000.00
19,303	1846 D	325.00	725.00	7000.00
66,000	1846 O	250.00	325.00	2500.00
29,814	1847	200.00	300.00	2250.00
23,226	1847 C	300.00	525.00	5000.00
15,784	1847 D	375.00	575.00	6250.00
124,000	1847 O	185.00	325.00	2250.00
8,886	1848	400.00	750.00	5250.00
	1848 CAL over			
	eagle (rare)	4500.00	6500.00	32,000.00
16,788	1848 C	450.00	625.00	6750.00
13,771	1848 D	500.00	650.00	7250.00
23,294	1849	225.00	350.00	1750.00
10,220	1849 C	425.00	625.00	8250.00
10,945	1849 D	425.00	700.00	8500.00
252,923	1850	175.00	250.00	850.00
9,148	1850 C	400.00	600.00	8250.00
12,148	1850 D	325.00	500.00	5000.00
84,000	1850 O	275.00	325.00	2500.00
1,372,648	1851	175.00	235.00	700.00
14,923	1851 C	325.00	550.00	7500.00
11,264	1851 D	325.00	550.00	7500.00
148,000	1851 O	250.00	275.00	2250.00
1,159,681	1852	175.00	235.00	1750.00
9,772	1852 C	425.00	575.00	7000.00
4,078	1852 D	525.00	775.00	9000.00
140,000	1852 O	175.00	250.00	2750.00
1,404,668	1853	150.00	200.00	750.00
3,178	1853 D	625.00	1000.00	10,000.00
596,258	1854	175.00	235.00	625.00
7,295	1854 C	375.00	625.00	8000.00
1,760	1854 D	1400.00	3000.00	14,000.00
153,000	1854 O	175.00	285.00	1250.00

QUANTITY	YEAR	FINE	VERY FINE	UNC.
246	1854 S	13,000.00	27,500.00	75,000.00
235,480	1855	175.00	250.00	625.00
3,677	1855 C	750.00	1100.00	12,500.00
1,123	1855 D	1500.00	3500.00	20,000.00
384,240	1856	150.00	200.00	600.00
7,913	1856 C	475.00	750.00	10,000.00
874	1856 D	4000.00	7250.00	35,000.00
21,100	1856 O	175.00	250.00	2750.00
71,120	1856 S	175.00	265.00	2250.00
214,130	1857	165.00	235.00	600.00
2,364	1857 D	475.00	900.00	8500.00
34,000	1857 O	200.00	325.00	2850.00
68,000	1857 S	175.00	250.00	3000.00
47,377	1858	175.00	250.00	1250.00
9,056	1858 C	315.00	625.00	7500.00
39,444	1859	175.00	250.00	1250.00
2,244	1859 D	550.00	1250.00	10,000.00
15,200	1859 S	250.00	425.00	5000.00
22,675	1860	200.00	300.00	1100.00
7,469	1860 C	350.00	650.00	7500.00
35,600	1860 S	180.00	300.00	2750.00
1,272,518	1861	180.00	250.00	625.00
24,000	1861 S	250.00	375.00	2500.00
112,353	1862	175.00	250.00	1000.00
8,000	1862 S	400.00	750.00	9250.00
30	* 1863 very rare			
10,800	1863 S	225.00	425.00	5000.00
2,874	1864	1000.00	2500.00	17,500.00
1,545	1865	525.00	2500.00	16,500.00
23,376	1865 S	200.00	275.00	2850.00
3,110	1866	425.00	900.00	8000.00
38,960	1866 S	200.00	350.00	2750.00
3,250	1867	350.00	625.00	7250.00
28,000	1867 S	225.00	325.00	2750.00
3,625	1868	300.00	425.00	2500.00
34,000	1868 S	175.00	250.00	2750.00
4,345	1869	300.00	325.00	3000.00
29,500	1869 S	175.00	250.00	2750.00
4,555	1870	250.00	350.00	3000.00
16,000	1870 S	185.00	275.00	2500.00
5,350	1871	225.00	375.00	2800.00
22,000	1871 S	175.00	250.00	1750.00
3,030	1872	275.00	400.00	4500.00
178,025	1873	175.00	225.00	800.00
27,000	1873 S	185.00	250.00	1750.00
3,940	1874	235.00	325.00	3200.00
420	1875	1750.00	4500.00	18,500.00
11,600	1875 S	175.00	250.00	2000.00
4,221	1876	250.00	325.00	2800.00
5,000	1876 S	225.00	300.00	2000.00
1,652	1877	340.00	550.00	3750.00
35,400	1877 S	180.00	225.00	750.00
286,260	1878	165.00	215.00	500.00
178,000	1878 S	165.00	215.00	500.00
88,900	1879	165.00	215.00	500.00
43,500	1879 S	175.00	225.00	800.00
2,996	1880	250.00	325.00	1200.00
680	1881	600.00	1200.00	11,000.00
4,040	1882	250.00	300.00	1200.00
1,960	1883	225.00	275.00	1300.00
1,993	1884	225.00	300.00	1500.00
887	1885	500.00	750.00	5250.00
4,088	1886	200.00	275.00	1250.00
6,282	1887	175.00	250.00	1000.00
16,098	1888	150.00	225.00	700.00
17,648	1889	150.00	225.00	625.00
8,813	1890	165.00	250.00	700.00

* Proof-63 specimen sold for $80,000 at Aug. 1990 RARCOA auction.

QUARTER EAGLES ; CORONET TYPE WITHOUT MOTTO (continued)

QUANTITY	YEAR	FINE	VERY FINE	UNC.
11,040	1891	150.00	225.00	600.00
2,545	1892	200.00	275.00	1000.00
30,106	1893	150.00	225.00	500.00
4,122	1894	165.00	275.00	850.00
6,119	1895	165.00	275.00	625.00
19,202	1896	150.00	200.00	500.00
29,904	1897	150.00	200.00	500.00
24,165	1898	150.00	200.00	500.00
27,350	1899	150.00	200.00	500.00
67,205	1900	150.00	200.00	500.00
91,323	1901	150.00	200.00	500.00
133,733	1902	150.00	200.00	500.00
201,257	1903	150.00	200.00	500.00
160,960	1904	150.00	200.00	500.00
217,944	1905	150.00	200.00	500.00
176,490	1906	150.00	200.00	500.00
336,448	1907	150.00	200.00	500.00

INDIAN HEAD INCUSE TYPE

The mint mark is to the left of the eagle's claw on the reverse.

QUANTITY	YEAR	VERY FINE	EXT. FINE	UNC.
565,057	1908	$150.00	$200.00	$325.00
441,899	1909	150.00	200.00	340.00
492,682	1910	150.00	200.00	340.00
704,191	1911	150.00	200.00	340.00
55,680	1911 D	625.00	1000.00	3000.00
616,197	1912	150.00	200.00	340.00
722,165	1913	150.00	200.00	340.00
240,117	1914	150.00	200.00	375.00
448,000	1914 D	150.00	200.00	340.00
606,100	1915	150.00	200.00	340.00
578,000	1925 D	150.00	200.00	340.00
446,000	1926	150.00	200.00	340.00
388,000	1927	150.00	200.00	340.00
416,000	1928	150.00	200.00	340.00
532,000	1929	150.00	200.00	340.00

Three-Dollar Gold Pieces

Like the three-cent pieces, these coins were intended for buying three-cent stamps. However, the public remained indifferent to both types of coins. When the postal rate was changed, the coinage of these gold pieces came to an end.

THREE-DOLLAR GOLD PIECES

The mint mark is below the wreath on the reverse.

QUANTITY	YEAR	FINE	VERY FINE	UNC.
138,618	1854	$400.00	$625.00	$2500.00
1,120	1854 D	4000.00	6500.00	25,000.00
24,000	1854 O	475.00	675.00	3250.00
50,555	1855	450.00	625.00	3000.00
6,600	1855 S	600.00	1000.00	10,000.00
26,010	1856	450.00	600.00	2750.00
34,500	1856 S small S	450.00	650.00	3750.00
20,891	1857	450.00	800.00	3000.00
14,000	1857 S	550.00	825.00	6500.00
2,133	1858	550.00	800.00	5000.00
15,638	1859	450.00	750.00	3000.00
7,155	1860	465.00	800.00	3250.00
7,000	1860 S	550.00	800.00	6500.00
6,072	1861	550.00	750.00	3750.00
5,785	1862	550.00	700.00	3750.00
5,039	1863	550.00	800.00	4000.00
2,680	1864	550.00	800.00	4000.00
1,165	1865	625.00	825.00	7250.00
4,030	1866	500.00	700.00	4500.00
2,650	1867	600.00	850.00	4750.00
4,875	1868	550.00	700.00	4250.00
2,525	1869	575.00	850.00	4750.00
3,535	1870	550.00	750.00	4000.00
2	1870 S unique $687,500, Bowers & Ruddy Oct. 1982 "U.S. Gold Sale"			
1,330	1871	650.00	850.00	4500.00
2,030	1872	575.00	750.00	4250.00
25	1873 (only proofs were struck)			32,500.00
41,820	1874	425.00	550.00	3250.00
20	1875 (only proofs were struck) $159,000, RARCOA Aug. 1990 Sale			
45	1876 (only proofs were struck) $35,200 1984 Carter Sale			
1,488	1877	750.00	1100.00	7500.00
82,234	1878	375.00	550.00	2750.00
3,030	1879	450.00	750.00	3750.00
1,036	1880	500.00	800.00	4250.00
550	1881	800.00	1000.00	5000.00
1,540	1882	500.00	575.00	4250.00
940	1883	575.00	825.00	4500.00
1,106	1884	575.00	800.00	4750.00
910	1885	575.00	800.00	4750.00
1,142	1886	550.00	750.00	4000.00
6,160	1887	500.00	750.00	3000.00
5,291	1888	500.00	750.00	3000.00
2,429	1889	500.00	750.00	3000.00

Four-Dollar Gold Pieces

These coins are sometimes called "Stellas" because of the star on the obverse. Though struck as patterns in 1879 and 1880, they were never issued as regular coins. The decision not to use them was a sensible one, as three-dollar and five-dollar gold pieces were already in existence.

The "Stellas" were struck in very small quantities and are therefore among the highly prized rarities of American coinage.

FOUR-DOLLAR ("STELLA") GOLD PIECE PATTERNS

(only proofs were struck)

QUANTITY	YEAR	PROOF-63
415	1879 flowing hair	$55,000.00
10	1879 coiled hair	130,000.00
15	1880 flowing hair	75,000.00
10	1880 coiled hair	150,000.00

An 1879 "Quintuple Stella," or $20, brought $214,500 at the May 1996 Eliasberg sale.

Half Eagles ($5)

It is curious that up to 1807 these coins carried no indication of their value.

BUST TYPE FACING RIGHT

1795–1798   1795–1807

Half Eagles ($5 Gold Pieces)

QUANTITY	YEAR	FINE	VERY FINE	UNC.
8,707	1795 small eagle	$5000.00	$8500.00	$27,500.00
	1795 large eagle	5500.00	9000.00	37,500.00
3,399	1796 over 95 small eagle	6000.00	10,000.00	37,500.00
6,406	1797 over 95 large eagle	5000.00	8000.00	27,500.00
	1797 15 stars small eagle	6000.00	10,000.00	37,500.00
	1797 16 stars small eagle	5500.00	9000.00	32,500.00
24,867	1798 small eagle	6500.00	20,000.00	50,000.00
	1798 large eagle	2500.00	3000.00	15,000.00
7,451	1799	1000.00	2000.00	10,000.00
11,622	1800	1000.00	1750.00	8500.00
53,176	1802 over 1	1000.00	1750.00	8000.00
33,506	1803 over 2	1000.00	1750.00	8000.00
30,475	1804	1100.00	1750.00	8000.00
33,183	1805	1100.00	1850.00	9000.00
64,093	1806	1100.00	1800.00	8500.00
33,496	1807	1000.00	1800.00	8500.00

BUST TYPE FACING LEFT

1807–1812   **1813–1834**

QUANTITY	YEAR	FINE	VERY FINE	UNC.
50,597	1807	1100.00	1500.00	8000.00
55,578	1808 over 7	1200.00	1650.00	8500.00
	1808	1100.00	1400.00	8000.00
33,875	1809 over 8	1100.00	1400.00	8000.00
	1809	1100.00	1400.00	8000.00
100,287	1810	1100.00	1500.00	8500.00
99,581	1811	1100.00	1500.00	8500.00
58,087	1812	1000.00	1400.00	8000.00
95,428	1813 larger head	1100.00	1400.00	8750.00
15,454	1814	1750.00	2800.00	12,500.00
635	1815		65,000.00	125,000.00
45,588	1818	1500.00	2500.00	10,000.00
51,723	1819	7500.00	10,000.00	45,000.00
263,806	1820	1250.00	2000.00	10,000.00
34,641	1821	3000.00	6250.00	20,000.00
17,796	1822 an outstanding rarity; proof			687,500.00
14,485	1823	2750.00	4250.00	15,000.00
17,340	1824	4500.00	8000.00	32,500.00
29,060	1825 over 21	4000.00	6500.00	24,000.00
	1825 over 24 $148,500 Bowers & Merena, March 1989 Sale			
18,069	1826	5000.00	5500.00	20,000.00
24,913	1827	10,000.00	20,000.00	50,000.00
28,029	1828 over 27	5000.00	7000.00	20,000.00
	1828	7500.00	10,000.00	28,500.00
57,442	1829 $104,500, Superior July 1985 Sale			
126,351	1830	2250.00	3650.00	16,500.00
140,594	1831	2250.00	3650.00	16,500.00
157,487	1832 curled 2, 12 stars	5500.00	7500.00	25,000.00
	1832 square-based 2, 13 stars	3500.00	6750.00	20,000.00
193,630	1833	2200.00	3750.00	16,000.00
50,141	1834	2250.00	3800.00	15,000.00

RIBBON TYPE WITHOUT MOTTO

The mint mark—only on 1838—is above the date on the obverse.

QUANTITY	YEAR	FINE	VERY FINE	UNC.
682,028	1834	250.00	300.00	3000.00
371,534	1835	235.00	285.00	3000.00
553,147	1836	235.00	285.00	3000.00
207,121	1837	265.00	325.00	3250.00

HALF EAGLES: RIBBON TYPE WITHOUT MOTTO (continued)

QUANTITY	YEAR	FINE	VERY FINE	UNC.
286,588	1838	265.00	325.00	3250.00
12,913	1838 C	800.00	1250.00	6500.00
20,583	1838 D	800.00	1250.00	7000.00

CORONET TYPE

1839–1865 **1866–1908**

The mint mark is below the eagle on the reverse.

118,143	1839	235.00	300.00	3250.00
17,205	1839 C	475.00	800.00	8500.00
18,939	1839 D	475.00	800.00	7500.00
137,382	1840	225.00	265.00	3500.00
19,028	1840 C	500.00	750.00	8250.00
22,896	1840 D	500.00	750.00	8250.00
30,400	1840 O	300.00	475.00	6250.00
15,833	1841	275.00	450.00	4750.00
21,511	1841 C	425.00	650.00	8750.00
30,495	1841 D	425.00	650.00	8500.00
8,350	1841 O (2 known)			
27,578	1842	225.00	325.00	4500.00
27,480	1842 C	375.00	700.00	7500.00
59,608	1842 D	375.00	700.00	6500.00
16,400	1842 O	325.00	500.00	5000.00
611,205	1843	185.00	200.00	1750.00
44,353	1843 C	400.00	650.00	5000.00
98,452	1843 D	350.00	550.00	6250.00
101,075	1843 O	250.00	375.00	3750.00
340,330	1844	185.00	200.00	1850.00
23,631	1844 C	375.00	625.00	6750.00
88,982	1844 D	375.00	575.00	7000.00
364,600	1844 O	250.00	400.00	3750.00
417,099	1845	200.00	250.00	2000.00
90,629	1845 D	325.00	500.00	5000.00
41,000	1845 O	275.00	475.00	4500.00
395,942	1846	200.00	225.00	2000.00
12,995	1846 C	400.00	750.00	7500.00
80,294	1846 D	350.00	600.00	6750.00
58,000	1846 O	275.00	425.00	5000.00
915,981	1847	200.00	225.00	1750.00
84,151	1847 C	375.00	600.00	5250.00
64,405	1847 D	375.00	600.00	5500.00
12,000	1847 O	450.00	700.00	6750.00
260,775	1848	200.00	250.00	1800.00
64,472	1848 C	400.00	625.00	6000.00
47,465	1848 D	400.00	625.00	6250.00
133,070	1849	200.00	250.00	2250.00
64,823	1849 C	400.00	600.00	6500.00
39,036	1849 D	400.00	600.00	6500.00
64,491	1850	250.00	325.00	3750.00
63,591	1850 C	400.00	525.00	5500.00
43,950	1850 D	400.00	525.00	6250.00
377,505	1851	200.00	250.00	1800.00
49,176	1851 C	400.00	500.00	5750.00
62,710	1851 D	400.00	500.00	5750.00

QUANTITY	YEAR	FINE	VERY FINE	UNC.
41,000	1851 O	350.00	550.00	4250.00
573,901	1852	180.00	200.00	1500.00
72,574	1852 C	375.00	550.00	5500.00
91,452	1852 D	375.00	550.00	5000.00
305,770	1853	180.00	235.00	1850.00
65,571	1853 C	375.00	550.00	5000.00
89,678	1853 D	375.00	500.00	5000.00
160,675	1854	180.00	250.00	1800.00
39,291	1854 C	400.00	550.00	5750.00
56,413	1854 D	375.00	525.00	5000.00
46,000	1854 O	265.00	450.00	3850.00
268	1854 S	ext. rare Sold for $210,000.00 at 1983 auction		
117,098	1855	180.00	235.00	1650.00
39,788	1855 C	400.00	550.00	4500.00
22,432	1855 D	400.00	550.00	5000.00
11,100	1855 O	425.00	575.00	6250.00
61,000	1855 S	215.00	375.00	3750.00
197,990	1856	180.00	200.00	1650.00
28,457	1856 C	425.00	550.00	4750.00
19,786	1856 D	425.00	550.00	5000.00
10,000	1856 O	425.00	625.00	7250.00
105,100	1856 S	250.00	300.00	3850.00
98,188	1857	180.00	225.00	1850.00
31,360	1857 C	375.00	600.00	6000.00
17,046	1857 D	425.00	625.00	6750.00
13,000	1857 O	350.00	575.00	5750.00
87,000	1857 S	215.00	300.00	3250.00
15,136	1858	250.00	350.00	3000.00
38,856	1858 C	375.00	550.00	5000.00
15,362	1858 D	375.00	550.00	5500.00
18,600	1858 S	325.00	525.00	4250.00
16,814	1859	250.00	375.00	3500.00
31,847	1859 C	375.00	525.00	5000.00
10,366	1859 D	425.00	575.00	6250.00
13,220	1859 S	450.00	550.00	6000.00
19,825	1860	250.00	375.00	3750.00
14,813	1860 C	375.00	625.00	7500.00
14,635	1860 D	375.00	625.00	9000.00
21,200	1860 S	350.00	600.00	8500.00
639,950	1861	185.00	250.00	1650.00
6,879	1861 C	1000.00	1500.00	12,500.00
1,597	1861 D	3250.00	5000.00	27,500.00
18,000	1861 S	325.00	625.00	7500.00
4,465	1862	475.00	750.00	7500.00
9,500	1862 S	550.00	850.00	8500.00
2,472	1863	650.00	1000.00	10,000.00
17,000	1863 S	375.00	800.00	6850.00
4,220	1864	450.00	625.00	8250.00
3,888	1864 S	1300.00	2850.00	16,500.00
1,295	1865	575.00	1000.00	10,000.00
27,612	1865 S	375.00	800.00	8500.00
43,920*	1866 S no motto	400.00	1000.00	9500.00

CORONET TYPE WITH MOTTO

The mint mark is below the eagle on the reverse.

QUANTITY	YEAR	FINE	VERY FINE	UNC.
6,730	1866	375.00	525.00	3750.00
34,920	*1866 S	350.00	500.00	3500.00
6,920	1867	350.00	500.00	3000.00
29,000	1867 S	275.00	450.00	3000.00
5,725	1868	325.00	500.00	6250.00
52,000	1868 S	275.00	425.00	3750.00
1,785	1869	600.00	850.00	7250.00
31,000	1869 S	325.00	625.00	3750.00
4,035	1870	350.00	650.00	5750.00
7,675	1870 CC	1400.00	2500.00	17,500.00

*Includes 1866 S coins with motto.

HALF EAGLES: CORONET TYPE WITH MOTTO (continued)

QUANTITY	YEAR	FINE	VERY FINE	UNC.
17,000	1870 S	325.00	500.00	4250.00
3,230	1871	375.00	625.00	4250.00
20,770	1871 CC	525.00	825.00	7250.00
25,000	1871 S	300.00	500.00	4000.00
1,690	1872	500.00	725.00	4500.00
16,980	1872 CC	500.00	800.00	4750.00
36,400	1872 S	275.00	450.00	3850.00
112,505	1873	200.00	300.00	1100.00
7,416	1873 CC	625.00	1100.00	7500.00
31,000	1873 S	350.00	525.00	3750.00
3,508	1874	375.00	600.00	4750.00
21,198	1874 CC	375.00	600.00	5500.00
16,000	1874 S	325.00	525.00	5000.00
220	1875 rare $115,000, Akers 1990 Sale, Proof			
11,828	1875 CC	525.00	900.00	8250.00
9,000	1875 S	325.00	625.00	4750.00
1,477	1876	525.00	1000.00	8500.00
6,887	1876 CC	500.00	800.00	5750.00
4,000	1876 S	500.00	800.00	6500.00
1,152	1877	625.00	1000.00	9000.00
8,680	1877 CC	500.00	900.00	5750.00
26,700	1877 S	250.00	325.00	2000.00
131,740	1878	180.00	200.00	650.00
9,054	1878 CC	875.00	1600.00	13,500.00
144,700	1878 S	185.00	225.00	875.00
301,950	1879	175.00	200.00	500.00
17,281	1879 CC	300.00	400.00	3750.00
426,200	1879 S	200.00	250.00	625.00
3,166,436	1880	175.00	200.00	365.00
51,017	1880 CC	275.00	525.00	2850.00
1,348,900	1880 S	200.00	275.00	385.00
5,708,800	1881	175.00	200.00	300.00
13,886	1881 CC	325.00	500.00	4250.00
969,000	1881 S	175.00	200.00	365.00
2,514,560	1882	175.00	200.00	365.00
82,817	1882 CC	225.00	325.00	2250.00
969,000	1882 S	175.00	200.00	365.00
233,440	1883	175.00	200.00	365.00
12,598	1883 CC	250.00	425.00	2850.00
83,200	1883 S	200.00	275.00	825.00
191,048	1884	185.00	215.00	750.00
16,402	1884 CC	250.00	525.00	2750.00
177,000	1884 S	175.00	225.00	525.00
601,506	1885	175.00	200.00	375.00
1,211,500	1885 S	175.00	200.00	375.00
388,432	1886	175.00	200.00	375.00
3,268,000	1886 S	175.00	200.00	375.00
87	1887 rare (only proofs were struck) 28,500.00			
1,912,000	1887 S	175.00	225.00	365.00
18,296	1888	200.00	275.00	750.00
293,900	1888 S	200.00	275.00	1000.00
7,565	1889	300.00	400.00	1100.00
4,328	1890	325.00	550.00	1850.00
53,800	1890 CC	200.00	285.00	1100.00
61,413	1891	175.00	225.00	650.00
208,000	1891 CC	200.00	250.00	900.00
753,572	1892	175.00	225.00	350.00
82,968	1892 CC	200.00	250.00	1000.00
10,000	1892 O	450.00	700.00	3500.00
298,400	1892 S	175.00	215.00	650.00
1,528,197	1893	150.00	175.00	275.00
60,000	1893 CC	225.00	315.00	1250.00
110,000	1893 O	215.00	280.00	1000.00
224,000	1893 S	175.00	200.00	650.00
957,955	1894	175.00	200.00	425.00
16,600	1894 O	200.00	300.00	1100.00

QUANTITY	YEAR	FINE	VERY FINE	UNC.
55,900	1894 S	185.00	250.00	1000.00
1,345,936	1895	150.00	175.00	275.00
112,000	1895 S	185.00	215.00	850.00
59,063	1896	175.00	210.00	500.00
155,400	1896 S	175.00	200.00	625.00
867,883	1897	150.00	175.00	275.00
354,000	1897 S	150.00	175.00	500.00
633,495	1898	150.00	175.00	275.00
1,397,400	1898 S	150.00	175.00	275.00
1,710,729	1899	150.00	175.00	275.00
1,545,000	1899 S	150.00	175.00	275.00
1,405,730	1900	150.00	175.00	275.00
329,000	1900 S	150.00	175.00	525.00
616,400	1901	150.00	175.00	275.00
3,648,000	1901 S	150.00	175.00	275.00
172,562	1902	150.00	175.00	275.00
939,000	1902 S	150.00	175.00	275.00
227,024	1903	150.00	175.00	275.00
1,855,000	1903 S	150.00	175.00	275.00
392,136	1904	150.00	175.00	275.00
97,000	1904 S	190.00	215.00	625.00
302,308	1905	150.00	175.00	275.00
880,700	1905 S	150.00	175.00	500.00
348,820	1906	150.00	175.00	275.00
320,000	1906 D	150.00	175.00	275.00
598,000	1906 S	150.00	175.00	275.00
626,192	1907	150.00	175.00	275.00
888,000	1907 D	150.00	175.00	275.00
421,874	1908	150.00	175.00	275.00

INDIAN HEAD INCUSE TYPE

The mint mark is to the left of the eagle's claw on the reverse.

QUANTITY	YEAR	FINE	VERY FINE	UNC.
578,012	1908	$175.00	$200.00	$500.00
148,000	1908 D	175.00	200.00	500.00
82,000	1908 S	275.00	500.00	2750.00
627,138	1909	200.00	250.00	750.00
3,423,560	1909 D	175.00	225.00	700.00
34,200	1909 O rare	450.00	725.00	7000.00
297,200	1909 S	225.00	265.00	1500.00
604,250	1910	200.00	250.00	700.00
193,600	1910 D	200.00	250.00	625.00
770,200	1910 S	200.00	250.00	1500.00
915,139	1911	200.00	250.00	500.00
72,500	1911 D	300.00	400.00	4250.00
1,416,000	1911 S	200.00	250.00	900.00
790,144	1912	200.00	250.00	625.00
392,000	1912 S	200.00	275.00	1850.00
916,099	1913	200.00	215.00	550.00
408,000	1913 S	225.00	250.00	2600.00
247,125	1914	200.00	250.00	525.00
247,000	1914 D	200.00	250.00	525.00
263,000	1914 S	200.00	250.00	1250.00
588,075	1915	200.00	200.00	525.00
164,000	1915 S	215.00	225.00	2350.00

HALF EAGLES: INDIAN HEAD INCUSE TYPE (continued)

QUANTITY	YEAR	FINE	VERY FINE	UNC.
240,000	1916 S	225.00	250.00	825.00
662,000	1929 rare	2000.00	2750.00	6500.00

Eagles ($10)

No value appeared on these coins until 1838.

The eagles and double eagles first issued in 1907 were designed by the distinguished sculptor, Augustus Saint-Gaudens. They are generally considered the most beautiful of all United States coins. Theodore Roosevelt, who was President at the time, forbade the use of the motto "In God We Trust" on these coins. He felt that the appearance of this phrase on a coin was in bad taste. His successor, President Taft, had the motto restored in 1908.

BUST TYPE

1795–1797   1797–1804

Eagles ($10 Gold Pieces)

QUANTITY	YEAR	FINE	VERY FINE	UNC.
5,583	1795	$5500.00	$7500.00	$32,500.00
4,146	1796	5250.00	7250.00	35,000.00
14,555	1797 small eagle	4250.00	6750.00	37,500.00
	1797 large eagle	3000.00	5000.00	17,500.00
1,742	1798 over 97; 4 stars before bust	4500.00	7500.00	32,500.00
	1798 over 97; 6 stars before bust	10,000.00	22,500.00	62,500.00
37,449	1799	2000.00	3250.00	12,500.00
5,999	1800	2750.00	3500.00	14,000.00
44,344	1801	2250.00	3250.00	12,000.00
15,017	1803	2250.00	3250.00	13,500.00
3,757	1804	3000.00	5000.00	26,500.00

CORONET TYPE

1838–1865   1866–1907

The mint mark is below the eagle on the reverse.

QUANTITY	YEAR	VERY FINE	EXT. FINE	UNC.
7,200	1838	1300.00	2500.00	12,500.00
38,248	1839	900.00	1750.00	9500.00
47,338	1840	425.00	625.00	6750.00
63,131	1841	325.00	500.00	6500.00
2,500	1841 O	1000.00	2500.00	17,500.00
81,507	1842	325.00	625.00	6750.00
27,400	1842 O	375.00	650.00	10,000.00
75,462	1843	350.00	600.00	8250.00
175,162	1843 O	315.00	500.00	5750.00
6,361	1844	575.00	1300.00	8250.00
118,700	1844 O	300.00	500.00	8000.00
26,153	1845	375.00	650.00	8000.00
47,500	1845 O	375.00	650.00	8000.00
20,095	1846	425.00	800.00	8500.00
81,780	1846 O	375.00	525.00	6000.00
862,258	1847	350.00	450.00	3250.00
571,500	1847 O	325.00	450.00	3750.00
145,484	1848	300.00	450.00	4250.00
35,850	1848 O	425.00	750.00	5000.00
653,618	1849	300.00	425.00	3500.00
23,900	1849 O	450.00	725.00	8000.00
291,451	1850	325.00	450.00	3850.00
57,500	1850 O	350.00	625.00	5000.00
176,328	1851	300.00	425.00	4750.00
263,000	1851 O	300.00	425.00	5000.00
263,106	1852	300.00	425.00	4750.00
18,000	1852 O	525.00	1000.00	7500.00
201,253	1853	300.00	450.00	3500.00
51,000	1853 O	325.00	525.00	5500.00
54,250	1854	325.00	525.00	3850.00
52,500	1854 O	325.00	525.00	4250.00
123,826	1854 S	300.00	500.00	4000.00
121,701	1855	285.00	425.00	3500.00
18,000	1855 O	500.00	900.00	6500.00
9,000	1855 S	1000.00	1400.00	10,000.00
60,490	1856	300.00	450.00	3250.00
14,500	1856 O	500.00	1000.00	7500.00
68,000	1856 S	400.00	600.00	6500.00
16,606	1857	375.00	650.00	6750.00
5,500	1857 O	875.00	1650.00	10,000.00
26,000	1857 S	425.00	725.00	6250.00
2,521	1858 ext. rare	4750.00	8750.00	37,500.00
20,000	1858 O	350.00	650.00	7250.00
11,800	1858 S	625.00	1000.00	7500.00
16,093	1859	375.00	750.00	7250.00
2,300	1859 O	1650.00	6250.00	17,500.00
7,000	1859 S	1000.00	1750.00	10,000.00
11,783	1860	365.00	750.00	6750.00
11,100	1860 O	425.00	1000.00	10,000.00
5,000	1860 S	1100.00	1750.00	17,500.00
113,233	1861	285.00	400.00	3750.00
15,500	1861 S	425.00	1200.00	9250.00
10,995	1862	425.00	750.00	5500.00
12,500	1862 S	500.00	1250.00	12,500.00
1,248	1863	3250.00	6250.00	22,500.00
10,000	1863 S	825.00	1250.00	10,000.00
3,580	1864	1000.00	2500.00	12,500.00
2,500	1864 S	2650.00	7500.00	25,000.00
4,005	1865	1000.00	2750.00	12,500.00
16,700	1865 S	1000.00	2500.00	13,500.00
20,000*	1866 S	1350.00	3250.00	14,500.00

CORONET TYPE WITH MOTTO

The mint mark is below the eagle on the reverse.

QUANTITY	YEAR	VERY FINE	EXT. FINE	UNC.
3,780	1866	$625.00	$1250.00	$7500.00
*	1866 S	600.00	1100.00	6250.00

*Includes 1866 S coins with motto.

CORONET TYPE

QUANTITY	YEAR	VERY FINE	EXT. FINE	UNC.
3,140	1867	$1000.00	$1650.00	$9500.00
9,000	1867 S	750.00	1250.00	6500.00
10,655	1868	625.00	900.00	5250.00
13,500	1868 S	625.00	900.00	5250.00
1,855	1869	1000.00	2500.00	10,000.00
6,430	1869 S	1000.00	1500.00	7500.00
2,535	1870	825.00	1250.00	6250.00
5,908	1870 CC	1750.00	8750.00	17,500.00
8,000	1870 S	750.00	1250.00	7250.00
1,780	1871	1600.00	2250.00	8250.00
7,185	1871 CC	875.00	1750.00	6500.00
16,500	1871 S	650.00	850.00	5750.00
1,650	1872	1500.00	2500.00	7500.00
5,500	1872 CC	1000.00	1500.00	7250.00
17,300	1872 S	575.00	1000.00	4750.00
825	1873	3250.00	5000.00	17,500.00
4,543	1873 CC	1250.00	4250.00	12,500.00
12,000	1873 S	625.00	1100.00	6750.00
53,160	1874	300.00	450.00	1250.00
16,767	1874 CC	700.00	1250.00	7250.00
10,000	1874 S	650.00	1000.00	6250.00
120	1875	rare $115,000, Akers Aug. 1990 Auction, Proof		
7,715	1875 CC	825.00	1850.00	8250.00
732	1876	2000.00	6250.00	12,500.00
4,696	1876 CC	1250.00	2000.00	10,000.00
5,000	1876 S	875.00	1750.00	6750.00
817	1877	1250.00	4750.00	17,500.00
3,332	1877 CC	1100.00	3250.00	12,500.00
17,000	1877 S	525.00	825.00	5000.00
73,800	1878	300.00	425.00	1300.00
3,244	1878 CC	1250.00	2500.00	11,000.00
26,100	1878 S	400.00	750.00	3500.00
384,770	1879	275.00	325.00	675.00
1,762	1879 CC	2750.00	6250.00	17,500.00
1,500	1879 O	1750.00	3250.00	14,000.00
224,000	1879 S	265.00	375.00	825.00
1,644,876	1880	250.00	350.00	500.00
11,190	1880 CC	350.00	700.00	2250.00
9,200	1880 O	375.00	725.00	2500.00
506,250	1880 S	275.00	325.00	600.00

CORONET TYPE WITHOUT MOTTO

QUANTITY	YEAR	VERY FINE	EXT. FINE	UNC.
3,877,260	1881	$200.00	$235.00	$300.00
24,015	1881 CC	325.00	450.00	2250.00
8,350	1881 O	375.00	600.00	2850.00
970,000	1881 S	200.00	250.00	300.00
2,324,480	1882	200.00	250.00	285.00
6,764	1882 CC	425.00	875.00	4250.00
10,820	1882 O	350.00	625.00	2750.00
132,000	1882 S	275.00	350.00	750.00
208,740	1883	275.00	350.00	450.00
12,000	1883 CC	375.00	675.00	2850.00
800	1883 O rare	2500.00	4250.00	16,500.00
38,000	1883 S	325.00	400.00	800.00
76,905	1884	325.00	375.00	650.00
9,925	1884 CC	450.00	750.00	4750.00
124,250	1884 S	275.00	350.00	800.00
253,527	1885	275.00	325.00	525.00
228,000	1885 S	275.00	325.00	500.00
236,160	1886	300.00	325.00	500.00
826,000	1886 S	300.00	325.00	450.00
53,680	1887	350.00	375.00	750.00
817,000	1887 S	300.00	325.00	400.00
132,996	1888	300.00	325.00	675.00
21,335	1888 O	300.00	350.00	725.00

QUANTITY	YEAR	VERY FINE	EXT. FINE	UNC.
648,700	1888 S	225.00	325.00	425.00
4,485	1889	400.00	600.00	1650.00
425,400	1889 S	250.00	325.00	415.00
58,043	1890	285.00	350.00	825.00
17,500	1890 CC	350.00	415.00	1200.00
91,868	1891	275.00	340.00	500.00
103,732	1891 CC	275.00	400.00	750.00
797,552	1892	215.00	300.00	400.00
40,000	1892 CC	300.00	450.00	1200.00
28,688	1892 O	265.00	325.00	550.00
115,500	1892 S	250.00	300.00	525.00
1,840,895	1893	225.00	275.00	400.00
14,000	1893 CC	350.00	500.00	2000.00
17,000	1893 O	285.00	340.00	725.00
141,350	1893 S	275.00	320.00	550.00
2,470,778	1894	225.00	275.00	375.00
107,500	1894 O	285.00	315.00	800.00
25,000	1894 S	350.00	425.00	1250.00
567,826	1895	215.00	250.00	375.00
98,000	1895 O	285.00	325.00	525.00
49,00	1895 S	300.00	375.00	1650.00
76,348	1896	250.00	325.00	425.00
123,750	1896 S	285.00	350.00	1250.00
1,000,159	1897	200.00	275.00	350.00
42,500	1897 O	275.00	325.00	700.00
234,750	1897 S	265.00	320.00	750.00
812,197	1898	215.00	300.00	375.00
473,600	1898 S	250.00	320.00	575.00
1,262,305	1899	215.00	300.00	375.00
37,047	1899 O	285.00	340.00	750.00
841,000	1899 S	265.00	320.00	450.00
293,960	1900	250.00	320.00	400.00
81,000	1900 S	265.00	350.00	750.00
1,718,825	1901	215.00	300.00	400.00
72,041	1901 O	285.00	340.00	550.00
2,812,750	1901 S	215.00	300.00	375.00
82,513	1902	225.00	325.00	450.00
469,500	1902 S	215.00	300.00	375.00
125,926	1903	215.00	300.00	375.00
112,771	1903 O	265.00	300.00	450.00
538,000	1903 S	215.00	300.00	400.00
162,038	1904	215.00	300.00	375.00
108,950	1904 O	300.00	350.00	500.00
201,087	1905	250.00	300.00	375.00
369,250	1905 S	275.00	320.00	800.00
165,497	1906	285.00	320.00	425.00
981,000	1906 D	200.00	300.00	375.00
86,895	1906 O	285.00	350.00	550.00
457,000	1906 S	275.00	325.00	600.00
1,203,973	1907	200.00	275.00	375.00
1,030,000	1907 D	200.00	275.00	375.00
210,500	1907 S	320.00	365.00	825.00

INDIAN HEAD TYPE

Without Motto   With Motto

The mint mark is to the left of the eagle's claw on the reverse.

QUANTITY	YEAR	VERY FINE	EXT. FINE	UNC.
500	1907 Periods before and after legends. Wire edge			20,000.00
42	1907 As above, but with rolled edge			35,000.00
239,406	1907 No periods	400.00	450.00	1000.00
33,500	1908 No motto	425.00	650.00	1250.00
210,000	1908 D No motto	400.00	500.00	1000.00
341,486	1908 Motto	400.00	425.00	850.00
836,500	1908 D Motto	400.00	425.00	850.00
59,850	1908 S	450.00	750.00	3250.00
184,863	1909	425.00	450.00	750.00
121,540	1909 D	450.00	500.00	1000.00
292,350	1909 S	425.00	500.00	1100.00
318,704	1910	400.00	475.00	800.00
2,356,640	1910 D	385.00	450.00	700.00
811,000	1910 S	400.00	500.00	1000.00
505,595	1911	425.00	500.00	800.00
30,100	1911 D	525.00	800.00	425.00
51,000	1911 S	475.00	750.00	2000.00
405,083	1912	400.00	475.00	650.00
300,000	1912 S	400.00	500.00	1200.00
442,071	1913	400.00	500.00	725.00
66,000	1913 S	525.00	800.00	5000.00
151,050	1914	400.00	500.00	800.00
343,500	1914 D	400.00	500.00	650.00
208,000	1914 S	425.00	525.00	1000.00
351,075	1915	400.00	500.00	750.00
59,000	1915 S	500.00	575.00	2400.00
138,000	1916 S	425.00	550.00	1250.00
126,500	1920 S	800.00	8000.00	20,000.00
1,014,000	1926	400.00	500.00	700.00
96,000	1930 S	3500.00	5000.00	11,000.00
4,463,000	1932	400.00	500.00	700.00
312,500	1933	rare	25,000.00	100,000.00

Double Eagles ($20)

This denomination, the highest in American coinage, made its appearance when gold became plentiful after the discovery of gold in California.

The rarest double eagle is that of 1849. Only one was issued and it is in the collection of the United States Mint.

CORONET TYPE

Without Motto
1850–1865

With Motto
1866–1907

Double Eagles ($20 Gold Pieces)
The mint mark is below the eagle on the reverse.

QUANTITY	YEAR	VERY FINE	EXT. FINE	UNC.
1,170,261	1850	$550.00	$650.00	$3750.00
141,000	1850 O	650.00	825.00	7500.00
2,087,155	1851	525.00	600.00	2500.00
315,000	1851 O	600.00	825.00	7500.00
2,053,026	1852	550.00	635.00	2500.00
190,000	1852 O	600.00	800.00	6500.00
1,261,326	1853	500.00	600.00	5000.00
71,000	1853 O	650.00	1000.00	10,000.00
757,899	1854	525.00	750.00	5500.00
3,250	1854 O		50,000.00	
141,468	1854 S	600.00	725.00	3750.00
364,666	1855	550.00	1000.00	5250.00
8,000	1855 O	2500.00	5000.00	16,500.00
879,675	1855 S	525.00	600.00	5000.00
329,878	1856	525.00	600.00	4750.00
2,250	1856 O		60,000.00	
1,189,750	1856 S	525.00	600.00	4250.00
439,375	1857	550.00	650.00	5500.00
30,000	1857 O	800.00	1200.00	8250.00
970,500	1857 S	525.00	600.00	3750.00
211,714	1858	525.00	600.00	5750.00
32,250	1858 O	875.00	1650.00	11,000.00
846,710	1858 S	550.00	650.00	5000.00
43,597	1859	800.00	1400.00	12,500.00
9,100	1859 O	2000.00	4250.00	17,500.00
636,445	1859 S	550.00	750.00	5250.00
577,670	1860	550.00	650.00	4250.00
6,600	1860 O	2750.00	4500.00	18,500.00
544,950	1860 S	550.00	700.00	6750.00
2,976,453	1861	550.00	650.00	2500.00
5,000	1861 O	1500.00	3000.00	15,000.00
768,000	1861 S	550.00	650.00	6500.00
?	1861 S Paquet's reverse $660,000.00 Nov. 1988 Norweb Sale			
92,133	1862	750.00	950.00	7500.00
854,173	1862 S	600.00	700.00	6500.00
142,790	1863	600.00	675.00	5500.00
966,570	1863 S	525.00	625.00	4750.00
204,285	1864	600.00	750.00	4500.00
793,660	1864 S	525.00	625.00	4750.00
351,200	1865	600.00	650.00	4500.00
1,042,500	1865 S	575.00	650.00	4650.00
?	1866 S No motto	750.00	1200.00	8750.00
698,775	1866	525.00	625.00	4500.00
842,250	1866 S	525.00	625.00	3850.00
251,065	1867	525.00	625.00	1250.00
920,750	1867 S	525.00	625.00	3750.00
98,000	1868	550.00	650.00	4000.00
837,500	1868 S	525.00	750.00	3750.00
175,155	1869	525.00	650.00	4650.00
686,750	1869 S	525.00	625.00	3850.00
155,185	1870	525.00	650.00	3850.00
3,789	1870 CC		45,000.00	
982,000	1870 S	525.00	625.00	3750.00
80,150	1871	550.00	650.00	4000.00
14,687	1871 CC	1850.00	3500.00	17,500.00
928,000	1871 S	525.00	625.00	3750.00
251,880	1872	550.00	650.00	2500.00
29,650	1872 CC	750.00	1500.00	8500.00
780,000	1872 S	525.00	625.00	2000.00
1,709,825	1873	525.00	625.00	900.00
22,410	1873 CC	750.00	1250.00	8500.00
1,040,600	1873 S	525.00	625.00	1300.00
366,800	1874	525.00	625.00	1400.00
115,085	1874 CC	625.00	875.00	6500.00
1,214,000	1874 S	525.00	650.00	1200.00
295,740	1875	525.00	625.00	1000.00
111,151	1875 CC	600.00	750.00	2000.00
1,230,000	1875 S	525.00	625.00	900.00

CATALOG OF UNITED STATES COINS **93**

DOUBLE EAGLES: CORONET TYPE (continued)

QUANTITY	YEAR	VERY FINE	EXT. FINE	UNC.
583,905	1876	525.00	625.00	900.00
138,441	1876 CC	625.00	750.00	3250.00
1,597,000	1876 S	525.00	625.00	1000.00
397,670	1877	525.00	625.00	850.00
42,565	1877 CC	650.00	850.00	6250.00
1,735,000	1877 S	525.00	625.00	800.00
543,645	1878	525.00	625.00	750.00
13,180	1878 CC	775.00	1200.00	7500.00
1,739,000	1878 S	525.00	625.00	800.00
207,630	1879	525.00	625.00	1000.00
10,708	1879 CC	900.00	1800.00	9500.00
2,325	1879 O	2600.00	4500.00	18,500.00
1,223,800	1879 S	525.00	625.00	800.00
51,456	1880	525.00	650.00	1750.00
836,000	1880 S	525.00	625.00	1500.00
2,260	1881	3500.00	8500.00	20,000.00
727,000	1881 S	475.00	550.00	1250.00
630	1882 rare	5000.00	8500.00	37,500.00
39,140	1882 CC	675.00	850.00	4750.00
1,125,000	1882 S	525.00	625.00	1000.00
40	1883 very rare (only proofs were struck)			95,000.00
59,962	1883 CC	650.00	850.00	3750.00
1,189,000	1883 S	475.00	550.00	650.00
71	1884 very rare (only proofs)			$71,500.00
	Stack's Nov. 1989 Sale			
81,139	1884 CC	675.00	850.00	2850.00
916,000	1884 S	425.00	500.00	600.00
828	1885	5000.00	8500.00	27,500.00
9,450	1885 CC	1100.00	1750.00	7500.00
683,500	1885 S	525.00	625.00	700.00
1,106	1886	6000.00	12,000.00	27,500.00
121	1887 rare (only proofs were struck)			42,500.00
283,000	1887 S	425.00	500.00	750.00
226,266	1888	425.00	500.00	700.00
859,600	1888 S	425.00	500.00	650.00
44,111	1889	525.00	675.00	900.00
30,945	1889 CC	625.00	800.00	3250.00
774,700	1889 S	500.00	625.00	750.00
75,995	1890	500.00	625.00	800.00
91,209	1890 CC	625.00	775.00	3250.00
802,750	1890 S	500.00	625.00	850.00
1,442	1891	2400.00	3750.00	12,500.00
5,000	1891 CC	1850.00	2750.00	10,000.00
1,288,125	1891 S	475.00	550.00	600.00
4,523	1892	1000.00	1500.00	5250.00
27,265	1892 CC	650.00	1200.00	3750.00
930,150	1892 S	475.00	550.00	600.00
344,339	1893	475.00	550.00	600.00
18,402	1893 CC	675.00	900.00	2750.00
996,175	1893 S	475.00	550.00	600.00
1,368,990	1894	425.00	500.00	550.00
1,048,550	1894 S	425.00	500.00	550.00
1,114,656	1895	425.00	500.00	550.00
1,143,500	1895 S	425.00	500.00	550.00
792,663	1896	450.00	525.00	575.00
1,403,925	1896 S	425.00	525.00	550.00
1,383,261	1897	425.00	525.00	550.00
1,470,250	1897 S	425.00	525.00	550.00
170,470	1898	475.00	575.00	750.00
2,575,175	1898 S	425.00	525.00	550.00
1,669,384	1899	425.00	525.00	550.00
2,010,300	1899 S	425.00	525.00	550.00
1,874,584	1900	425.00	525.00	550.00
2,459,500	1900 S	425.00	525.00	550.00
111,526	1901	475.00	550.00	700.00
1,596,000	1901 S	425.00	550.00	625.00

QUANTITY	YEAR	VERY FINE	EXT. FINE	UNC.
31,254	1902	600.00	675.00	850.00
1,753,625	1902 S	450.00	525.00	600.00
287,428	1903	500.00	600.00	700.00
954,000	1903 S	450.00	550.00	600.00
6,256,797	1904	425.00	550.00	600.00
5,134,175	1904 S	425.00	550.00	600.00
59,011	1905	500.00	600.00	1100.00
1,813,000	1905 S	450.00	525.00	600.00
69,600	1906	500.00	600.00	850.00
620,250	1906 D	425.00	500.00	600.00
2,065,750	1906 S	425.00	500.00	600.00
1,451,864	1907	425.00	500.00	600.00
842,250	1907 D	450.00	600.00	700.00
2,165,800	1907 S	450.00	500.00	600.00

LIBERTY STANDING (SAINT-GAUDENS) TYPE

Without Motto
1907–1908

With Motto
1908–1933

The mint mark is above the date on the reverse.

QUANTITY	YEAR	VERY FINE	EXT. FINE	UNC.
16	* 1907 very high relief (ext. rare)		$400,000.00	
11,250	1907 MCMVII date high relief			
	with wire edge	$3500.00	$4500.00	$10,000.00
	1907 same			
	with flat edge	4000.00	5000.00	11,000.00
361,667	1907 Arabic date	525.00	600.00	700.00
4,271,551	1908 no motto	500.00	575.00	650.00
663,750	1908 D no motto	500.00	600.00	675.00
156,359	1908 motto	500.00	600.00	675.00
349,500	1908 D motto	500.00	600.00	675.00
22,000	1908 S motto		1100.00	4000.00
161,282	1909 over 8	500.00	700.00	1250.00
	1909	500.00	600.00	700.00
52,500	1909 D	600.00	650.00	1750.00
2,774,925	1909 S	500.00	575.00	675.00
482,167	1910	525.00	600.00	700.00
429,000	1910 D	525.00	600.00	700.00
2,128,250	1910 S	525.00	600.00	700.00
197,350	1911	525.00	600.00	700.00
846,500	1911 D	525.00	600.00	700.00
775,750	1911 S	525.00	600.00	700.00
149,824	1912	550.00	625.00	725.00
168,838	1913	500.00	600.00	700.00
393,500	1913 D	500.00	600.00	700.00
34,000	1913 S	550.00	650.00	1100.00
95,320	1914	525.00	625.00	725.00
453,000	1914 D	500.00	575.00	700.00
1,498,000	1914 S	500.00	575.00	700.00
152,050	1915	525.00	650.00	725.00
567,500	1915 S	500.00	600.00	700.00

DOUBLE EAGLES: LIBERTY STANDING (SAINT-GAUDENS) TYPE (continued)

QUANTITY	YEAR	VERY FINE	EXT. FINE	UNC.
796,000	1916 S	500.00	600.00	675.00
228,250	1920	500.00	600.00	675.00
558,000	1920 S	4500.00	10,000.00	16,500.00
528,500	1921	7000.00	12,500.00	30,000.00
1,375,500	1922	500.00	600.00	675.00
2,658,000	1922 S	550.00	600.00	1000.00
566,000	1923	525.00	600.00	700.00
1,702,000	1923 D	500.00	600.00	675.00
4,323,500	1924	500.00	600.00	700.00
3,049,500	1924 D	700.00	800.00	1850.00
2,927,500	1924 S	750.00	900.00	1800.00
2,831,750	1925	500.00	600.00	700.00
2,938,500	1925 D	800.00	1000.00	3200.00
3,776,500	1925 S	750.00	850.00	2000.00
816,750	1926	600.00	700.00	800.00
481,000	1926 D	900.00	1250.00	2750.00
2,041,500	1926 S	750.00	900.00	2000.00
2,946,750	1927	525.00	600.00	675.00
180,000	1927 D $522,500 Stacks March 1991 Sale, MS-65			
3,107,000	1927 S	2000.00	4000.00	11,000.00
8,816,000	1928	500.00	550.00	650.00
1,779,750	1929	3000.00	4500.00	11,000.00
74,000	1930 S		10,000.00	25,000.00
2,938,250	1931		8500.00	18,500.00
106,500	1931 D		10,000.00	20,000.00
1,101,750	1932		9000.00	19,000.00
445,500	1933 not officially released			

*The very high relief experimental pieces show 14 rays extending from the sun on the reverse side.
The regular issue high relief coins have only 13 rays.

BULLION COINS

The United States struck its first gold bullion coin, the American Eagle, on September 8, 1986 at the West Point, NY Bullion Depository. The American Eagle is being issued in four sizes with nominal dollar values inscribed upon them. The $50 denomination contains 1 troy ounce of bullion, while the 1/2, 1/4, and 1/10 ounce sizes are denominated at $25, $10, and $5, respectively. All coins will be sold at prices according to prevailing market quotations for bullion. The appearance of the $50 bullion coin in particular has resulted in a declining collector interest in the St. Gaudens $20 gold piece of 1907–33 since the designs are so similar.

1986 U.S. $50 gold bullion coin

The U.S. also issued its first silver bullion coin in 1986, the "Silver Eagle," denominated at $1. It contains one troy ounce of silver. The obverse features Adolph A. Weinman's "Walking Liberty" design used on the half-dollar coins from 1916 to 1947, while the reverse design is a rendition of a heraldic eagle by John Mercanti, a Mint sculptor and engraver.

1986 U.S. $1 silver bullion coin

COMMEMORATIVE COINS

American commemorative coins make up the handsomest and most varied series in all our coinage. Almost all buying and selling of these coins are in the uncirculated state; the commemoratives have never been intended for general use. To date there are over 125 major varieties of silver commemorative coins and some 70 gold commemorative coins.

Several of these coins have been issued in a considerable variety of dates and mint marks. The Texas Centennial coin, for example, has 13 such varieties. For the collector who is not a specialist, the advisable course is to limit himself to the cheapest variety of such a coin. In this way he will be able to acquire the largest number of commemorative coins.

The gold commemorative coins are of course more expensive than the silver coins which make up the bulk of the commemorative coinage. The two outstanding rarities among commemorative coins are the 1915 S Panama-Pacific $50 gold pieces.

SILVER COMMEMORATIVE COINS
(Half Dollars unless otherwise specified)

QUANTITY	YEAR	UNC.
950,000	1892 Columbian Exposition	$65.00
1,550,405	1893 Columbian Exposition	60.00
24,191	1893 Isabella Quarter	550.00
36,000	1900 Lafayette Dollar	1200.00
27,134	1915 S Panama-Pacific Exposition	400.00
100,058	1918 Illinois Centennial	125.00
50,028	1920 Maine Centennial	150.00
152,112	* 1920 Pilgrim Tercentenary	85.00

1892 Columbian
Exposition

SILVER COMMEMORATIVE COINS (continued)

1920 Pilgrim Tercentenary

QUANTITY	YEAR	UNC.
20,053	*1921 Pilgrim Tercentenary (1921 on obverse)	125.00
5,000	1921 Missouri Centennial (2 [mult] 4)	500.00
15,400	1921 Missouri Centennial (no 2 [mult] 4)	450.00
6,006	1921 Alabama Centennial (with 2 [mult] 2)	300.00
49,038	1921 Alabama Centennial (no 2 [mult] 2)	250.00
4,250	1922 Grant Memorial (with star)	825.00
67,411	1922 Grant Memorial (no star)	125.00
274,077	1923 S Monroe Doctrine Centennial	75.00
142,080	1924 Huguenot-Walloon Tercentenary	125.00
162,099	1925 Lexington-Concord Sesquicentennial	80.00
1,314,709	1925 Stone Mountain Memorial	50.00
86,594	1925 S California Diamond Jubilee	175.00
14,994	1925 Fort Vancouver Centennial	400.00
141,120	1926 Sesquicentennial of American Independence	75.00
48,030	1926 Oregon Trail Memorial	125.00
86,354	1926 S Oregon Trail Memorial	125.00
6,028	1928 Oregon Trail Memorial	200.00
5,008	1933 D Oregon Trail Memorial	225.00
7,006	1934 D Oregon Trail Memorial	175.00
10,006	1936 Oregon Trail Memorial	125.00
5,006	1936 S Oregon Trail Memorial	185.00
12,008	1937 D Oregon Trail Memorial	135.00
6,006	1938 Oregon Trail Memorial	
6,005	1938 D Oregon Trail Memorial	
6,006	1938 S Oregon Trail Memorial	
	1938 P-D-S (set of three)	500.00
3,004	1939 Oregon Trail Memorial	
3,004	1939 D Oregon Trail Memorial	
3,005	1939 S Oregon Trail Memorial	
	1939 P-D-S (set of three)	1000.00
28,142	1927 Vermont Sesquicentennial	250.00
10,008	1928 Hawaiian Sesquicentennial	1200.00
25,015	1934 Maryland Tercentenary	175.00
61,350	1934 Texas Centennial	125.00
9,994	1935 Texas Centennial	
10,007	1935 D Texas Centennial	
10,008	1935 S Texas Centennial	
	1935 P-D-S (set of three)	325.00
8,911	1936 Texas Centennial	
9,039	1936 D Texas Centennial	
9,064	1936 S Texas Centennial	
	1936 P-D-S (set of three)	325.00
6,571	1937 Texas Centennial	
6,605	1937 D Texas Centennial	
6,637	1937 S Texas Centennial	
	1937 P-D-S (set of three)	425.00
3,780	1938 Texas Centennial	
3,775	1938 D Texas Centennial	
3,816	1938 S Texas Centennial	
	1938 P-D-S (set of three)	650.00
10,007	1934 Daniel Boone Bicentennial	125.00
10,010	1935 Daniel Boone Bicentennial	
5,005	1935 D Daniel Boone Bicentennial	
5,005	1935 S Daniel Boone Bicentennial	
	1935 P-D-S (set of three)	325.00
10,008	*1935 Daniel Boone Bicentennial	
2,003	*1935 D Daniel Boone Bicentennial	
2,004	*1935 S Daniel Boone Bicentennial	
	1935 P-D-S (set of three)	875.00
12,012	1936 Daniel Boone Bicentennial	
5,005	1936 D Daniel Boone Bicentennial	
5,006	1936 S Daniel Boone Bicentennial	
	1936 P-D-S (set of three)	325.00

Oregon Trail Memorial

Texas Centennial

*Of the total 1920–1921 issue, 148,000 coins were melted down by the Mint.

QUANTITY	YEAR	UNC.
9,810	1937 Daniel Boone Bicentennial	
2,506	1937 D Daniel Boone Bicentennial	
2,506	1937 S Daniel Boone Bicentennial	
	1937 P-D-S (set of three)	650.00
2,100	1938 Daniel Boone Bicentennial	
2,100	1938 D Daniel Boone Bicentennial	
2,100	1938 S Daniel Boone Bicentennial	
	1938 P-D-S (set of three)	1200.00
25,018	1935 Connecticut Tercentenary	225.00
13,012	1935 Arkansas Centennial	100.00
5,505	1935 D Arkansas Centennial	100.00
5,506	1935 S Arkansas Centennial	100.00
9,660	1936 Arkansas Centennial	
9,660	1936 D Arkansas Centennial	
9,662	1936 S Arkansas Centennial	
	1936 P-D-S (set of three)	300.00
5,505	1937 Arkansas Centennial	
5,505	1937 D Arkansas Centennial	
5,506	1937 S Arkansas Centennial	
	1937 P-D-S (set of three)	400.00
3,156	1938 Arkansas Centennial	
3,155	1938 D Arkansas Centennial	
3,156	1938 S Arkansas Centennial	
	1938 P-D-S (set of three)	550.00
2,104	1939 Arkansas Centennial	
2,104	1939 D Arkansas Centennial	
2,105	1939 S Arkansas Centennial	
	1939 P-D-S (set of three)	1100.00
10,008	1935 Hudson, N. Y. Sesquicentennial	700.00
70,132	1935 S California-Pacific Exposition	100.00
30,092	1936 D California-Pacific Exposition	135.00
10,008	1935 Old Spanish Trail	850.00
20,013	1936 Rhode Island Tercentenary	
15,010	1936 D Rhode Island Tercentenary	
15,011	1936 S Rhode Island Tercentenary	
	1936 P-D-S (set of three)	325.00
50,030	1936 Cleveland, Great Lakes Exposition	125.00
25,015	1936 Wisconsin Territorial Centennial	250.00
5,005	1936 Cincinnati Musical Center	
5,005	1936 D Cincinnati Musical Center	
5,006	1936 S Cincinnati Musical Center	
	1936 P-D-S (set of three)	1000.00
81,773	1936 Long Island Tercentenary	125.00
25,015	1936 York County, Maine Tercentenary	250.00
25,015	1936 Bridgeport, Conn. Centennial	200.00
20,013	1936 Lynchburg, Va. Sesquicentennial	250.00
20,015	1936 Elgin, Illinois Centennial	275.00
16,687	1936 Albany, N. Y. Charter	325.00
71,369	1936 S San Francisco-Oakland Bay Bridge	135.00
9,007	1936 Columbia, S. C. Sesquicentennial	
8,009	1936 D Columbia, S. C. Sesquicentennial	
8,007	1936 S Columbia, S. C. Sesquicentennial	
	1936 P-D-S (set of three)	750.00
25,265	1936 Arkansas Centennial-Robinson	125.00
25,015	1936 Delaware Tercentenary	275.00
26,928	1936 Battle of Gettysburg (1863–1938)	300.00
15,000	1936 Norfolk, Va. Bicentennial500.00	
29,030	1937 Roanoke Island, N. C. (1587–1937)	250.00
18,028	1937 Battle of Antietam (1862–1937)	500.00
15,266	1938 New Rochelle, N. Y. (1688–1938)	500.00
100,057	1946 Iowa Centennial	125.00
1,000,546	1946 Booker T. Washington Memorial	12.50
200,113	1946 D Booker T. Washington Memorial	15.00
500,279	1946 S Booker T. Washington Memorial	12.50
	1946 P-D-S (set of three)	50.00
100,017	1947 Booker T. Washington Memorial	

*Small "1934" added on reverse.

Daniel Boone Bicentennial

Arkansas Centennial

Old Spanish Trail

San Francisco-Oakland Bay Bridge

SILVER COMMEMORATIVE (continued)

QUANTITY	YEAR	UNC.
100,017	1947 D Booker T. Washington Memorial	
100,017	1947 S Booker T. Washington Memorial 1	
	947 P-D-S (set of three)	65.00
8,005	1948 Booker T. Washington Memorial	
8,005	1948 D Booker T. Washington Memorial	
8,005	1948 S Booker T. Washington Memorial	
	1948 P-D-S (set of three)	130.00
6,004	1949 Booker T. Washington Memorial	
6,004	1949 D Booker T. Washington Memorial	
6,004	1949 S Booker T. Washington Memorial	
	1949 P-D-S (set of three)	200.00
6,004	1950 Booker T. Washington Memorial	
6,004	1950 D Booker T. Washington Memorial	
512,091	1950 S Booker T. Washington Memorial	
	1950 P-D-S (set of three)	160.00
510,082	1951 Booker T. Washington Memorial	
12,004	1951 D Booker T. Washington Memorial	
12,004	1951 S Booker T. Washington Memorial	
	1951 P-D-S (set of three)	110.00
110,018	1951 Carver-Washington	12.50
10,004	1951 D Carver-Washington	
10,004	1951 S Carver-Washington	
	1951 P-D-S (set of three)	100.00
2,006,292	1952 Carver-Washington	12.50
6,003	1952 D Carver-Washington	
6,003	1952 S Carver-Washington	
	1952 P-D-S (set of three)	115.00
8,003	1953 Carver-Washington	
8,003	1953 D Carver-Washington	
108,020	1953 S Carver-Washington	
	1953 P-D-S (set of three)	165.00
12,006	1954 Carver-Washington	·
12,006	1954 D Carver-Washington	
122,024	1954 S Carver-Washington	
	1954 P-D-S (set of three)	90.00
2,210,502	1982 D George Washington	
	(250th anniversary of birth)	12.50
4,894,044	1982 S George Washington (proof)	15.00

Booker T. Washington Memorial

Carver-Washington

GOLD COMMEMORATIVE COINS
(Dollars unless otherwise specified)

QUANTITY	YEAR	UNC.
17,375	1903 Louisiana Purchase (Jefferson)	$800.00
17,375	1903 Louisiana Purchase (McKinley)	800.00
9,997	1904 Lewis and Clark Exposition	1250.00
10,000	1905 Lewis and Clark Exposition	1500.00
25,000	1915 S Panama-Pacific Exposition	1000.00
6,749	1915 S Panama-Pacific Exposition ($2.50)	2500.00
483	1915 S Panama-Pacific Exposition ($50 round)	45,000.00
645	1915 S Panama-Pacific Exposition ($50 octagonal)	30,000.00
9,977	1916 McKinley Memorial	875.00
10,000	1917 McKinley Memorial	825.00
5,000	1922 Grant Memorial (with star)	1750.00
5,000	1922 Grant Memorial (no star)	1750.00
46,019	1926 Philadelphia Sesquicentennial ($2.50)	675.00

1915 S Panama-Pacific Exposition

1984 LOS ANGELES OLYMPICS
COMMEMORATIVE COIN SET

One Dollar Silver

QUANTITY	YEAR	BU-65
920,485	1983 Ancient Greek Discus Thrower	$35.00
597,157	1983 D Same Type	40.00
662,837	1983 S Same Type	40.00
4,575,837	1983 S Same Type (proof)	35.00
470,131	1984 Olympic Coliseum Dollar	35.00
316,778	1984 D Same Type	40.00
339,970	1984 S Same Type	40.00
2,623,609	1984 S Same Type (proof)	35.00

Ten Dollars Gold

QUANTITY	YEAR	BU-65
40,000	1984 Two Runners Bearing Olympic Torch Aloft	$385.00
44,000	1984 D Same Type	385.00
55,000	1984 S Same Type	385.00
100,000	1984 W (West Point Mint) Same Type	385.00
661,000	1984 W (proof)	385.00

STATUE OF LIBERTY CENTENNIAL SET

50 Cents Clad

QUANTITY	YEAR	MS-65	PROOF-65
928,008	1986 D	$7.50	—
6,925,627	1986 S (Proof)	—	12.50

One Dollar Silver

723,635	1986 P	27.50	—
6,414,638	1986 S (Proof)	—	35.00

Five Dollars Gold

95,248	1986 W (West Point)	250.00	—
404,013	1986 W (Proof)	—	200.00

Statue of Liberty

CONSTITUTIONAL BICENTENNIAL

One Dollar Silver

451,629	1987 P	$35.00	—
2,747,116	1987 S (Proof)	—	40.00

Five Dollars Gold

214,225	1987 W	250.00	—
651,659	1987 W (Proof)	—	200.00

1988 SEOUL, KOREA OLYMPICS
COMMEMORATIVE COIN SET

One Dollar Silver

QUANTITY	YEAR	MS-65	PROOF-65
191,368	1988 D	$25.00	—
1,359,366	1988 S (Proof)	—	30.00

Five Dollars Gold

	YEAR	MS-65	UNC.
62,913	1988 W	225.00	—
281,465	1988 W (Proof)	—	200.00

U.S. CONGRESS
BICENTENNIAL SET

50 Cents Clad

163,753	1989 D	$7.50	—
767,897	1989 S (Proof)	—	10.00

One Dollar Silver

135,203	1989 D	25.00	—
762,198	1989 S (Proof)	—	30.00

U.S. Congress Bicentennial Set

QUANTITY	YEAR	Five Dollars Gold MS-65	PROOF-65
		200.00	
46,899	1989 W	200.00	—
281,456	1989 W (Proof)	—	225.00

DWIGHT D. EISENHOWER CENTENNIAL SILVER DOLLAR

Dwight D. Eisenhower Centennial

QUANTITY	YEAR	MS-65	PROOF-65
241,669	1990 W	$27.50	—
1,144,461	1990 (Proof)	—	35.00

Future Commemorative Issues

U.S. Mint Plans Elaborate Coin Program to Commemorate the 26th International Summer Olympic Games Scheduled for Atlanta in 1996.

As this book goes to press, the United States Mint is in the midst of elaborate preparations to strike an ambitious set of coins to commemorate the 26th International Summer Olympic Games scheduled for Atlanta, an affair that will mark the centennial of the modern Olympic Games.

At the moment, plans are to mint two $5 gold coins in each of 1995 and 1996, four silver dollars in 1995–96, and two clad (copper-nickel) half-dollars in each of those two years as well.

Since each of those 16 major varieties of coins is to be produced in both Proof and Uncirculated, there will be 32 types in all, making this the longest commemorative set ever released by the U.S. Mint.

MOUNT RUSHMORE GOLDEN ANNIVERSARY

One Dollar Silver

QUANTITY	YEAR	Half Dollar Copper-Nickel MS-65	PROOF-65
172,754	1991 D	$12.00	—
753,257	1991 S	—	15.00
		One Dollar Silver	
133,139	1991	27.50	—
738,419	1991 S	—	35.00
		Five Dollars Gold	
31,959	1991 W	200.00	225.00

Five Dollars Gold

KOREAN WAR MEMORIAL

QUANTITY	YEAR	One Dollar Silver MS-65	PROOF-65
213,049	1991 D	$22.00	—
618,488	1991 S	—	25.00

UNITED SERVICE ORGANIZATIONS GOLDEN ANNIVERSARY

		One Dollar Silver	
124,958	1991 D	$22.00	—
321,275	1991 S	—	25.00

USO Golden One Dollar Silver

1992 BARCELONA SUMMER OLYMPICS COMMEMORATIVE COIN SET

Olympic Half Dollar Clad

		Half Dollar Clad	
161,619	1992 ("The graceful gymnast")	$8.00	—
519,699	1992 S (Proof)	—	10.00

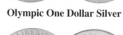

		One Dollar Silver	
187,562	1992 ("The focused pitcher")	$30.00	—
504,544	1992 S (Proof)	—	32.00

Olympic One Dollar Silver

		Five Dollars Gold	
127,732	1992 W ("The deter-mined sprinter")	$200.00	—
77,313	1992 W (Proof)	—	225.00

Olympic Five Dollars Gold

CHRISTOPHER COLUMBUS QUINCENTENARY COMMEMORATIVE COIN SET

		Half Dollar	
135,718	1992	$12.50	—
390,255	1992 S (Proof)	—	15.00

		Silver Dollar	
106,962	1992	$25.00	—
385,290	1992 S (Proof)	—	35.00

		Five Dollars Gold	
24,331	1992	$225.00	—
79,734	1992 S (Proof)	—	250.00

Columbus Half Dollar

Columbus Five Dollars Gold

Columbus One Dollar Silver

Proof Sets

In modern times the Mint has issued specially struck proof coins in the cent, nickel, dime, quarter, and half dollar denominations. Premium values are as follows:

YEAR	VALUE	YEAR	VALUE	YEAR	VALUE
1936	$4250.00	1961	17.50	1983 S	15.00
1937	2500.00	1962	17.50	1984 S	15.00
1938	1250.00	1963	17.50	1984 S	
1939	1100.00	1964	15.00	(Olympic dollar)	85.00
1940	850.00	1968 S	8.00	1985 S	12.50
1941	875.00	1969 S	15.00	1986 S	10.00
1942*	900.00	1970 S	12.50	1987 S	10.00
1950	425.00	1971 S	10.00	1988 S	10.00
1951	300.00	1972 S	10.00	1989 S	10.00
1952	150.00	1973 S	12.50	1990 S	22.50
1953	125.00	1974 S	9.00	1991 S	22.50
1954	75.00	1975 S	15.00	1992 S	22.50
1955	75.00	1976 S	15.00	1993 S	25.00
1956	40.00	1977 S	12.00	1994 S	25.00
1957	25.00	1978 S	12.50	1995 S	25.00
1958	30.00	1979 S	12.50	1996 S	25.00
1959	22.00	1980 S	12.50	1997 S	25.00
1960 Large date	$20.00	1981 S	12.50		
1960 Small date	35.00	1982 S	10.00		

*Includes both types of nickels issued in 1942.

RECENT COMMEMORATIVE ISSUES

White House
Bicentennial Commemorative
One Dollar Silver

QUANTITY	YEAR	MS-65	PROOF-65
123,803	1992	$75.00	—
375,849	1992 S (Proof)	—	85.00

One Dollar Silver

Bill of Rights
Commemorative Coin Set

		Silver Half Dollar	
173,224	1993	$17.50	—
559,758	1993 S (Proof)	—	20.00
		One Dollar Silver	
92,415	1993 D	$27.50	—
515,038	1993 S (Proof)	—	27.50
		Five Dollars Gold	
22,897	1993 W	$225.00	—
79,422	1993 P (Proof)	—	225.00

Thomas Jefferson,
250th Anniversary of Birth
Commemorative Silver Dollar

	1993 (1994) (P)	$27.50	—
	1993 (1994) S (Proof)	—	32.50

(Note: The Jefferson coins were struck in 1993, but dated 1994.)

One Dollar Silver

WORLD WAR II 50TH ANNIVERSARY COMMEMORATIVE COIN SET

(The coins are dated 1991–95, but were all struck in 1992.)

Half Dollar Clad

QUANTITY	YEAR	MS-65	PROOF-65
192,968	1993	$10.00	—
290,343	1993 (Proof)	—	12.00

Silver Dollar

94,700	1993 D	25.00	—
515,038	1993 W (Proof)	—	30.00

Five Dollars Gold

23,089	1993 W	180.00	—
65,461	1993 W (Proof)	—	200.00

Clad Half Dollar

THOMAS JEFFERSON, 250TH ANNIVERSARY OF BIRTH
Commemorative Silver Dollar

1993 (1994) (P)	$27.50	—
1993 (1994) S (Proof)	—	32.50

(Note: The Jefferson coins were struck in 1993, but dated 1994.)

Silver Dollar

VIETNAM VETERANS MEMORIAL
One Dollar Silver

1994 W	$27.50	—
1994 P (Proof)	—	32.50

Five Dollars Gold

NATIONAL PRISONER OF WAR MUSEUM
One Dollar Silver

1994 W	$27.50	—
1994 P (Proof)	—	32.50

One Dollar Silver

WOMEN IN MILITARY SERVICE FOR AMERICA MEMORIAL
One Dollar Silver

1994 W	$27.50	—
1994 P (Proof)	—	32.50

One Dollar Silver

1994 WORLD CUP SOCCER TOURNAMENT HELD IN THE UNITED STATES COMMEMORATIVE COIN SET
Clad Half Dollar

1994 W	$10.00	—
1994 (P) (Proof)	—	12.50

Silver Dollar

1994 D	27.50	—
1994 S (Proof)	—	35.00

Five Dollars Gold

1994 W	180.00	—
1994 W (Proof)	—	200.00

One Dollar Silver

UNITED STATES CAPITOL, WASHINGTON, D.C., BICENTENNIAL
Commemorative Silver Dollar

QUANTITY	YEAR	MS-65	PROOF-65
	1994 (P)	$27.50	—
	1994 S (Proof)	—	32.50

U.S. Capitol Silver Dollar

CIVIL WAR
BATTLEFIELD COMMEMORATIVE

Half Dollar Clad
(Drummer/Cannon)

1995 S	$10.00	—
1995 S (Proof)	—	12.00

Silver Dollar
(Medical corpsman with soldier/Inscription)

1995 P	30.00	—
1995 S (Proof)	—	35.00

Five Dollars Gold
(Bugler on horseback/U.S. Eagle)

1995 W	200.00	—
1995 W (Proof)	—	225.00

CENTENNIAL OF THE MODERN OLYMPIC GAMES COMMEMORATIVE COIN SET

Since each of the 16 major varieties of coins in the 1996 26th International Summer Olympic Games, set for Atlanta, Georgia, is being produced in both Proof and Uncirculated, there will be 32 types in all, making this the longest commemorative set ever released by the U.S. Mint.

According to the U.S. Mint, the coins were to be released four at a time—one gold, two silver and one clad (eight in all counting the proofs)—in February 1995, July 1995, January 1996 and spring 1996.

Clad Half Dollars

i and ii Clad Half Dollars

i—Baseball

1995 D	$12.50	—
1995 S (Proof)	—	15.00

ii—Basketball

1995 D	12.50	—
1995 S (Proof)	—	15.00

(Note: Common reverse for the two 1995 clad half dollars: a Panoramic Globe.)

Silver Dollars

iii—Gymnastics

1995 D	30.00	—
1995 S (Proof)	—	37.50

iii, iv, v and vi Silver Dollars

QUANTITY	YEAR	MS-65	PROOF-65

iv—Paralympics, Blind Runner
1995 D	$30.00	—
1995 S (Proof)	—	37.50

v—Athletics, Track and Field
1995 D	30.00	—
1995 S (Proof)	—	37.50

vi—Cycling
1995 D	30.00	—
1995 S (Proof)	—	37.50

(Note: Common reverse for all 1995 dollar coins: Clasped Hands.)

Five Dollars Gold

vii, viii Five Dollars Gold

vii—Torch Runner
1995 D	250.00	—
1995 S (Proof)	—	275.00

viii—Olympic Stadium
1995 D	250.00	—
1995 S (Proof)	—	275.00

(Note: Common reverse for the two 1995 gold coins: the American Eagle design by the noted engraver Frank Gasparro.)

Clad Half Dollars

ix—Swimming
1996 D	12.50	—
1996 S (Proof)	—	15.00

ix, x Clad Half Dollars

x—Soccer
1996 D	12.50	—
1996 S (Proof)	—	15.00

(Note: Common reverse for the two 1996 clad half dollars: "Atlanta Centennial Olympic Games" logo designed by Clint Hansen.)

Silver Dollars

xi—Tennis
1996 D	30.00	—
1996 S (Proof)	—	37.50

xi, xii, xiii, and xiv Silver Dollars

xii—Paralympics—Wheelchair Athlete
1996 D	30.00	—
1996 S (Proof)	—	37.50

xiii—Rowing
1996 D	30.00	—
1996 S (Proof)	—	37.50

xv, xvi Five Dollars Gold

QUANTITY	YEAR	MS-65	PROOF-65

Franklin D. Roosevelt

Commemorates the opening of the F.D.R. Memorial in Washington, D.C.

Five Dollars Gold

1997			—
1997 (Proof)	—		

QUANTITY	YEAR	MS-65	PROOF-65

Jackie Robinson

(50th Anniversary of Major League Debut)

Silver Dollar

1997		—
1997 S (Proof)	—	

Five Dollars Gold

1997		—
1997 S (Proof)	—	

National Law Enforcement Officers Memorial

Silver Dollar

1997		—
1997 S (Proof)	—	

Black Revolutionary War Patriots

Silver Dollar

1998		—
1998 S (Proof)	—	

George Washington Bicentennial Memorial

Five Dollars Gold

1999		—
1999 S (Proof)	—	

Yellowstone National Park

Silver Dollar

1999		—
1999 S (Proof)	—	

Dolley Madison Sesquicentennial Memorial

Silver Dollar

1999		—
1999 S (Proof)	—	

(Note: Mints for the striking of the commemorative issues from 1997 to 1999 may be changed.)

Smithsonian Silver Dollar

Smithsonian Gold Five Dollar

National Community Service

3

CATALOG OF
CANADIAN COINS

The coinage of Canada is much less ramified than United States coinage. The Province of Canada had its first coinage in 1858, and the Dominion's issues began in 1870. These coins have always carried the portrait of the reigning British monarch on the obverse:

Victoria	1858–1901	George VI	1937–1952
Edward VII	1902–1910	Elizabeth II	1953 to date
George V	1911–1936		

Up to 1948, the monarch's title read *Rex et Ind: Imp* ("King and Emperor of India"). In Victoria's reign, the legend read *Regina et Ind: Imp* for "Queen and Empress of India." In 1948, *et Ind: Imp* was deleted because of the change in India's status.

In Canadian coinage, mint marks play a less important role than they do in United States coinage. Canadian coins have been struck at three different mints, but it has rarely happened that different mints have issued the identical denomination in the same year. Thus, Canadian coinage has practically none of those sensational variations in value that come about frequently when several mints turn out coins in the same year.

As far as mint marks are concerned, Canadian coins are classified as follows: H coins were struck at the Heaton Mint in Birmingham, England. Coins dated between 1858 and 1907, which bear no mint mark, were struck at the Royal Mint at London. Coins dated after 1907, with the C mint mark or no mint mark, were struck at the Royal Canadian Mint at Ottawa.

Two years of Canadian coinage were struck with special marks after the regular coinage for those years had already been completed. In 1937, a tiny dot was punched on the 1936 dies for the cent, 10-cent piece, and 25-cent piece. The resulting "dot" coinage resulted in the outstanding Canadian rarities as far as the cents and 10-cent coins were concerned.

In 1948, some coins were struck from the 1947 dies, with a tiny maple leaf added after the date to indicate that 1948 was the year of issue. In the tables, the notation "ML" indicates this.

For many years, the reverses of Canadian coins were quite plain, being limited to values and wreaths. But the first dollar, issued in 1935, was a radical departure. The first coinage of George VI in 1937 extended the change to all the other denominations. The colorful reverses that have appeared since that time place modern Canadian coins among the most picturesque and attractive coins ever issued.

The five-cent piece has gone through a number of transformations. Its silver content was dropped in 1922 in favor of nickel. During World War II, nickel was needed so badly that the coin was struck in tombac brass, an alloy of 88 percent copper and 12 percent zinc. As this alloy is easily confused with bronze, the new coin was given a twelve-sided shape.

In 1943, the tombac was retained, but the beaver on the reverse gave way to a torch and a "V" for victory. This design was continued in 1944 and 1945, but chromium-finished steel replaced tombac. In 1946, nickel was again used and the beaver reappeared. However, the new coins were still twelve sided.

From 1973 to 1976, Canada issued a long series of coins to commemorate and help finance the 1976 International Olympic Summer Games staged at Montreal. The series consisted of 28 sterling silver coins in $5 and $10 denominations and two gold pieces in $100 denominations.

Since 1977, Canada has issued on an annual basis $100 gold commemorative coins in proof condition. In October 1985, the Royal Canadian Mint began striking a series of ten $20 silver coins to publicize and help raise funds for the 1988 International Olympic Winter Games scheduled for Calgary, Alberta. In 1990, Canada began issuing $200 gold commemorative coins on an annual basis.

The 1994 $200 "Anne of Green Gables" coin pays tribute to the famous character in the novel by Lucy Maud Montgomery, while 1995 $200 gold publicizes maple syrup production in Canada.

CANADIAN LARGE CENTS
PROVINCE OF CANADA

QUANTITY	YEAR	VERY GOOD	FINE	VERY FINE	UNC.
421,000	1858	$25.00	$30.00	$60.00	$200.00
9,579,000	1859	1.25	2.00	5.00	35.00
	1859 re-engraved date	20.00	25.00	50.00	125.00
	1859 over 58, wide 9	25.00	30.00	60.00	150.00
	1859 over 58, narrow 9	30.00	45.00	60.00	200.00

DOMINION OF CANADA
Mint marks on 1876, 1881, 1882, 1890, and 1907 issues are under date on reverse. Mint marks on 1898 and 1900 issues are above bottom rim on reverse.
QUEEN VICTORIA

4,000,000	1876 H	1.25	2.25	5.00	45.00
2,000,000	1881 H	1.75	3.00	10.00	55.00
4,000,000	1882 H	1.25	2.00	3.00	35.00
2,500,000	1884	1.50	2.25	5.00	40.00
1,500,000	1886	3.00	3.50	6.00	65.00
1,500,000	1887	2.50	3.00	5.50	50.00
4,000,000	1888	1.25	2.00	2.50	35.00
1,000,000	1890 H	4.00	7.00	10.00	125.00
1,452,537	1891 large date	4.00	6.00	10.00	80.00
	1891 small date, small leaves	30.00	40.00	65.00	325.00

QUANTITY	YEAR	VERY GOOD	FINE	VERY FINE	UNC.
	1891 small date,				
	large leaves	40.00	50.00	85.00	350.00
1,200,000	1892	2.50	4.00	8.00	45.00
2,000,000	1893	1.75	2.75	4.00	30.00
1,000,000	1894	6.00	8.00	10.00	85.00
1,200,000	1895	3.00	5.00	6.00	45.00
2,000,000	1896	1.50	2.00	2.75	30.00
1,500,000	1897	1.50	2.00	2.75	35.00
1,000,000	1898 H	3.50	5.00	7.50	75.00
2,400,000	1899	1.25	2.00	3.00	35.00
1,000,000	1900	5.50	7.50	10.00	80.00
2,600,000	1900 H	1.50	2.50	3.50	37.50
4,100,000	1901	1.00	1.50	2.25	30.00
	KING EDWARD VII				
3,000,000	1902	1.10	1.50	2.75	20.00
4,000,000	1903	1.25	1.75	2.50	20.00
2,500,000	1904	1.50	2.50	3.50	32.50
2,000,000	1905	3.00	4.50	6.50	45.00
4,100,000	1906	1.25	2.00	3.00	20.00
2,400,000	1907	1.75	2.75	4.00	32.00
800,000	1907 H	7.50	11.00	20.00	125.00
2,401,506	1908	2.25	3.25	4.50	35.00
3,973,329	1909	1.25	1.75	2.50	25.00
5,146,487	1910	1.00	1.50	2.00	20.00
	KING GEORGE V				
4,663,486	1911	1.25	2.00	3.50	32.50
5,107,642	1912	.75	1.00	1.75	20.00
5,735,405	1913	.75	1.00	1.75	20.00
3,405,958	1914	1.25	1.75	2.50	37.50
4,932,134	1915	.85	1.35	2.25	20.00
11,022,367	1916	.50	1.00	1.50	17.50
11,899,254	1917	.50	1.00	1.25	15.00
12,970,798	1918	.50	.85	1.25	15.00
11,279,634	1919	.50	.85	1.25	15.00
6,762,247	1920	.50	1.00	1.35	17.50

CANADIAN SMALL CENTS

QUANTITY	YEAR	VERY GOOD	FINE	VERY FINE	UNC.
15,483,923	1920	.25	.40	1.50	15.00
7,601,627	1921	.25	.65	1.25	20.00
1,243,635	1922	7.50	10.00	20.00	135.00
1,019,002	1923	12.00	15.00	30.00	225.00
1,593,195	1924	3.00	5.50	8.50	100.00
1,000,622	1925	9.50	12.50	25.00	225.00
2,143,372	1926	2.00	3.50	5.00	85.00
3,553,928	1927	1.00	1.50	3.00	35.00
9,144,860	1928	.20	.35	.80	12.50
12,159,840	1929	.20	.35	.75	12.50
2,538,613	1930	1.50	2.00	3.50	37.50
3,842,776	1931	1.00	1.25	3.50	35.00
21,316,199	1932	.15	.25	.45	12.50
12,079,310	1933	.15	.25	.50	12.50
7,042,358	1934	.20	.30	1.00	15.00
7,526,400	1935	.15	.25	1.00	12.50
8,768,769	1936	.15	.25	1.00	12.50
678,823	1936 dot (outstanding rarity; only 5 known)				
	KING GEORGE VI				
10,040,231	1937	.75	3.50		
18,365,608	1938	.50	3.50		
21,600,319	1939	.40	3.00		
85,740,532	1940	.25	2.00		
56,336,011	1941	.25	10.00		
76,113,708	1942	.30	12.50		
89,111,969	1943	.30	6.50		
44,131,216	1944	.25	5.00		
77,268,591	1945	.20	2.50		

CANADIAN SMALL CENTS (continued)

QUANTITY	YEAR	VERY GOOD	FINE
56,662,071	1946	.20	2.00
31,093,901	1947	.20	2.00
43,855,488	1947 ML	.20	2.50
25,767,779	1948	.50	2.75
32,190,102	1949	.15	1.75
60,444,992	1950	.15	1.50
80,430,379	1951	.15	1.25
67,633,553	1952	.15	.75

QUEEN ELIZABETH II

QUANTITY	YEAR	MS-65	QUANTITY	YEAR	MS-65
72,293,723	1953	1.00	329,695,772	1968	.20
21,898,646	1954	7.50	335,240,929	1969	.20
56,686,307	1955	1.00	311,145,010	1970	.10
78,685,535	1956	1.00	298,228,936	1971	.10
100,422,054	1957	.50	451,304,591	1972	.10
57,827,413	1958	.50	457,059,852	1973	.10
83,615,343	1959	.30	692,058,489	1974	.10
75,772,775	1960	.30	642,318,000	1975	.10
139,598,404	1961	.30	701,122,890	1976	.05
227,244,069	1962	.30	453,762,670	1977	.05
279,076,334	1963	.25	911,170,647	1978	.05
484,655,322	1964	.15	754,394,064	1979	.05
304,441,082	1965	.15	911,800,000	1980	.05
183,644,388	1966	.15	1,219,465,254	1981	.05
345,140,645	1967 dove reverse	.15	876,029,450	1982	.05

Beginning in 1982, the shape of the Canadian cent was changed from a round to a 12-sided coin in order to make it easier for the blind to identify.

QUANTITY	YEAR	MS-65	QUANTITY	YEAR	MS-65
997,820,210	1983	.05	696,629,000	1991	.05
838,235,000	1984	.05	—	1992	.05
782,752,500	1985	.05	752,034,000	1993	.05
740,335,000	1986	.05	146,424	1994	.05
918,549,000	1987	.05	50,000	1995	.05
482,676,752	1988	.05	(Copper-plated steel replaces copper.)		
1,066,628,200	1989	.05		1996	.05
205,377,000	1990	.05		1997	.05

CANADIAN 5 CENTS SILVER
PROVINCE OF CANADA

QUANTITY	YEAR	VERY GOOD	FINE	VERY FINE	UNC.
1,500,000	1858 small date	$9.00	$15.00	$30.00	$250.00
	1858 large date	125.00	200.00	350.00	1100.00

DOMINION OF CANADA

The mint marks are below center of ribbon tying wreath on reverse.

QUEEN VICTORIA

QUANTITY	YEAR	VERY GOOD	FINE	VERY FINE	UNC.
2,800,000	1870	10.00	15.00	35.00	225.00
1,400,000	1871	7.50	14.00	30.00	250.00
2,000,000	1872 H	6.50	9.00	25.00	235.00
800,000	1874 H	8.00	12.50	35.00	350.00
1,000,000	1875 H	35.00	85.00	300.00	1500.00
3,000,000	1880 H	4.00	7.00	20.00	175.00
1,500,000	1881 H	4.50	8.00	20.00	200.00
1,000,000	1882 H	5.00	9.00	30.00	225.00
600,000	1883 H	10.00	16.00	50.00	350.00
200,000	1884	85.00	100.00	200.00	2000.00
1,000,000	1885	7.00	10.00	35.00	350.00
1,700,000	1886	4.00	8.00	20.00	275.00
500,000	1887	10.00	17.50	45.00	325.00
1,000,000	1888	4.00	6.50	15.00	175.00
1,200,000	1889	15.00	30.00	60.00	500.00
1,000,000	1890 H	4.50	7.00	20.00	200.00
1,800,000	1891	3.00	5.50	9.00	140.00
860,000	1892	5.00	10.00	15.00	200.00
1,700,000	1893	3.00	5.50	9.00	140.00
500,000	1894	10.00	15.00	37.50	275.00
1,500,000	1896	4.00	5.50	15.00	250.00
1,319,283	1897	4.00	5.50	15.00	200.00
580,717	1898	8.00	14.00	25.00	225.00
3,000,000	1899	2.50	4.00	7.00	130.00
1,800,000	1900 oval O	2.50	4.50	7.00	130.00
	1900 round O	14.00	35.00	50.00	350.00
2,000,000	1901	2.50	4.00	10.00	125.00

KING EDWARD VII

QUANTITY	YEAR	VERY GOOD	FINE	VERY FINE	UNC.
2,120,000	1902	1.50	2.50	3.00	65.00
2,200,000	1902 H (small H)	7.50	10.00	20.00	175.00
	1902 H (large H)	2.00	2.50	5.00	65.00
1,000,000	1903	4.00	6.50	20.00	200.00
2,640,000	1903 H	2.50	4.00	10.00	125.00
2,400,000	1904	2.50	4.00	10.00	150.00
2,600,000	1905	2.50	4.00	10.00	125.00
3,100,000	1906	2.00	3.00	7.50	100.00
5,200,000	1907	1.75	3.00	7.50	100.00
1,220,524	1908	7.50	10.00	17.50	125.00
1,983,725	1909	2.50	3.50	10.00	150.00
5,850,325	1910	1.50	2.50	3.00	80.00

KING GEORGE V

QUANTITY	YEAR	VERY GOOD	FINE	VERY FINE	UNC.
3,692,350	1911	2.50	4.00	10.00	125.00
5,863,170	1912	1.50	2.50	5.00	65.00
5,588,048	1913	1.50	2.50	5.00	50.00
4,202,179	1914	1.50	2.50	5.00	65.00
1,172,258	1915	10.00	12.50	25.00	325.00
2,481,675	1916	2.50	3.00	5.00	100.00
5,521,373	1917	1.25	2.00	3.50	65.00
6,052,298	1918	1.25	2.00	3.50	50.00
7,835,400	1919	1.25	2.00	3.00	50.00
10,649,851	1920	1.50	2.25	4.00	50.00
2,582,495	1921 rare—only about 50 known				
		1500.00	2000.00	3000.00	16,500.00

Note: Choice BU specimen, finest known, sold at Stack's Dec. 1989 sale for $57,200.

CANADIAN 5 CENTS NICKEL

KING GEORGE V

QUANTITY	YEAR	VERY GOOD	FINE	VERY FINE	UNC.
4,794,119	1922	$.40	$1.00	$3.50	$65.00
2,502,279	1923	.65	1.50	5.00	100.00
3,105,839	1924	.50	1.00	4.50	90.00
201,921	1925	30.00	40.00	90.00	800.00
938,162	1926 Near 6	3.00	4.50	30.00	350.00
	1926 Far 6	80.00	125.00	200.00	1500.00

CANADIAN 5 CENTS NICKEL (continued)

QUANTITY	YEAR	VERY GOOD	FINE	VERY FINE	UNC.
5,285,627	1927		1.00	3.50	60.00
4,577,712	1928		1.00	3.50	60.00
5,611,911	1929		1.00	3.50	60.00
3,704,673	1930		1.00	3.50	80.00
5,100,830	1931		.75	3.00	80.00
3,198,566	1932		.75	3.00	100.00
2,597,867	1933		1.00	3.50	125.00
3,827,304	1934		.75	3.00	100.00
3,900,000	1935		.75	3.00	100.00
4,400,450	1936		.75	3.00	65.00
	KING GEORGE VI				
4,593,263	1937			2.50	27.50
3,898,974	1938			3.25	95.00
5,661,123	1939			1.75	55.00
13,920,197	1940			1.25	30.00
8,681,785	1941			1.00	37.50
6,847,544	1942			1.00	32.50
3,396,234	1942 tombac			1.50	5.00
24,760,256	1943 tombac			.75	4.00
11,532,784	1944 chrome steel			.50	3.50
18,893,216	1945 chrome steel			.40	3.50
6,952,684	1946			.60	9.00
7,603,724	1947			.60	9.00
9,595,124	1947 ML			.60	9.00
1,810,789	1948			2.50	25.00
12,750,002	1949			.40	6.00
4,970,520	1950			.40	6.00
8,329,321	1951 nickel commemorative			.25	3.50
4,313,410	1951 steel			.35	7.00
10,892,877	1952 steel			.25	5.00
	QUEEN ELIZABETH II				MS-65
16,638,218	1953 steel			.25	5.00
6,998,662	1954 steel			.25	10.00
5,356,020	1955 nickel			.15	4.00
9,399,854	1956 nickel				3.50
7,329,862	1957 nickel				3.50
7,592,000	1958 nickel				1.50
11,552,523	1959 nickel				.85
37,157,433	1960				.50
47,889,051	1961				.35
46,307,305	1962				.25
43,970,320	1963				.25
78,075,068	1964				.25
84,876,019	1965				.20
27,678,469	1966				.50
58,884,849	1967 rabbit reverse				.25
99,253,330	1968				.25
27,830,229	1969				.15
5,726,010	1970				.15
27,312,609	1971				.15
62,417,387	1972				.15
53,507,435	1973				.15
94,704,645	1974				.15
138,882,000	1975				.10
55,140,213	1976				.10
89,120,791	1977				.10
137,079,273	1978				.10
186,295,825	1979				.10
134,878,000	1980				.10
99,104,272	1981				.10
105,532,450	1982 copper nickel				.10
33,220,210	1983 copper nickel				.10
84,088,000	1984 copper nickel				.10

QUANTITY	YEAR	MS-65		QUANTITY	YEAR	MS-65
126,168,000	1985 copper nickel	.10		46,693,000	1991 copper nickel	.10
148,158,000	1986 copper nickel	.10			1992 copper nickel	.10
106,299,000	1987 copper nickel	.10		86,877,000	1993 copper nickel	.10
75,025,000	1988 copper nickel	.10			1994 copper nickel	.10
141,435,538	1989 copper nickel	.10			1995 copper nickel	.10
42,402,000	1990 copper nickel	.10			1996 nickel-plated steel	.10
					1997	.10

CANADIAN 10 CENTS SILVER

The mint marks are below center on ribbon tying wreath on reverse.

QUEEN VICTORIA

Quantity	Year				
1,250,000	1858	$11.00	$17.50	$45.00	$325.00
1,600,000	1870	8.00	14.00	35.00	350.00
800,000	1871	11.00	20.00	50.00	400.00
1,870,000	1871 H	16.50	25.00	55.00	500.00
1,000,000	1872 H	55.00	100.00	200.00	750.00
600,000	1874 H	7.00	12.50	30.00	350.00
1,000,000	1875 H	150.00	225.00	500.00	3500.00
1,500,000	1880 H	5.50	12.50	20.00	300.00
950,000	1881 H	7.50	17.50	35.00	375.00
1,000,000	1882 H	6.00	12.50	30.00	350.00
300,000	1883 H	17.50	35.00	125.00	1000.00
150,000	1884	100.00	250.00	425.00	4500.00
400,000	1885	17.50	25.00	100.00	1200.00
800,000	1886	12.00	25.00	65.00	425.00
350,000	1887	20.00	40.00	125.00	1500.00
500,000	1888	5.00	9.00	30.00	375.00
600,000	1889	350.00	550.00	1200.00	8000.00
450,000	1890 H	10.00	20.00	50.00	475.00
800,000	1891	9.00	20.00	40.00	400.00
520,000	1892	8.50	15.00	30.00	350.00
500,000	1893 round top				
		3400.00	700.00	1300.00	8750.00
	1893 flat top	312.00	25.00	65.00	475.00
500,000	1894	6.50	11.00	50.00	400.00
650,000	1896	6.50	11.00	25.00	325.00
720,000	1898	6.50	11.00	25.00	325.00
1,200,000	1899	4.00	7.00	20.00	275.00
1,100,000	1900	3.00	6.25	25.00	225.00
1,200,000	1901	3.00	6.25	25.00	225.00

KING EDWARD VII

Quantity	Year				
720,000	1902	4.00	7.00	20.00	250.00
1,100,000	1902 H	3.00	5.00	12.50	150.00
500,000	1903	7.00	12.50	60.00	800.00
1,320,000	1903 H	3.00	5.00	20.00	300.00
1,000,000	1904	7.00	12.50	35.00	325.00
1,000,000	1905	5.00	10.00	35.00	325.00
1,700,000	1906	4.00	7.00	25.00	250.00
2,620,000	1907	3.00	5.00	15.00	215.00
776,666	1908	4.00	11.00	25.00	350.00
1,697,200	1909 with				
	1908 leaves	5.00	10.00	35.00	325.00
	1909 broad				
	leaves	6.00	12.00	40.00	400.00
4,468,331	1910	2.50	5.50	12.50	175.00

KING GEORGE V

Quantity	Year				
2,737,584	1911	10.50	15.00	30.00	225.00
3,235,557	1912	1.50	2.50	10.00	200.00
3,613,937	1913 broad				
	leaves	90.00	150.00	300.00	4250.00
	1913 (1914				
	leaves)	1.25	2.50	12.50	200.00
2,549,811	1914	1.50	3.00	10.00	175.00
688,057	1915	6.50	12.50	35.00	650.00

10 CENTS SILVER: KING GEORGE V (continued)

QUANTITY	YEAR	VERY GOOD	FINE	VERY FINE	UNC.
4,218,114	1916	1.00	1.50	5.00	150.00
5,011,988	1917	1.00	1.50	3.50	100.00
5,133,602	1918	1.00	1.50	3.50	100.00
7,877,722	1919	1.00	1.50	3.50	100.00
6,305,345	1920	1.00	1.50	4.00	100.00
2,469,562	1921	1.25	2.00	4.00	125.00
2,458,602	1928	1.25	1.75	4.50	100.00
3,253,888	1929	1.25	1.75	4.50	100.00
1,831,043	1930	1.50	3.00	5.50	100.00
2,067,421	1931	1.50	2.75	6.00	100.00
1,154,317	1932	1.75	3.00	7.50	125.00
672,368	1933	2.00	5.00	8.50	135.00
409,067	1934	3.50	5.00	9.00	225.00
384,056	1935	3.50	7.50	20.00	375.00
2,460,871	1936	1.50	2.00	4.00	90.00
192,194	1936 dot (4 known)				37,500.00

KING GEORGE VI

QUANTITY	YEAR	VERY GOOD	FINE	VERY FINE	UNC.
2,499,138	1937	2.50	3.50	5.25	27.50
4,197,323	1938	1.50	2.75	5.00	70.00
5,501,748	1939	1.50	2.00	8.00	50.00
16,526,470	1940	1.50	1.75	3.50	25.00
8,716,386	1941	1.50	1.75	4.50	75.00
10,214,011	1942	1.50	1.75	3.00	50.00
21,143,229	1943	1.50	1.75	3.00	20.00
9,383,582	1944	1.50	1.75	3.00	32.50
10,979,570	1945	1.50	1.75	2.00	20.00
6,300,066	1946		1.75	2.00	35.00
4,431,926	1947		1.75	3.50	50.00
9,638,793	1947 ML		1.75	2.00	20.00
422,741	1948	4.50	8.00	12.50	90.00
11,120,006	1949			2.00	10.00
17,823,595	1950			2.00	10.00
15,079,265	1951			2.00	10.00
10,476,340	1952			2.00	7.50

QUEEN ELIZABETH II

QUANTITY	YEAR	VERY FINE	MS-65
18,467,020	1953	1.50	7.50
4,435,795	1954	2.50	15.00
12,294,649	1955	1.50	6.00
16,732,844	1956	1.75	12.50
15,631,952	1957		2.00
10,908,306	1958		3.00
19,691,433	1959		1.50
45,446,835	1960		1.50
26,850,859	1961		1.50
41,864,335	1962		1.50
41,916,208	1963		1.50
49,518,549	1964		1.50
56,965,392	1965		1.50
34,330,199	1966		1.50
63,012,417	1967 mackerel reverse		1.50
70,460,000	1968 .500 fine silver		1.00
172,582,930	1968 pure nickel		.75
55,833,929	1969		.65
5,249,296	1970		.50
41,016,968	1971		.35
60,169,387	1972		.35
167,715,435	1973		.35
201,566,565	1974		.35
207,680,000	1975		.35
95,018,533	1976		.20
128,452,206	1977		.20

QUANTITY	YEAR	UNC.	QUANTITY	YEAR	UNC.
170,366,431	1978	.20	162,998,558	1988	.20
236,910,479	1979	.20	198,695,414	1989	.20
169,742,000	1980	.20	64,400,000	1990	.20
123,899,272	1981	.20	46,693,000	1991	.20
93,953,450	1982	.20		1992	.20
111,920,210	1983	.20		1993	.20
119,080,000	1984	.20		1994	.20
143,025,000	1985	.20		1995	.20
156,400,000	1986	.20		1996 nickel-plated steel	.20
147,309,000	1987	.20		1997	

CANADIAN 20 CENTS SILVER

750,000	1858	$60.00	$85.00	$125.00	$1250.00

CANADIAN 25 CENTS SILVER

The mint marks are below center of ribbon tying wreath on reverse.

QUEEN VICTORIA

900,000	1870	12.00	20.00	60.00	650.00
400,000	1871	12.00	20.00	70.00	950.00
748,000	1871 H	15.00	25.00	85.00	850.00
2,240,000	1872 H	6.50	11.00	30.00	500.00
1,600,000	1874 H	6.50	11.00	30.00	500.00
1,000,000	1875 H	175.00	450.00	1000.00	6500.00
400,000	1880 H narrow "O"	20.00	50.00	125.00	1000.00
	1880 H wide "O"	70.00	125.00	350.00	2500.00
820,000	1881 H	10.00	20.00	60.00	650.00
600,000	1882 H	14.00	25.00	80.00	750.00
960,000	1883 H	8.50	14.00	60.00	650.00
192,000	1885	70.00	130.00	300.00	3000.00
540,000	1886	10.00	20.00	75.00	1000.00
100,000	1887	55.00	100.00	250.00	2750.00
400,000	1888	10.00	20.00	60.00	650.00
66,324	1889	65.00	110.00	400.00	4000.00
200,000	1890 H	15.00	27.50	80.00	1100.00
120,000	1891	35.00	65.00	185.00	1400.00
510,000	1892	8.50	18.00	50.00	650.00
100,000	1893	45.00	90.00	300.00	1750.00
220,000	1894	12.50	25.00	80.00	900.00
415,580	1899	5.00	9.00	30.00	475.00
1,320,000	1900	5.00	7.50	20.00	350.00
640,000	1901	5.00	7.50	17.50	350.00

KING EDWARD VII

464,000	1902	6.00	10.00	35.00	500.00
800,000	1902 H	5.00	7.50	20.00	325.00
846,150	1903	5.00	12.00	35.00	450.00
400,000	1904	10.00	25.00	80.00	900.00

25 CENTS SILVER: KING EDWARD VII (continued)

QUANTITY	YEAR	VERY GOOD	FINE	VERY FINE	UNC.
800,000	1905	6.00	12.00	40.00	700.00
1,237,843	1906	5.00	12.00	35.00	450.00
2,088,000	1907	5.00	10.00	25.00	375.00
495,016	1908	6.50	12.00	50.00	500.00
1,335,929	1909	5.00	8.00	25.00	450.00
3,577,569	1910	4.00	9.00	20.00	300.00

KING GEORGE V

QUANTITY	YEAR	VERY GOOD	FINE	VERY FINE	UNC.
1,721,341	1911	15.00	28.00	70.00	550.00
2,544,199	1912	3.50	6.50	15.00	300.00
2,213,595	1913	3.50	6.50	15.00	275.00
1,215,397	1914	3.50	6.00	15.00	350.00
242,382	1915	10.00	22.50	100.00	2500.00
1,462,566	1916	3.25	5.00	15.00	250.00
3,365,644	1917	3.25	4.50	12.50	150.00
4,175,649	1918	3.25	4.50	12.50	130.00
5,852,262	1919	3.25	4.50	12.50	130.00
1,975,278	1920	3.50	5.00	16.00	150.00
597,337	1921	9.00	20.00	80.00	1250.00
468,096	1927	20.00	40.00	100.00	1500.00
2,114,178	1928	3.25	4.50	11.00	200.00
2,690,562	1929	3.25	4.50	11.00	200.00
968,748	1930	4.00	5.50	12.50	300.00
537,815	1931	3.75	6.50	18.00	375.00
537,994	1932	4.00	7.00	18.00	350.00
421,282	1933	4.00	7.50	20.00	325.00
384,350	1934	4.00	7.50	20.00	400.00
537,772	1935	4.00	6.50	15.00	325.00
972,094	1936	3.25	6.00	12.50	150.00
153,685	1936 dot	30.00	65.00	175.00	1750.00

KING GEORGE VI

QUANTITY	YEAR	VERY GOOD	FINE	VERY FINE	UNC.
2,689,813	1937	3.25	5.25	12.50	30.00
3,149,245	1938	3.25	5.25	12.50	100.00
3,532,495	1939	3.25	5.25	12.50	90.00
9,583,650	1940	3.25	5.25	9.00	27.50
6,654,672	1941	3.25	5.25	9.00	27.50
6,935,871	1942	3.25	5.25	9.00	27.50
13,559,575	1943		4.75	7.00	27.50
7,216,237	1944		4.75	7.00	35.00
5,296,495	1945		4.75	7.00	30.00
2,210,810	1946		4.75	7.00	55.00
1,524,554	1947		4.75	8.00	500.00
4,393,938	1947 ML		5.25	8.00	25.00
2,564,424	1948			9.00	65.00
7,864,002	1949			6.00	17.50
9,673,335	1950			6.00	15.00
8,285,599	1951			6.00	15.00
8,861,657	1952			6.00	15.00

QUEEN ELIZABETH II

QUANTITY	YEAR	MS-65
11,141,851	1953	$10.00
2,318,891	1954	50.00
9,552,505	1955	12.50
11,269,353	1956	8.00
12,364,001	1957	4.50
9,743,033	1958	4.50
13,503,461	1959	3.50
22,835,327	1960	3.25
18,164,368	1961	3.25
29,559,266	1962	3.25
21,180,652	1963	3.25
36,479,343	1964	3.25
44,708,869	1965	3.00
25,388,892	1966	3.00
48,863,764	1967 wildcat reverse	3.00
71,500,000	1968 .500 silver	3.00

QUANTITY	YEAR	MS-65
88,686,931	1968 pure nickel	1.00
133,037,929	1969	1.00
10,300,000	1970	1.00
48,100,000	1971	1.00
43,743,387	1972	1.00

QUANTITY	YEAR	MS-65	QUANTITY	YEAR	MS-65
134,958,587	1973 RCMP Comm.	1.00	119,280,000	1986	.50
192,360,598	1974	.85	53,408,000	1987	.50
141,148,000	1975	.85	80,368,475	1988	.50
86,898,261	1976	.50	119,624,307	1989	.50
99,634,555	1977	.50	31,140,000	1990	.50
176,475,408	1978	.50	459,000	1991	.50
131,042,905	1979	.50	73,758,000	1992	.50
76,178,000	1980	.50		1993	.50
131,580,272	1981	.50	75,015,000	1994	.50
167,414,450	1982	.50		1995	.50
13,920,210	1983	.50		1996 nickel-plated steel	.50
119,212,000	1984	.50		1997	.50
158,734,000	1985	.50			

CANADIAN 50 CENTS SILVER

The mint marks are below center of ribbon tying wreath on reverse.

QUEEN VICTORIA

QUANTITY	YEAR	VERY GOOD	FINE	VERY FINE	UNC.
450,000	1870	$200.00	$750.00	$1000.00	$12,500.00
200,000	1871	50.00	120.00	300.00	4000.00
45,000	1871 H	80.00	165.00	375.00	4500.00
80,000	1872 H	37.50	70.00	250.00	4500.00
150,000	1881 H	35.00	60.00	200.00	4000.00
60,000	1888	90.00	185.00	500.00	6500.00
20,000	1890 H	550.00	1000.00	2250.00	18,500.00
151,000	1892	40.00	80.00	200.00	5000.00
29,036	1894	165.00	300.00	1000.00	12,000.00
100,000	1898	40.00	80.00	300.00	5000.00
50,000	1899	80.00	160.00	425.00	8000.00
118,000	1900	35.00	70.00	175.00	3500.00
80,000	1901	40.00	80.00	215.00	3500.00

KING EDWARD VII

120,000	1902	20.00	50.00	135.00	1500.00
140,000	1903 H	30.00	65.00	200.00	2000.00
60,000	1904	85.00	175.00	425.00	5000.00
40,000	1905	100.00	200.00	500.00	6500.00
350,000	1906	17.50	37.50	100.00	1600.00
300,000	1907	17.50	37.50	100.00	1500.00
128,119	1908	25.00	60.00	180.00	1500.00
203,118	1909	17.50	50.00	125.00	1500.00
649,521	1910	12.50	30.00	100.00	1350.00

KING GEORGE V

209,972	1911	17.50	85.00	350.00	2000.00
285,867	1912	10.00	18.50	70.00	1750.00
265,889	1913	10.00	18.50	70.00	1750.00
160,128	1914	22.50	65.00	185.00	2850.00
459,070	1916	10.00	17.50	55.00	900.00
752,213	1917	8.50	15.00	30.00	750.00
854,989	1918	8.50	15.00	30.00	625.00
1,113,429	1919	8.50	15.00	30.00	700.00
584,691	1920	8.50	15.00	30.00	850.00
206,398	1921*	8000.00	10,000.00	14,000.00	37,500.00
228,328	1929	8.50	15.00	37.50	800.00
57,581	1931	12.50	22.50	70.00	1500.00
19,213	1932	50.00	80.00	225.00	2000.00
39,539	1934	17.50	32.50	85.00	1500.00
38,550	1936	17.50	32.50	70.00	1000.00

*Note: Outstanding rarity. Choice MS-65 specimen sold at Bowers-Merena Sept. 1989 sale for $110,000.

KING GEORGE VI

192,016	1937		10.00	12.50	60.00
192,018	1938		12.00	20.00	265.00
287,976	1939		10.00	12.50	160.00
1,996,566	1940		9.00	10.00	35.00
1,974,165	1941		9.00	10.00	35.00
1,974,165	1942		9.00	10.00	35.00
3,109,583	1943		9.00	10.00	32.50

50 CENTS SILVER: KING GEORGE VI (continued)

QUANTITY	YEAR	FINE	VERY FINE	UNC.
2,460,205	1944	$9.00	$10.00	$32.50
1,959,528	1945	9.00	10.00	32.50
950,235	194	9.00	10.00	80.00
424,885	1947			
	straight 7	10.00	12.50	135.00
	1947			
	curved 7	9.00	12.00	125.00
38,433	1947 ML			
	straight 7	35.00	50.00	200.00
	1947 ML			
	curved 7	100.00	1500.00	3500.00
37,784	1948	60.00	100.00	250.00
858,002	1949	9.00	12.00	50.00
2,384,179	1950	8.50	10.00	30.00
2,421,010	1951	8.50	10.00	17.50
2,598,337	1952	8.50	10.00	17.50

QUEEN ELIZABETH II

QUANTITY	YEAR	MS-65	QUANTITY	YEAR	MS-65
1,781,191	1953	20.00	3,710,000	1975	1.25
506,305	1954	50.00	2,940,719	1976	1.00
753,511	1955	25.00	709,839	1977	5.50
1,379,499	1956	15.00	3,341,892	1978	1.00
2,171,689	1957	10.00	3,425,000	1979	1.00
2,957,200	1958	10.00	1,574,000	1980	1.00
3,095,535	1959	10.00	2,692,272	1981	1.00
3,488,897	1960	8.50	2,877,124	1982	1.00
3,584,417	1961	8.50	1,920,210	1983	1.00
5,208,030	1962	8.50	1,502,989	1984	1.00
8,348,871	1963	8.50	2,188,374	1985	1.00
9,377,676	1964	8.50	779,400	1986	1.00
12,629,974	1965	8.50	373,000	1987	1.00
7,683,228	1966	8.50	220,000	1988	1.00
4,221,135	1967 wolf reverse	10.00	266,419	1989	1.00
3,966,932	1968 pure nickel		207,000	1990	1.00
	(smaller planchet)	1.25	490,000	1991	1.00
7,113,929	1969	1.25	143,065	1992	1.00
2,429,526	1970	1.25		1993	1.00
2,166,444	1971	1.25	146,424	1994	1.00
2,515,632	1972	1.25		1995	1.00
2,546,096	1973	1.25			
3,436,650	1974	1.25			

CANADIAN SILVER DOLLARS

KING GEORGE V

QUANTITY	YEAR	FINE	VERY FINE	UNC.
428,707	1935	$20.00	$25.00	$75.00
306,100	1936	17.50	22.50	70.00

A Gem Proof of the 1935 dollar brought $12,100 at the November 1996 Norweb sale.

QUANTITY	YEAR	FINE	VERY FINE	UNC.
		KING GEORGE VI		
241,002	1937	17.50	25.00	60.00
90,304	1938	28.50	35.00	135.00

QUANTITY	YEAR	FINE	VERY FINE	UNC.
1,363,816	1939 Parliament buildings	11.00	12.50	28.50
38,391	1945	150.00	200.00	350.00
93,055	1946	30.00	40.00	150.00
65,595	1947 blunt 7	50.00	75.00	165.00
	1947 pointed 7	100.00	175.00	500.00
21,135	1947 ML	125.00	200.00	475.00
18,780	1948	375.00	600.00	1000.00
641,840	1949 ship (Newfoundland commem.)	17.50	25.00	45.00
261,002	1950	12.50	14.00	37.50
411,395	1951	12.00	13.50	22.50
408,835	1952	12.00	13.50	22.50

QUANTITY	YEAR		VERY FINE	MS-65
		QUEEN ELIZABETH II		
1,087,265	1953		12.50	17.50
242,815	1954		13.50	27.50
274,810	1955		13.50	27.50
209,092	1956		15.00	35.00
496,389	1957		12.50	17.50
3,390,564	1958 Totem Pole (British Columbia Commem.)		20.00	
1,443,502	1959			12.50
1,420,486	1960			12.50
1,262,231	1961			12.50
1,884,789	1962			12.50
4,179,981	1963			12.50
7,296,832	1964			12.50
10,768,569	1965			12.50
9,912,178	1966			12.50

QUANTITY	YEAR	UNC.
6,694,571	1967 goose reverse	20.00
5,579,714	1968 pure nickel (smaller planchet)	3.50
4,809,313	1969	3.50
4,140,058	1970 (Manitoba Centennial)	4.00
4,260,781	1971 (British Columbia Centennial) nickel	4.00
555,564	1971 (British Columbia Centennial) silver	20.00
2,676,041	1972 nickel	4.00
350,109	1972 Voyageurs silver	20.00
3,196,452	1973 (Prince Edward Island Centennial) nickel	4.00
904,795	1973 (Royal Canadian Mounted Police Centennial) silver	17.50
2,799,363	1974 (Winnipeg Centennial) nickel	4.00
628,183	1974 (Winnipeg Centennial) silver	17.50
833,095	1975 (Calgary Centennial) silver	17.50

CANADIAN SILVER DOLLARS (continued)

QUANTITY	YEAR	UNC.	PROOF-65
2,498,204	1976 Voyageurs nickel	4.00	
483,722	1976 (Parliament Library) silver	22.50	
1,393,745	1977 Voyageurs nickel	17.50	
847,194	1977 (Elizabeth II Silver Jubilee) silver	17.50	
744,655	1978 (XI Commonwealth Games) silver	17.50	
2,954,842	1979 Voyageurs nickel	5.00	
913,818	1979 (The *Griffon*) silver	15.00	
		MS-65	
3,291,221	1980 Voyageurs nickel	3.00	
552,439	1980 (Arctic Territories) silver	17.50	
2,775,272	1981 Voyageurs nickel	3.00	
699,494	1981 (Railroad) silver	15.00	
3,391,624	1982 Voyageurs nickel	2.50	
903,888	1982 (Regina Centennial) silver	15.00	
11,812,000	1982 (Constitution Centennial) nickel	2.50	
2,720,210	1983 Voyageurs nickel	2.50	
159,450	1983 (World University Games, Edmonton) silver	12.50	
340,068	1983 (World University Games, Edmonton)		17.50
7,009,323	1984 (Jacques Cartier 400th anniversary of the voyage to Canada) nickel	2.50	
87,760	1984 (Jacques Cartier 400th anniversary of the voyage to Canada)		10.00
133,610	1984 (Toronto Sesquicentennial) silver	12.50	
570,940	1984 (Toronto Sesquicentennial)		17.50
162,873	1985 (National Parks, Moose) silver	12.50	
727,247	1985 (National Parks, Moose)		17.50
124,574	1986 (Centennial of Vancouver) silver	12.50	
672,642	1986 (Centennial of Vancouver)		17.50
117,147	1987 (Davis Straits) silver	12.50	
587,102	1987 (Davis Straits)		17.50
199,300,000	1987 (Common Loon) nickel		2.00
178,120	1987 (Common Loon)		20.00
106,702	1988 (St. Maurice ironworks) silver	12.50	
259,230	1988 (St. Maurice ironworks)		17.50
138,893,539	1988 (Common Loon) nickel	2.00	
	1988 (Common Loon)		12.50
110,650	1989 (Bicentennial of Mackenzie River discovery) silver	12.50	
272,319	1989 (Bicentennial of Mackenzie River discovery)		17.50
184,773,902	1989 (Common Loon) nickel	2.00	
	1989 (Common Loon)		12.50
99,206	* 1990 (300th anniversary of exploration of the Canadian prairies by Henry Kelsey) silver	12.50	
254,634	1990 (300th anniversary of the exploration of the Canadian prairies by Henry Kelsey)		17.50
68,402,000	1990 (Common Loon) nickel	2.00	
140,649	1990 (Common Loon)		12.50
73,843	1991 ("S.S. Frontenac") silver	15.00	
195,824	1991 ("S.S. Frontenac")		22.50
23,156,000	1991 (Common Loon) nickel	2.00	
187,160	1991 (Common Loon)		20.00
78,160	1992 (Stagecoach Service) silver	15.00	
4,242,085	1992 (Stagecoach Service)		22.50
	1992 (Common Loon) nickel	2.00	
	1992 (Common Loon)		22.50
23,915,000	1992 (Parliament, 125th Anniversary of Confederation) nickel	2.00	
	1992 (Parliament, 125th Anniversary of Confederation)		22.50
	1993 (Common Loon) nickel	2.00	
	1993 (Common Loon)		22.50
88,160	1993 (Stanley Cup Hockey Centennial)	17.50	
294,314	1993 (Stanley Cup Hockey Centennial) silver		25.00

*The obverse of Canada's Henry Kelsey 1990 commemorative silver dollar bears a new effigy of Queen Elizabeth II by Dora dePedery Hunt (replacing the previous design by Arnold Machin used from 1965 to 1989). This is the first time an effigy of Elizabeth II by a Canadian artist has appeared on coinage.

QUANTITY	YEAR	UNC.	PROOF-65
	1994 (Common Loon) nickel	2.00	
	1994 (Common Loon)		22.50
	1994 (Royal Canadian Mounted Police		
170,374	Dog Team Patrol)	17.50	25.00
15,000,000	1994 (National War Memorial)		
	bronze/nickel	15.00	20.00
	1995 (Common Loon) nickel	2.00	
	1995 (Common Loon)		22.50
	1995 (325th Anniversary of the Hudson's		
	Bay Company in Canada)	17.50	25.00
	1995 (Peacekeeping, 50th Anniversary		
	of the United Nations)	15.00	20.00
	1996 (200th Anniversary of John McIntosh,		
	developer of the apple)	15.00	20.00
	1997 (25th Anniversary team Canada's		
	hockey victory over the U.S.S.R.)		

CANADIAN 2 DOLLARS

1996 Nickel/Aluminum/Bronzel	4.00	
1996 Gold		22.50

CANADIAN SILVER 5 DOLLARS
QUEEN ELIZABETH II

One Dollar Hockey

	UNC	PROOF-65
1973 (Olympic Games Commemorative—sailboats)	$20.00	
1973 (Map of North America)	20.00	
Series II		
1974 (Olympic Games Commemorative—Olympic Rings)	$20.00	$35.00
1974 (Athlete with torch)	20.00	35.00
Series III		
1974 (Rowing)	20.00	35.00
1974 (Canoeing)	20.00	35.00
Series IV		
1975 (Marathon)	20.00	35.00
1975 (Ladies' javelin throwing)	20.00	35.00
Series V		
1976 (Swimmer)	20.00	35.00
1976 (Diver)	20.00	35.00
Series VI		
1976 (Fencing)	20.00	35.00
1976 (Boxing)	20.00	35.00
Series VII		
1976 (Olympic Village)	20.00	35.00
1976 (Olympic flame)	20.00	35.00

CANADIAN SILVER 10 DOLLARS

Two Dollar Polar Bear

Series I		
1973 (Olympic Games Commemorative—Montreal skyline)	35.00	50.00
1973 (Map of World)	35.00	50.00
Series II		
1974 (Head of Zeus)	35.00	50.00
1974 (Temple of Zeus)	35.00	50.00
Series III		
1974 (Cycling)	35.00	50.00
1974 (Lacrosse)	35.00	50.00
Series IV		
1975 (Men's hurdles)	35.00	50.00
1975 (Ladies' shot put)	35.00	50.00
Series V		
1975 (Sailing)	35.00	50.00
1975 (Paddler)	35.00	50.00
Series VI		
1976 (Football)	35.00	50.00
1976 (Field Hockey)	35.00	50.00

	1976 (Olympic Stadium)	35.00	50.00
	1976 (Olympic Velodrome)	35.00	50.00

COMMEMORATIVE $100 GOLD COINS

QUANTITY	YEAR	PROOF
650,000	1976 (.583 gold) (Olympic)	$150.00
350,000	1976 (.917 gold, reduced size) (Olympic)	200.00
180,396	1977 (Elizabeth II Silver Jubilee)	275.00
200,000	1978 (Canadian Unification)	250.00
250,000	1979 (Year of the Child)	250.00
300,000	1980 (Arctic Territories)	250.00
102,000	1981 (National Anthem)	250.00
122,000	1982 (New Constitution)	250.00
83,000	1983 (St. John's Newfoundland, 400th Anniversary)	275.00
200,000	1984 (Jacques Cartier, 400th anniversary of voyage to Canada)	250.00
200,000	1985 (National Parks)	250.00
200,000	1986 (International Year of Peace)	250.00
145,175	1987 (1988 Summer Olympics Torch and Rings)	250.00
52,239	1988 (Bowhead Whale)	250.00
63,881	1989 (350th Anniversary of Ste. Marie Among the Hurons)	250.00
49,518	1990 *(International Literacy Year)	250.00
33,966	1991 (S.S. *Empress of India*)	250.00
	1992 (Montreal 350th Anniversary)	250.00
28,162	1993 (The Horseless Carriage)	250.00
25,971	1994 (Home Front World War II)	250.00
35,000	1995 (Louisbourg—275th Anniversary)	250.00
	1996 (Klondike Gold Rush Centennial)	250.00
	1997 (150th Anniversary of Alexander Graham Bell)	250.00

CANADIAN GOLD SOVEREIGNS

QUANTITY	YEAR	VERY FINE	UNC.
636	1908 C	1850.00	3750.00
16,273	1909 C	300.00	900.00
28,012	1910 C	260.00	700.00
KING GEORGE V			
3,715	1913 C	600.00	1250.00
14,891	1914 C	325.00	850.00
6,111*	1916 C	20,000.00	32,500.00
58,845	1917 C	130.00	225.00
106,516	1918 C	130.00	225.00
135,889	1919 C	130.00	225.00

The mint marks are above the date on the reverse.

* Rare, about 20 known. Choice BU specimen, finest known, sold for $82,500 at Stack's Dec. 1989 sale. A Gem Unc. specimen brought $16,500 at the Nov. 1996 Norweb sale.

5 DOLLARS GOLD
KING GEORGE V

165,680	1912	200.00	400.00
98,832	1913	200.00	400.00
31,122	1914	500.00	950.00

10 DOLLARS GOLD
KING GEORGE V

74,759	1912	450.00	900.00
149,232	1913	450.00	900.00
140,068	1914	550.00	1200.00

20 DOLLARS GOLD
QUEEN ELIZABETH II

337,512	1967 (proof only)	250.00

20 Dollars Gold

1988 WINTER OLYMPIC GAMES, CALGARY

$20 Silver Set of Ten

QUANTITY	ITEM	EVENT	RELEASE DATE	PROOF
359,522	(1)	Downhill Skiing	Oct. 1985	$40.00
311,830	(2)	Speed Skating	Oct. 1985	40.00
345,203	(3)	Ice Hockey	March 1986	40.00
280,188	(4)	Biathlon	March 1986	40.00
267,790	(5)	Cross-Country Skiing	Sept. 1986	40.00
263,820	(6)	Free-Style Skiing	Sept. 1986	40.00
283,720	(7)	Figure Skating	March 1987	40.00
253,220	(8)	Curling	March 1987	40.00
246,651	(9)	Ski-Jumping	Sept. 1987	40.00
216,709	(10)	Bobsledding	Sept. 1987	40.00

Gold Bullion Trade ("Maple Leaf")

Since 1979, Canada has annually issued a gold bullion trade coin containing exactly one troy ounce of gold. Called the "Maple Leaf" it has a nominal denomination of $50. Beginning in 1982, fractional Maple Leafs were minted: a $5 denomination containing $1/10$ troy ounce of gold and a $10 denomination containing $1/4$ troy ounce of pure bullion.

On July 29,1993, during the American Numismatic Association Convention at Baltimore, the Royal Canadian Mint unveiled two new members of its Maple Leaf bullion coin investment program: the $1/20$ ounce gold and platinum coins. Both are denominated at $1.

Then on Sept. 9, 1994, the Royal Canadian Mint inaugurated two new values in its bullion coin investment family: the $1/15$ ounce gold and platinum coins. Both are denominated at $2.

1987 Canadian $50 "Maple Leaf" Gold Bullion Coin

Platinum Bullion and Collectors Coins

Since 1988 Canada has annually issued a series of platinum bullion trade coins which are nominally denominated at $5, $10, $20, and $50 and contain $1/10$, $1/4$, $1/2$ and 1 troy ounce of pure bullion, respectively. Prices vary according to bullion quotations, which in early-to-mid-1995 fluctuated between $405/450 per ounce.

Starting in 1990, the Royal Canadian Mint has been producing sets of four platinum coins designed especially for collectors. These carry nominal denominations of $30, $75, $150, and $300 and contain $1/10$, $1/4$, $1/2$ and 1 troy ounce of pure bullion, respectively.

The 1990 set depicts polar bears, while the 1991 set portrays the snowy owls native to Canada. All platinum coins bear the obverse portrait of Elizabeth II. The 1992 set portrays Cougars, the 1993 set depicts Arctic Foxes, the 1994 set features Sea Otters, while the 1995 set depicts the female lynx.

Mintage for each coin has been limited to 3,500 or less.

Silver Bullion Coins

Since 1988 Canada has annually issued a silver bullion coin nominally denominated at $5. The coin, containing exactly one troy ounce of silver, portrays Elizabeth II on obverse and the Canadian Maple leaf on reverse.

Canadian Confederation 125th Anniversary Issue

In 1992 Canada issued a set of 13 coins commemorating the 125th anniversary of Confederation. Reverse designs for all 13 coins in the "Canada 125" coin program were chosen in an open competition. Obverse of each coin has the Elizabeth II portrait.

Throughout 1992 the Royal Canadian Mint issued one quarter dollar coin in silver from January through December, one for each of the country's 12 provinces and territories. In July, RCM issued a "Confederation Dollar" in nickel-plated silver in proof. Though legal tender, the coins are not intended to circulate. Mintage for each coin was set at 10 million.

25 CENTS SILVER

ITEM	NAME	RELEASE DATE	BU PROOF
(l)	New Brunswick	Jan. 1992	$10.00
(2)	Northwest Territories	Feb. 1992	10.00
(3)	Newfoundland	March 1992	10.00
(4)	Manitoba	April 1992	10.00
(5)	Yukon	May 1992	10.00
(6)	Alberta	June 1992	10.00
(7)	Prince Edward Island	July 1992	10.00
(8)	Ontario	August 1992	10.00
(9)	Nova Scotia	Sept. 1992	10.00
(10)	Quebec	Oct. 1992	10.00
(11)	Saskatchewan	Nov. 1992	10.00
(12)	British Columbia	Dec. 1992	10.00

$20 SILVER/GOLD

1992 First 50 Years

Powered Flight: CF-100 and CF-105 Avro Arrow

QUANTITY	YEAR	PROOF
29,162	1990 (Powered Flight in Carada/The First 50 Years, "Anson" "Harvard," Pilot Robert Leckie)	$50.00
28,997	1990 (Powered Flight in Canada/The First 50 Years, "Lancaster," Pilot John Fauquier)	50.00
28,791	1991 (Powered Flight in Canada/The First 50 Years, "A.E.A. Silver Dart," Designer John A.D. McCurdy and Pilot Casey Baldwin)	50.00
29,399	1991 (Powered Flight in Canada/The First 50 Years, The "de Havilland Canada Beaver," Pilot Phillip C. Garratt)	50.00
56,000	1992 (Powered Flight in Canada/The First 50 Years)	50.00
50,000	1992 (Powered Flight in Canada/The First 50 Years)	50.00
32,199	1993 ("Fairchild 71C," Powered Flight in Canada/The First 50 Years)	50.00
32,550	1993 ("Lockheed 14 Super Electra," Powered Flight in Canada/The First 50 Years)	50.00
28,835	1994 ("Curtiss HS-2L," Powered Flight in Canada/The First 50 Years)	50.00
28,520	1994 (Canadian "Vickers Vedette," Powered Flight in Canada/The First 50 Years)	50.00
	1995 C-Fea 1 Fleet Cannuck	50.00
	1995 DHC-1 Chipmunk	50.00
	1996 (Powered Flight in in Canada/CF-100; cameo,Jan Zurakowski)	50.00
	1996 (Powered Flight in in Canada/CF-105 Avro Arrow; cameo, James Chamberlain)	50.00

The Powered Flight in Canada Coins are unusual because the cameo portraits are .999 gold and are superimposed over .999 sterling silver.

PLATINUM SETS

1996 Peregrine Falcon   375.00

COMMEMORATIVE 50¢ SILVER COINS

QUANTITY	YEAR	PROOF
	1996 "Little Wild Ones" series four-coin sterling silver series)	$50.00

"Little Wild Ones" Bear, Moose, Cougar, and Wood Duck

CATALOG OF CANADIAN COINS **127**

18,040	1990 Canadian flag carried aloft, Honors the Spirit and Promise of Canada's Youth	$375.00
8,741	1991 ("Hockey—a National Passion" Celebrates Canada's Youth)	375.00
9,465	1992 (Niagara Falls)	375.00
25,000	1993 (Royal Canadian Mounted Police)	375.00
8,017	1994 (Anne of Green Gables)	375.00
25,000	1995 (Maple Syrup Production)	
	1996 (Transcontinental Railroad)	
	1997 (Native Cultures Haida Totemic Art)	

Maple Syrup

1992 Olympic Centennial Set

Canada has joined forces with four other countries (Australia, France, Austria and Greece) to commemorate the centennial of the modern Olympic Games, the five nations agreeing to strike three coins each, one in gold and two in silver.

Totemic Art

The modern Olympic games were started in Athens in 1896, and thus all 15 coins carry the "1896–1996" dates underneath the interlocking-rings Olympic emblem.

Canada took the honor of commencing the five-nation series of coins in 1992 and was to be followed by Australia, France, Austria and Greece from 1993 to 1996.

The Canadian gold coin (containing approximately a ½ troy ounce of bullion) is nominally denominated at $175, while the two silver coins (containing a troy ounce of bullion each) are denominated at $15.

All 15 coins are inscribed with the Latin motto "Citius Altius Fortius" (faster, higher, stronger).

Olympic Silver

QUANTITY	YEAR	PROOF-65
	1992 Speed Skater, Pole Vaulter and Gymnast $15 Silver	
	1992 "Spirit of the Generations of Athletes" $15 Silver	$400.00
35,000	1992 The Olympic Flame $175 Gold	

The Royal Canadian mint for the first time in its history began striking $2 coins for circulation in 1996.

Olympic Gold